306.485

CAUSEWAY INSTITUTE OF FURTHER & HIGHER EDUCATION

BALLYMONEY CAMPUS
2 COLERAINE ROAD
BALLYMONEY BT53 6BP

Return on or be

Deconstructing Disney

Eleanor Byrne and Martin McQuillan

Pluto  Press

LONDON • STERLING, VIRGINIA

First published 1999 by Pluto Press
345 Archway Road, London N6 5AA
and 22883 Quicksilver Drive,
Sterling, VA 21066–2012, USA

British Library Cataloguing in Publication Data
A catalogue record for this book is available from
the British Library

ISBN 0 7453 1456 2 hbk

Library of Congress Cataloging in Publication Data
Byrne, Eleanor.
    Deconstructing Disney / Eleanor Byrne and Martin McQuillan.
      p.   cm.
    Includes bibliographical references.
    ISBN 0–7453–1456–2 (hc.)
    1. Walt Disney Company. I. McQuillan, Martin. II. Title.
PN1999.W27 B97 1999
384'.8'6579494—dc21   99–34635
                                                           CIP

Designed and produced for Pluto Press by
Chase Production Services, Chadlington OX7 3LN
Typeset from disk by Stanford DTP Services, Northampton
Printed in the EC by T.J. International, Padstow

Contents

Acknowledgements

For their invaluable suggestions and unfailing good humour we would like to thank Peter Buse, Nuria Triana-Toribio, Adrian Plant (a star is born!), Jason Cleverly, Cathy Nicholls, Marq Smith, Joanne Morra, Phil Rothsfield, Eric Woehrling, Scott McCracken, Robert Eaglestone, Bryan Cheyette, Sharon Kivland, Giles Peaker, Kirsten Waechter, Nicholas Royle, Willy Maley, our friends and colleagues at University College Worcester and Staffordshire University, and our editor Anne Beech. We would also like to thank Jeremy Gilbert and Timothy Bewes for allowing us to present the introduction to this book at the conference 'Cultural Politics/Political Cultures' at the University of Sussex, 25 September 1998. Finally, we would like to thank the staff of Blockbuster Video in Chorlton, Manchester, for always smiling.

This book is respectfully dedicated to Ariel Dorfman and Armand Mattelart who first taught us how to read Donald Duck.

Introduction

Duckology: Political Narrative in the Age of Deconstruction

Reading Disney is like having one's own exploited condition rammed with honey down one's throat.

Dorfman and Mattelart

Reading for Socialism

At this late stage in the process of 'Advanced' Capitalism, the conditions of 'postmodernity', the construction of the Disney *oeuvre*, and the practice of 'poststructuralist' inquiry, what is there left to say about the feature-length animations of the Disney corporation? As early as 1971 Ariel Dorfman and Armand Mattelart concluded in their seminal study *How to Read Donald Duck: Imperialist Ideology in the Disney Comic*, that 'attacking Disney is no novelty'.[1] Dorfman and Mattelart aside, works such as the biographies by Richard Schickel and Marc Eliot (published 25 years apart) or critical editions like Elizabeth Bell, Lynda Haas and Laura Sells's *From Mouse to Mermaid* have consistently recorded, analysed and critiqued the right-wing agenda more or less implicit in Disney films.[2] The most frequent criticisms include sexism, racism, conservatism, heterosexism, andro-centricism, imperialism (cultural), imperialism (economic), literary vandalism, jingoism, aberrant sexuality, censorship, propaganda, paranoia, homophobia, exploitation, ecological devastation, anti-union repression, FBI collaboration, corporate raiding, and stereotyping. It would seem only a matter of time before conclusive proof is discovered linking Walt Disney to the assassination of J. F. Kennedy and the production of anti-personnel landmines. Even if such a baroque critical strategy as this were to be pursued it would have long since lost any power to surprise let alone illuminate. Disney has become synonymous with a certain conservative, patriarchal,

1

heterosexual ideology which is loosely associated with American cultural imperialism. As such Disney films (never mind the merchandise, theme parks, and media conglomerate) might be thought of as not in need of 'deconstruction' because they are self-evidently reactionary parables of the American Right.

Disney (man, films, or corporation) is therefore beyond the political pale, having been exposed by a series of devastating ideological incursions which have demolished Disney's claims to political neutrality and to be a purveyor of mere innocent entertainment. At this late stage there ought to be nothing left to say. Disney has been well and truly 'deconstructed', there must be more urgent topics to address. And yet there is still much to say about Disney and the terms of such a criticism are as valid as ever even if they are now open to negotiation. Disney's powerful hegemonic hold over children's literature, family entertainment, mainstream taste, and Western popular culture remains intact and indeed continues to grow. Alongside Disneyland, Walt Disney World and the EPCOT centre (these sites are linked by Disney Cruises) it is now possible to visit Disney Safari World, Disneyland (Paris) and soon Disneyland (Tokyo) and Disneyland (Beijing). Not only can we watch Walt Disney Pictures (with six feature-length animations due to be released in the two years between 1999 and 2000) but we can also enjoy Touchstone, Hollywood, Caravan, Miramax, Henson, and Merchant Ivory Productions, as well as Buena Vista Television and the Disney Channel. This adds up to a production facility and media and entertainment group with a truly global reach and an estimated worth of $4.7 billion.[3] Despite consistent and clear denunciations of the ideological inscriptions of Disney the evil empire continues to grow and one must assume (the popularity of semiotics aside) continues to work its reactionary magic across the globe.

In the face of Disney's wilful refusal to lie down and allow itself to be analysed out of existence perhaps the self-knowing yawn of 'postmodern' criticism, bored with yet another 'deconstruction' of Disney, is an inappropriate response. Equally, another impassioned condemnation of Disney's hetero-andro-conservatism might not cut the mustard either. Such criticism valuable as it may be merely occupies and unquestioningly reproduces a position allotted to it by the Disney text as a condition of that text's existence. A Disney text (film, video, comic book, shop, theme park, cruise ship) only functions ideologically within the wider contextual frame of the entire Disney corporation, which in turn is representative of a set of overdetermined cultural values, as a result, in part, of the existence of critics prepared to question those values. In other words, if denunciations of Disney did not exist, Disney would have to invent them. They are precisely what keeps Disney going. Attacks on the religio-politico-socio-economic values of Disney have from the very beginning (whenever we might like to date this) enabled the corporation to construct and defend its ideological machinery. The fact that a Disney text is so open to the charge of ideological conservatism (as any child can see) allows it to exercise those very conservative values in the face of an imagined external 'leftist' critical agenda. The blatantness of Disney is what makes it so resistant to the challenge of ideological exposure.

This is not to imply that a critical response to the determinate political effects of the Disney Corporation is a necessarily closed interpretation. Instead it is to point out that the so-called conservative and therefore *ipso facto* reactionary ideology of Disney (based as it seems to be around questions of nation, capital and race) is predicated on an opposition to a pre-existing and fixed set of 'leftist' values which it opposes. Disney is able to do what it does ideologically because it is a 'justifiable' bulwark against a caricatured (one might say ideologically determined) set of identifiably left-wing and therefore *ipso facto* subversive values. Disney's critics pre-exist Disney (or at least occupy a necessary position for the continued successful functioning of Disney as an ideological event) and so legitimise its actions in the field of ideology. What is at stake in this configuration is the very serious question of whether we know what we mean when we attempt to criticise Disney from a left-wing point of view.

As an *a priori* of post-structuralist criticism (this term will need to be unpacked later) we accept that texts are radically indeterminate with respect to their meaning, therefore any reading of a text must be determined by factors not prescribed by the text itself. These factors are, so the logic runs, political and it is therefore an obligation of those of us on the Left 'to read for socialism'.[4] This implies, contrary to our initial suggestion, that the readings such a criticism produces are determinate with respect to their meaning: we know what it means to be on the Left, we know what we want and we know what socialism is. However, it is not disrespectful to either party to suggest that the historically rooted concerns of Dorfman and Mattelart (writing in 1971 as part of an educational programme sponsored by Allende's Popular Unity government) and the anxieties of the liberal-left American academics of 1995 contributing to *From Mouse to Mermaid* are not one and the same. The Chilean revolutionary process is not reducible to the North American academic apparatus.

The identification of this contradiction must open a way for a consideration of the terms of criticism as a prior responsibility to any analysis of the Disney text. This engagement with a 'self-evidently' reactionary text poses certain difficulties in relation to our understanding of the reading process and our appreciation of the political space. This is not to repeat a tired rhetoric about the current redundancy of terms such as Right and Left (which is itself a depoliticising gesture invoked in the name of various political interests) but rather to ask whether these terms have not in fact always been importantly undecidable sites of ideological contest, and what have been the political effects of their supposed stability? The ultimate stake in such an analysis might be a questioning of the ways in which terms such as 'the Left' or 'socialism' have been determined by the metaphysical sedimentation of historically constituted political discourses. To continue to say that we know what we want and that we want socialism will necessarily involve a displacement of the terms 'socialism' and 'Left' from the metaphysical discourse of politics. In other words these terms will have to resist the temptation to reassert themselves in a transcendental position in a reading strategy which denies the possibility of transcendentality altogether.

As a first principle of this inquiry then, it will be necessary to assume that we might not be certain of what we mean by 'Left' or 'Right' or indeed that the meaning of the space denoted by the term 'the political' is fixed. The contextual operation of these terms is what is at stake in, and what will emerge as a result of, the encounter with the Disney text. Our analysis of Disney will only be able to make an effective intervention in the field of political oppositions it criticises by offering the double gesture of overturning the classical oppositions which surround Disney and displacing the conceptual order which predicates these oppositions. This conceptual order ('Left', 'Right', 'socialist', 'imperialist' etc.) is articulated through a non-conceptual order of non-discursive forces. This order must also be overturned and displaced and that finally is what has always been at stake in the deconstruction of Disney.

It is equally important to start from a position of openness to the question of what we mean when we use the term 'Disney' itself. Walt Disney is a man who died in 1967. This man was a film-maker, FBI informant, strike breaker, propagandist, television presenter, before his death about to be proposed as a recipient of the Nobel Peace Prize, and according to urban myth, is cryogenically frozen in a vault under Sleeping Beauty's castle in Disneyland. Disney is a studio system and a classically Fordian chain of filmic production. Disney is an entertainment and leisure complex with global interests from brand endorsement to satellite television. Disney is an *oeuvre* of audio-visual publications (including feature-length animation, short animation, pedagogical material, nature films, and live action films, not to mention home videos, CD-ROMs and computer games). Furthermore, the name 'Disney' is a signifier which has come to represent a set of contradictory and unstable ideological codes. This entire signifying complex (which incorporates all the anxieties and conflicts of national and international cultural development in the twentieth century) is inscribed in the signature 'Walt Disney' which accompanies every Disney product. This recognisable signature simultaneously implies the bodily non-presence of Walt Disney and establishes him as the origin of the text by suggesting he was present in some moment in the past. This moment of past-presence becomes a moment of future-presence when the signature is repeated after Disney's death (as it was during his life) as a copyrighted trade-mark. Walt is always with us; he is the origin of all that the corporation produces. However, as we have suggested above, the signature gathers a multiplicity of meanings around it and inscribes them in the pure singularity of Disney's autograph. It is the very reproducibility of the pure event of Disney's signature which means that it can be detached from 'the singular intention of its production'.[5] This citational structure means that on every occasion the Disney signature does not necessarily signify the same thing. The possibility of its legibility as a marker of a certain right-wing ideology depends upon the impossibility of the 'rigorous purity' of such an ideological mark. Alterity takes place and reading is possible.

In other words the ideological event of Disney is never saturated. Accordingly, it is not enough to rehearse the same textual exegesis which explained *Snow White* in 1937 (or the Duckburg comics in early 1970s Chile) when confronted by each new Disney text. This is not to say that *How to Read Donald Duck* is 'out of date' but rather to suggest that the form and space in which it was written are no longer the same conditions under which we write today. So much has changed: the space of public discussion, the means of communication and the channels of information, the relation these have to the question of authority, the place of the intellectual, the form of critique, the ideological meanings currently in circulation and so forth. *How to Read Donald Duck* should never be forgotten but it cannot be exactly repeated.[6] Just as these changes affect the terms of involvement open to the critic they also affect the production of the Disney text.

For example, how can we explain an event like Gayday at Walt Disney World in Orlando? Every year since 1991 on the first Saturday in June a lesbian and gay fun day has been held in the park and celebrated as a stand against intolerance. The day is not organised or sponsored by Disney but they profit greatly by it and Disney Chairman Michael Eisner has given it his official blessing on national television.[7] While the Disney camp has been keen to benefit from the strength of the pink dollar at home,[8] it has simultaneously made inroads into exploiting 'red' China as a new foreign market (with two prospective theme parks and a collection of factories). The National Association for the Advancement of Coloured

People objected to the representation of happy plantation workers in *Song of the South* when the film was released in 1946 (and on each of its re-releases in 1956, 1972, 1980 and 1986).[9] However, the space and scope of Disney's filmic racism has since widened to include a letter of reprimand from the General Secretariat of the Arab League, suggesting a proposed Arab boycott of Disney products in response to persistent 'negative portrayals of Arabs' in Disney films.[10] How can we reconcile exactly the Walt Disney who was a social correspondent for the FBI with the 'Team Disney' executive of Michael Eisner, Jeffrey Katzenberg and Frank Wells who offered open support to the democratic presidency of Bill Clinton? Quasimodo is not Pinocchio and Pocahontas is not Snow White.

If the Disney text has changed then so too must the terms of critical engagement. This book must not only ask questions about Disney but it must also ask questions about the questions we have been taught to ask about Disney. It is necessary to question the form of the critique as a pre-condition of making an intervention into the conceptual and non-conceptual order which predicates the Disney empire. On its own such a gesture would not constitute 'reading for socialism' but it cannot impede commitment. Quite the reverse.

Keeping Up With the Paula Joneses

'It depends what the meaning of "is" is.'
Bill Clinton

The 1996 film *The Hunchback of Notre Dame* gives an indication of the ways in which the Disney text might be said to have changed in the mediatic space of the 1990s (the feature-length animations produced since 1989 are this book's object of study). Disney's films have always (with varying degrees of success) incorporated songs as a formal component of the text. Much of the cultural capital of Disney has been based upon the mnemonic quality of this music: 'Whistle While You Work', 'One Day My Prince Will Come', 'When

You Wish Upon A Star', 'Bare Necessities', 'The Circle of Life' and so forth. Far from being mere adjuncts to the animated narrative, musical interludes between anthropomorphic action, these songs represent some of the decisive indices in which the Disney ideology is most securely embedded. They structure the films and carry the weight of the Disney signature. The above list reads like New Labour's pre-election pledges. Disney songs have produced a lucrative sideline in the merchandise catalogue of sing-along videos, soundtracks and songbooks. In the 1996 film two songs stand out as the same but different from their predecessors in the Disney canon. The first is 'A Gypsy's Prayer', sung by Esmerelda, the second is 'Beata Maria', sung by Minister Frollo. Curiously both are addressed to *notre dame*.

Esmerelda has become trapped in the cathedral after falling foul of the city guard when rescuing Quasimodo from ridicule at the 'Festival [*sic*] of Fools'. In a perfect Californian accent she asks the Archdeacon of Notre-Dame, 'What have they got against people who are different anyway?' The Archdeacon ponderously tells her, 'You can't right all the wrongs of this world by yourself', and with evangelical opportunism suggests, 'Perhaps there is someone in here who can [help].' Esmerelda turns into a side chapel, evidently amazed to see figures kneeling in prayer. She looks up to a curiously un-Catholic Madonna (if there were to be a puritan statue of the Virgin Mary this would be it) and sings, 'I don't know if you can hear me, or if you're even there.' There is a last doubtful equivocation when she sings, 'I don't know if you would listen to a gypsy's prayer.' What is remarkable here for Disney is not the postmodern scepticism but the very evidence of religion at all. With the exception of weddings and christenings to open or end a narrative there are no other explicitly religious representations in any of the feature-length animations (spanning a period of 60 years), perhaps unusual for a production company whose ideological values are so closely associated, as a critical commonplace, with the American Right. Esmerelda's opening lines might be not so much a songwriter's embarrassment in a secular age but rather a sop to and apology for that secularism. One might argue that it is now only possible for Disney to make religion visible because it is only now necessary for Disney to make it visible.

The camera pans out into a sumptuous tracking shot of Esmerelda walking through the swirling tendrils of light in the cathedral, illuminated by a forest of candles. With admirable invocation of the politically correct she sings, 'God help the outcast hungry from birth. / Show them the mercy they don't find on earth.' The lyrical content of the song is at a considerable remove from the comic gusto of previous Disney offerings. However, the tune bears a striking family resemblance to the homogenous Disney lover's ballad of its later films. As the audience is offered a head-and-shoulder shot of Esmerelda walking through the candles we are reminded of the numerous pop videos for sound-alike ballads which invoke the same waxy conceit. Esmerelda is recognisable as Janet Jackson and/or Celine Dion (a neat trick, given the racial implications of such ambiguity). The set-piece operates through the conventions of pop video (in which a young contemporary audience would be highly literate) rather than the choreographed routines of previous Disney vaudeville. The song is tearing in two directions then: firstly, as an introduction of one of the few quasi-religious sentiments in the entire film (and Disney canon); secondly, offering a consumerist conceptual frame to secularise unfamiliarly and unhealthily Catholic material. Esmerelda walks in the opposite direction to a processing chorus of the Parisian Catholic bourgeoisie, their passing shadows cast across Esmerelda's face as they sing contrapuntally, 'I ask for wealth, I ask for fame' etc. The bourgeois Catholics kneel at the feet of a giant stained-glass window of the stigmatic Christ (again specifically puritan in outline) while Esmerelda turns away from such patriarchal idolatry to sing to Our Lady of Self-Reliance, 'I ask for nothing, I can get by. I know so many less lucky than I.' Along with the frontiers of the state it would seem that Disney would like to roll back the interventionist powers of the Almighty as well.

Esmerelda walks into a circle of light cast by a high stained-glass window dedicated to the Virgin; as the camera pans away and a solo piano reaches its diminuendo, she concludes, 'Please help my people poor and downtrod. / I thought we all were children of God.' Previously Disney have approached the name of God with an almost Hebraic zeal (that it should never be stated) yet here it is invoked in a manner both pious and puritan in a suggestively Christian (almost 'socialist') sentiment which concludes another production-line pop song. The play of secular and religious frames and discourses is particularly striking. What is important here is not the ethics of political correctness (only a very superficial analysis of the text would stop here) but the peculiar ways in which religious discourse permeates the politico-ideological conceptual frame of what remains a deeply conservative film. This configuration is important because it demonstrates all the contradictions which constitute contemporary American political discourse here and now in the second term of the Clinton presidency. There will be much to say about this situation later as there will be about this particular text as well. However, we offer it now in this introduction as an example of the historical specificity of these later Disney films.

The second song, 'Beata Maria', sung by Minister Frollo, is also problematic in terms of a conventional critical vocabulary about Disney. Esmerelda's song is immediately preceded by a singular scene in which Frollo surprises her from behind, twists her arm, sniffs her hair and runs his hand over her face. Little is left to our childish imaginations. Frollo tells her, 'I was just imagining a noose around this pretty neck.' She retorts, 'I know what you were imagining' – just in case anyone has missed the point. 'How typical of your kind to twist the truth to cloud the mind with unholy thoughts', replies Frollo, with a studied air of prurience as he makes the only reference to the 'holy' in the film. This religious discourse ('un/holy', which opens the text onto theological and philosophical considerations as well) is linked to sexuality. Specifically it is linked to an expression of desire inappropriate for a public official, tempted by poor gypsy trash. This is the only physical proximity between Frollo and Esmerelda (until he stands before her to burn her at the stake during the film's denouement) and yet unexpectedly it produces the uncontrollable lust which gives rise to Frollo's operatic set-piece, 'Beata Maria', and provides the motivation for the narrative which follows.

Frollo looks out towards Notre-Dame and sings, 'Beata Maria, you know I am a righteous man. Of my virtue I am justly proud.' The audience are confirmed in their suspicions regarding the pomposity and hypocrisy of this pantomime villain. However, what follows is an extraordinarily powerful piece of computer animation which uniquely for the film seems to have more in common with Victor Hugo than with Walt Disney. Frollo turns towards his stylish and contemporary fireplace which has a suitably grand cross above it. He sings, 'Beata Maria, you know I am much purer than the common, vulgar, weak, licentious crowd.' It is hard to imagine previous Disney villains using the word 'licentious'. The camera moves to Frollo staring into the flames: 'Then tell me, Maria, why I see her dancing there. Why her smouldering eyes still scorch my soul.' There is an explicit sexual tension here between the song addressed to the Virgin and Frollo's carnal desire. There has always been a sexualised agenda in Disney films but always encoded and never as explicitly religious in its constitution. Frollo continues, 'I feel her, I see her, the sun caught in her raven hair is blazing in me out of all control.' As he stares into the fire the outline of the figure of Esmerelda appears in the flames, her body further sexualised by the lack of detail: her breasts and lips exaggerated, her hair let loose, her body language erotic and flirtatious like a cartoon lap-dancer, her shift is tight and cut lower; perhaps most significantly her features seem blacker than the previous full-colour Demi-Moore-with-a-suntan character this woman in the flames represents. Frollo is terrified and clasps his arms tightly when confronted by this sudden explosion of repressed sexuality. This is a very different representation of sexuality from the platonic chasteness of Mr and Mrs Pongo or Lady and Tramp (none of which were actually human and could therefore allow sexuality to be obliquely legible in their narrative) and rests in an entirely different country of meaning from the celibate world of Disney (Mickey and Minnie, Donald and Daisy, Mary Poppins and Bert, etc.).

Frollo struggles with his desires, he rubs Esmerelda's scarf over his face, singing, 'Like fire, hell fire, this fire in my skin. This burning desire is turning me to sin.' The lyrics imply that Frollo does not want to desire Esmerelda but he simply cannot help himself. We surely do not need to push the point about the historical specificity of an American audience prepared to understand the temptations which beset certain publicly devout government officials. With a heavy ending on the word 'sin' the melody switches to Frollo's pleas of, 'It's not my fault, I'm not to blame', counterpointed by rows of faceless, red-cowled figures sitting in a chorus on either side of the kneeling Frollo, intoning '*Mea culpa*'. There is perhaps nothing new in finding a scene in Disney which is designed to frighten (the witch in *Snow White*, Monstro the whale, Mowgli's fight with Shere Khan) but it is certainly unusual to find a horror scene explicitly linked to a character's sexuality.

We might again suggest that such a sequence is only possible in the later Disney features because the mediatic space which produces them allows for such a representation. The red figures are heavily encoded, their seating patterns resemble the monastery interior in *The Name of the Rose*, while their garments point towards the Imperial guard in *Return of the Jedi* and their facelessness offers them a likeness to the traditional representation of the ghost of Christmas Future in filmic adaptations of *A Christmas Carol*. Again the historical Catholic context is mediated through a consumerist intertextual frame of supposed media literacy. Similarly, it may be argued that sexuality becomes legible in this conservative narrative only because it is necessary to make it legible in this age of moral relativism. Women are to blame for men's desires and men in positions of authority are constantly tempted to keep up with the Paula Joneses. Frollo makes an increasingly desperate plea to the Virgin; 'Protect me, Maria, don't let this siren cast her spell. Don't let her fires seer my flesh and bone.' The sexual innuendo of 'flesh and bone' lingers as the hooded figures melt into one flow of swirling red which surrounds Frollo before turning to flame and returning to the fireplace. With his arm raised and the scarf in his clenched fist, Frollo's aria reaches its misogynist climax; 'Destroy Esmerelda and let her taste the fires of hell.' At this point there is a disturbingly operatic scream on the soundtrack and we can see the bricks at the back of the fireplace for the first time through the re-emergent outline of Esmerelda. But Frollo is a man torn; 'or else let her be mine and mine alone', he sings, as the outline of Esmerelda comes out of the fire only to evaporate into purple haze when Frollo moves to embrace her. This episode has more in keeping with *Tosca* or *Don Giovanni* than with *Fantasia*.

The tension and music are broken by a guard who enters to tell Frollo that Esmerelda has escaped from Notre-Dame. 'Get out, you idiot', screams Frollo, and continues, 'I'll find her if I have to burn down all of Paris.' The remaining narrative is therefore not predicated on the plight of the gypsy Quasimodo as outcast and his journey to acceptance (*Dumbo* with bells on) but through the libidinal economy of Frollo's competition for Esmerelda, not necessarily with Quasimodo or Captain Phoebus, but with his own codes of sexual repression. It is hard to think of a previous example in the Disney *oeuvre* of such a situation existing between fully human characters. The song ends in dramatic fashion when Frollo moves to the back wall of his chamber, pursued by shadows from the fire. He turns to face the wall as the shadows encroach upon him (crosses are clearly visible here) and intones, 'God have mercy on her, God have mercy on me', as the shadows reply, '*Kyrie eleison*'. This is the second and last mention of the name of God in the film: like Esmerelda's Protestant ethics it provides an authoritative closure to the song. Frollo is now on his knees as the shadows smother him, turning from red to black. He sings finally, 'But she will be mine or she will burn', as the fire is blown out and Frollo collapses, creating a cross on the stone floor where he falls. His body is now only illuminated by moonlight as the camera fades to black.

One of the striking things about *The Hunchback of Notre Dame* is its commitment to making its central characters play it straight. With very few exceptions it is only the anthropo-morphised gargoyles Victor, Hugo and Laverne who are allowed any comic licence. What follows on from Frollo's song is then a more or less faithful animated remake of the popularly received iconography of the classic Charles

Laughton hunchback. Such a narrative might be in keeping with a certain Hollywood vogue for remaking classic films but it has little to do with the 'traditions' of Disney (the past-presence of Walt himself) promised by the Walt Disney signature which appeared in the sky above Notre-Dame cathedral at the start of the film. There is something going on in this film (and we would argue the entire period of Disney films dating from *The Little Mermaid* in 1989) which cannot be satisfactorily explained by the reapplication of old coats of critical paint (imperialism, sexism, etc.). No doubt the expected list of Disney crimes are there but quite a few more besides and in some unexpected places. The singularity of these texts and their relation to the specifically American, specifically international, historical and political order of today which informs them must be respected if we are to achieve an effective deconstruction of them.

How to Read Donald Trump

> SCHOOL TEACHER: This is irregular, irregular, irregular!
> NORA: But he [Pete] needs an education, education, education!
>
> *Pete's Dragon*

In the film *Husbands and Wives* Woody Allen's student lover writes an essay entitled 'Oral Sex in the Age of Deconstruction'. This use of the term 'deconstruction' has as much to do with the theoretico-political reading practice of Jacques Derrida or Gayatri Spivack as *The Hunchback of Notre Dame* has to do with Victor Hugo's novel. That is to say, very little but not absolutely nothing. Here the term refers to a socio-mediatic zeitgeist of a kind of self-conscious ethical and epistemological relativism that is accompanied by the popularity of notions of critical relativism which propose that all readings are equally valid and any reading can say whatever you want it to say. This image of deconstruction has been established by academic and journalistic interests which do not or cannot read it. On the one hand, it would be a mistake to talk of 'the age of deconstruction', particularly since such a phrase seems to take no account of a deconstructive understanding of time and seems to imply a present-now of deconstruction. Furthermore, it would be wrong to think that a deconstructive discourse could invade the entire social field and replace other practices to produce a recognisable historically constituted discursive field whose cause and effect can easily be identified as identical with themselves. We might call this lazy use of the term 'deconstruction*ism*' and remind ourselves of the risks of such complacent thinking. On the other hand, there is something equally worrying about the fetishistic tyranny of critics and philosophers who attempt to preserve the purity of meaning in the term 'deconstruction' as if they had missed the point of every word Derrida ever wrote. We can object to Allen's loose synonymisation of deconstruction with postmodernism (his equation of deconstruction with pre-Barthes liberal humanist literary criticism in *Deconstructing Harry* is even more reprehensible) but should not be afraid to recognise that deconstruction as a sign is also iterable.

We have used the phrase 'the age of deconstruction' in the title of this introduction to illustrate one of a series of double-binds which inform this book. Our argument is that the feature-length animations made by Disney in the historically specific mediatic space of the last two decades cannot be subject to the same terms of critique as the other equally historically specific Disney productions. The changes in technology, distribution, audience and cultural context mean that a new set of criteria must be found to carry on the task of distinguishing and analysing these later films. With a due sense of irony we have called this mediatic space 'the age of deconstruction', if only to wrest such an abusive phrase from those who have too often found it easier to criticise deconstruction than to read it. However, deconstruction is also the philosophico-theoretical strategy open to us at the time of writing. Having set out on the premiss that we do not necessarily know what we mean by the term 'Disney', it would be a mistake to imagine that we know what we mean by the term 'deconstruction'. Certainly the authors of this book have very different experiences of what deconstruction might be (one a Heideggerian-by-way-of-de-Man-Bennington-

and-a-tradition-of-indigenous-socialism, the other a post-colonialist-Bhabha-Spivack-Young-turning-left-at-feminism). Furthermore, if we propose to follow a strategy that seeks to displace the conceptual order which predicates the metaphysical inscription of the political then it follows as a matter of course that the meaning of the term 'deconstruction' will come under review during this process. Deconstruction might be showing its age and is in need of overturning and displacement from its place as a quasi-transcendental term in a conceptual order of its own. A discussion of the later animated features of the Disney Corporation seems as good a place as any for such a political gesture, rather than an explication of Hegel (as if the two were separable). That is unless some margins are more marginal than others.

The case made against Dorfman and Mattelart by the Disney Corporation in their attempt to ban the importation of their book into America was not a legal objection to the critical acuity of the text or to the Marxist values which underpinned it but to the 'fair use' of the cartoons the authors choose to exemplify their argument. Disney claimed that the unauthorised use of these pictures deprived the company of reasonable income and was an attempt to deceive unsuspecting readers into buying a Disney product. Disney also claimed that illustrations were not necessary to demonstrate the authors' point and that mere précis, description and quotation would suffice. To their eternal credit the US Customs department rejected Disney's claims on two grounds, just as it shamefully invoked the manufacturing clause of the copyright regulations to limit importation to 1500 copies. Firstly, 'the questioned item, priced at $3.25, and consisting overwhelmingly of ponderous text, could not be confused for a Disney'[11] and secondly, in concurrence with Dorfman and Mattelart's lawyers at the Centre for Constitutional Rights, use of the cartoons was not piratical because it constituted fair use. In other words, what is important about Disney and what makes their products ultimately irreducible to questions of literary style or musical merit is the illustrations themselves. The plot alone does not make *Dumbo* an effective parable of tactical aerial bombing but the visual matter in conjunction with the story does. The story and songs from *Aladdin* do not make it a successful representation of Operation Desert Storm by themselves; only their relation to the illustrations can do this. Accordingly, this book must be sensitive to what is ultimately irreducible in Disney, namely the filmic experience of feature-length animation, and not a mere analysis of screenplays or songbooks. This will be difficult because for obvious reasons we are unable to reproduce here any of the images we discuss in this book (instead they are transposed into detailed descriptions of scenes and stills). We hope that the visual material under consideration here is already familiar enough to the reader to make reproduction, while not unnecessary, certainly not a bar to understanding. The familiarity of the images will at least prove one of our points about the permeation of the social fabric by Disney. We trust these images are as close to the hearts and minds of our readers as our concerns are.

In this respect our analysis is bound to be inadequate and the phrase 'Deconstructing Disney' might take on an alternative meaning based upon Glaswegian dialect in which 'disney' is a homonym of 'disnae', meaning 'does not'.[12] Hence the perhaps over-familiar Glasgow pun 'What's the difference between Bing Crosby and Walt Disney? Bing sings but Walt disnae.' Deconstructing disnae dae enough. Perhaps this is true and a more materialist response may be required – we make no claims to anything other than opening a move in a wider strategy of criticism. However, as the above entrance to these later Disney texts demonstrates, the canon of films we are studying encompasses questions of the self, (un)consciousness, reason, desire, ethics, freedom, social responsibility, the body, sexual difference, death, the state, the law, perception, the image, international relations, the proper, theology, childhood, class, race, time, the historical, the political and so forth. In short these films incorporate the entire philosophical and theoretical field of inquiry and must be thought through as part of a more comprehensive process of questioning before an analysis of the material effects of Disney might be properly engaged.

This, then, is a study in 'Duckology', to use Dorfman and Mattelart's phrase. It comprises a consideration of specifically those feature-length animations produced from 1989 (inclusive) onwards in order to understand their singular relation to the cultural context of contemporary culture in the United States of America which gave rise to them. The chapters which follow alternate between readings of individual texts and wider thematic concerns such as race and gender. At this late stage they are not quite the iconoclastic polemic they might once have been. Instead, they are an attempt to show that if we are interested in the political circumstances which oppress us then we can never know too much about Disney.[13]

Eleanor Byrne
Martin McQuillan

1

A Spectre is Haunting Europe: Disney Rides Again

Hauls me through air—
Thighs, hair;
Flakes from my heels.
  Sylvia Plath, 'Ariel'

'I believe we are on an irreversible trend toward more
freedom and democracy – but that could change.'
  Dan Quayle, Speech 22 May 1989

Speculating on Disney

To suggest that the fall of the Berlin Wall and the simultane-
ous, financial and artistic resurgence of Disney in *The Little
Mermaid* (1989) is not mere coincidence might be condemned
as wild speculation. We could be accused of floating an idea
which was not verifiable by any material fact. Certainly it
seems unlikely that Disney artists, directors and management
sat around a table and consciously worked out a plan in
which all feature-length animations (the flagships of the
Disney corporation) would in covert ways represent the
interests of United States foreign policy at the time of
production. However, the fact that we may never know
whether records of such a meeting are stored away in the
vaults under the Disney castle does not mean that such a
conclave did not happen, just that it is unlikely. What we can
say, with a fundamental and irreducible uncertainty as to its
reasonableness, is that it is not unreasonable to suggest that
the Disney text (associated in the popular imagination with
the vanguard of American Cultural Imperialism and as a
defining condition of postmodernism) is a site for the *representation* of the conflicting ideologies in operation in Western

19

society at the time of production and so therefore has a non-simple relation to American cultural and economic imperialism. The value of this speculation, which will constitute the thematic backbone of this book, therefore does not depend upon the authorial intentions of directors, screenwriters, lyricists and animators but upon the system of signification put in play by the Disney *oeuvre*. We are all too aware of the fate of those animators who worked for Disney to produce some of the studios' most interesting and most conservative films during the 'Golden Age', only to be sacked for organising their labour and subsequently blacklisted during the dark age of 'un-American activities'. Positive vetting and personnel aptitude tests aside, there is no reason to assume that the Disney corporation of the 1990s does not consist of an equally exploited workforce. Consequently, this book is not concerned with naming and shaming individuals but in the totality of a system which puts in play a set of privileged ideological operators only to have them returned against that system by the text which it produces.

If this reasoning looks like mere speculation then that may prove to be the most suitable form of analysis for Disney because speculation is the mode of writing which constitutes the Disney text. Speculation is the mode of our research not only because Disney makes speculation the object of its texts but also because the Disney text follows a structure of speculation. Speculation is what Disney does in writing, that which makes Disney write and that which Disney causes to be written.[1] The construction of EuroDisney was well under way when *The Little Mermaid* was released in 1989. 'EuroDisney', as this portmanteau name has come to suggest, is an attempt to open up a space for the Disney corporation in the European single market. Its location in Marne outside Paris (the site of the first battle of World War I) is not without significance as it lays siege to the cultural and historical 'heart' of Europe. Every year since it opened EuroDisney has been running at a loss and the Disney company have been underwriting this failing subsidiary in the belief that the Disneyfication of Europe is inevitable. Disney's speculative venture outside the French capital follows a Fukuyama-esque logic which suggests that the continued deregulation of world markets will result in a political and cultural homogenisation around the values of liberal democracy in which the United States will occupy a privileged position as both commodity and value (pure gold).[2] While Disney may yet recuperate its losses and continental Europe succumb to the alluring insistence of EuroDisney (the United Kingdom has been irredeemably Disneyfied since at least *Snow White*), to date this adventure of Late Capitalism has proven to be too late for a continent quite at ease with its own complacent brand of liberal democracy and its related cultural *machins-bidules*. This may explain why the proposed Disney theme-parks (evidently places where themes are parked) in Shanghai and near Guangzhov in Southern China will coincide with the introduction of market reforms but precede democracy. If speculating on EuroDisney has been profitless for the corporation then it might not be so for us because this attempt to make economic inroads into Europe was underwritten by two Disney texts which took Europe as their source, content and target: *The Little Mermaid* and *Beauty and the Beast*.

If these films constitute the latest landing of the barbarian longboats on the shores of Europe then their speculative nature is also a challenge to the speculative-philosophical tradition which constitutes Europe as a category, from Socrates to Freud and beyond. History having been so undialectical as to have produced EuroDisney rather than the New Jerusalem, we might read the Disney text as the latest neon bulb of the Enlightenment. Disney's encampment on the borders of Paris means that the corporation begins its presencing in Europe at the edge of the overdetermined site of European revolution, socialism, democracy, enlightenment and culture. EuroDisney is not only a challenge to the Smurfs, Asterix and Tintin but also to Hegel, Kant and Heidegger. The cultural imperialism of EuroDisney demonstrates that the West is not homogeneous and self-identical but is in important respects set against itself. If European imperialism incorporated North America into the category of the West then Disney's cultural imperialism is an attempt to incorporate Europe categorically as the most easterly state of North America. What is at stake in this culture war is a contest over the very definition of what 'the West' might mean. It is not insignificant then that Western culture started this conflict in its own house at a time when certain forces within it believed they had just won a prolonged war in Europe against Marxist-Leninism. As yet it may be too early to say what will prove to be the most potent symbol of Western culture, Mickey Mouse or Hegel, or whether they can be separated, but this is the speculation which Disney thematises in *The Little Mermaid*.

When Shrimps Learn to Whistle

'If anyone believes that our smiles involve abandonment of the teaching of Marx, Engels, and Lenin he deceives himself. Those who wait for that must wait until a shrimp learns to whistle.'

Nikita Khrushchev[3]

There is something fishy about *The Little Mermaid*. At a very superficial level the plot, as extrapolated from Hans Christian Andersen, involves two ideologically opposed kingdoms separated by a supposedly impenetrable barrier. This barrier is one which is policed by interpellation and mythology rather than strictly repressive forces. 'Contact between the human world and the mer world is strictly forbidden', King Triton tells his headstrong teenage daughter who has fallen in love with a prince she saved from drowning. In Triton's view humans are 'all the same: spineless, savage, harpooning fish-eaters, incapable of any feeling'. Of course part of the drive of the Disney narrative is that Triton will inevitably learn his lesson, recant his ill-founded prejudice and not only come to accept his daughter's love for the human Prince Eric but also use his magic powers to give Ariel legs so that she might become human too. The détente that exists between the human and mer worlds at the end of the film is not based upon a partnership of equals but the appropriation of the mer world's most precious asset (King Triton's favourite daughter) by the humans. In the final scene Triton and his merpeople wave to Ariel and Eric as they slip off into the sunset but the ship has sailed and they are left behind. There is more than a hint here of the post-Cold War euphoria which disguised the Western annexation and asset-stripping of the East.

By the end of the film Ariel's prince has come but from the start this has been a story about a deprived dissident's desire for the amenities of the West. 'Ariel' literally means 'of the air' – she is only marginally of the sea. She cannot stand the repressive austerity of the mer world and longs for legs. In mer terms, being of the air means being out of the water and so being human. However, she is doubly marked by her name because 'Ariel' is also a popular brand of soap powder in Western Europe. An 'aerial' is also the receptive apparatus on a television, the part which absorbs and mediates signals from outside. In terms of the Eastern bloc this means picking up channels of communication from the West, in particular advertisements for consumer goods. She is then the very embodiment of consumer-fetishism and demonstrates this by collecting 'human stuff': cutlery, crockery, pipes, corkscrews, egg-timers, watches, thimbles, tankards, candelabras, figurines, jewellery, books, paintings. In the first great set-piece of the New Disney canon Ariel sings of the ways in which her desire is constructed not only as a woman but as a consumer. If we are to continue this speculative parallel between mer and human and East and West (the mapping is not quite exact but retains a relation of familiar foreignness to the idea of a map) then it should be noted that Ariel as a deprived citizen of a communistic bloc is not 'within a capitalist system' *per se* but shows that there are no limits to the effects of such a system. The failed prophylactic attempts of the Soviet politburo to seal its Eastern Empire from the effects of capitalist ideology suggest that the moment such totalizing boundaries are set up they will immediately begin to degenerate because the border of such hermeticism is the point at which the capitalist other begins its presencing. The point at which communism sets its boundary becomes a moment of contestation; the limit of interaction is the point of transaction where meanings and values come up against each other and are exchanged in an overrun of conceptual and cultural boundaries. Even if Ariel is outside the human system she is inscribed within that system by the knowledge of her exclusion from it. She is also aware of the human world as a more efficient system of capital than the mer world. It is not the case that the communist and capitalist systems are opposites but that the internal market of the Eastern bloc could be thought of as a system of 'state capitalism' which could not effectively manage the effects of capital because of its hermeticism and because of its reliance on heavy industry dictated by defence requirements. Khrushchev's 'Red Spring', Lenin's New Economic Policy and Gorbachev's *glasnost* demonstrate the ways in which consumer capitalism was always already implied within the Soviet model of communism. It is not that Ariel lacks consumer choice (she has a natty red handbag and cockleshell bra) but that the human world has better kitchen accessories on offer. Compared to the human world, hers is only a mere world.

Having been reprimanded by her father for visiting the surface, Ariel, like any Westernised teenager, sulks in her private space (not her bedroom which she shares with her six sisters but the cavern in which she stores the human things she salvages from shipwrecks). She sings of her relative material well-being (she is the daughter of a king): 'Look at this stuff, isn't it neat / Wouldn't you think my collection's complete? / Wouldn't you think I'm the girl, the girl who has everything?' She looks up to the camera with doe eyes and with enhanced breasts, which have more to do with animation than anatomy, to remind us of the mix of innocence and cupidity which predicates the assumption of the innate superiority of consumerism. We are made privy to the excellence of the commodities in her treasure trove ('I've got gadgets and gizmos a-plenty / I got whozits and whatzits galore') as the camera pans around the cavern to show the fine array of domestic items on display, before the melody rises to a crescendo: 'But who cares? No big deal, I want more!' The conceit of the heroine seeking a better world beyond the confinements of her present situation is not unique to *The Little Mermaid*, indeed in various ways it is the common trope of every film in the recent Disney *oeuvre*, but in Europe in 1989 it has a special resonance related to the consumerist deprivations of communism. The magic kingdom which lies beyond the 'untranscendable horizon' of the mer world (or

Belle's 'provincial life', Princess Jasmine's palace, Simba's troubles, Pocahontas's village, Quasimodo's bell tower, Hercules' farm, and Mulan's chores) is, unsurprisingly, Disney itself – a place which matches personal freedom with consumerist bounty and the pursuit of happiness.

Ariel longs to 'be part of that world', she wants to 'be where the people are / I wanna see, wanna see 'em dancin''. Dancing is not only a teenager's metonymic substitution for sex but the style of dancing suggested here by Ariel's musicbox points towards a desire for Western fashions and adolescent consumerism. Dancing, as Ariel reminds us, requires feet: 'Flippin' your fins you don't get too far / Legs are required for jumpin', dancin'.' Feet and/or shoes being the mark which leaves the trace of the all-too-human capitalist world. Here the West's consumer fetishism is mixed with Ariel's foot fetishism. However, Ariel realises if she is to be 'Up where they walk / Up where they run / Up where they stay all day in the sun', there will be a price to pay. After the song reaches its high point in which Ariel pirouettes to the top of her cavern and gazes longingly through her amorphous red hair and a shoal of fish, she speculates on the price to be paid: 'What would I give / if I could live / outta these waters? / What would I pay / to spend a day / warm on the sand?' The rest of the film is a speculation on these questions; who is to pay and at what price? Ariel's desire for the human world is mer(e) speculation based on the supposition that 'I just don't see ... how a world which makes such wonderful things could be bad.' Her collection, then, is the reserve on which she bases her speculation 'Betcha on land / They understand / Bet they don't reprimand their daughters.' Ariel equates this wager with wages, and the free market with freedom from parental authority. She plans to escape from the repressive patriarchy of her own family into the holy family of capitalism: 'Bright young women / Sick o' swimmin' / Ready to stand.' What is important here is not the rather glib assertion that being allowed to buy lipstick is a feminist issue but that there could be no enlightenment and no democracy without the idea of exchange value. Ariel's song conflates taking a stand against patriarchy with being part of the democratic West (the human world) and the Thatcher/Reaganite mentality of standing on one's own two feet. Starting with Ariel, Disney attempts to lay claim to the heritage of the enlightenment, what Derrida calls in *Specters of Marx* 'the state of the debt',[4] in which the Disney text represents the possibility of emancipation: 'And ready to know what the people know / Ask 'em my questions / And get some answers.' Disney's enlightenment ('What's a fire and why does it / (What's the word?) burn?') after 'the fall of the Berlin Wall', attempts to ensure 'the end of history' by turning the clock back and denying the marxist dialectic as an evolutionary phase in the history of the West.[5]

Like Lévi-Strauss and Freud before him, Disney associates technologies of fire with higher degrees of civilisation; one could also think of the monkey King Louie's attempt to 'become a man' by learning 'the secret of man's red fire' from Mowgli in *The Jungle Book*.[6] The human world is not only a more efficient system of capital than the mer world but is also culturally superior because Ariel believes it respects human freedoms. But this is a mer-made fantasy since the human world does indeed respect human freedoms but not mer(e) freedom: they are after all fish-eaters. When Ariel becomes human we assume that she eats fish on a fry-day; at one point in Eric's palace she in fact sits down to a meal which consists of her chaperone Sebastian the crab.[7] Ariel's new consumption is related to both the West's incorporation and ingestion of the East and to its previous vomiting and expulsion of that term. The category 'the West' presupposes its opposite 'the East', which is constructed not as a historical and cultural part of Europe (the mirror image of an inverted dialectic) but as the Evil Empire which threatens the stability of Europe's borders. The later appropriation of East by West at one and the same time erases that history of division and airbrushes out communism from the history of the West. Disney's designs on Europe not only involve a pervasive presence in its developing market but also a rewriting of its narrative with a feelgood, happy ending of history in which the Disney text is the prophylactic which seals up all in rest.

There is a reprise of Ariel's song after she has saved Eric from drowning in which she repeats her speculation by singing over the unconscious body of the prince 'What would

I give to live where you are? / What would I pay to stay here beside you?' In this film, as in the capitalist system, everything begins with debt. There is the debt to Hans Christian Andersen and so to Europe as such; there is also the debt to the bodily non-presence of Walt Disney and so to America as such. Just as Disney's incursion into Europe with EuroDisney as a loss-leader is predicated on debt, so too the West's incorporation of the Soviet bloc is also based on debt, paid for by loans and unification bonds issued by the *Bundesbank*. Such bonds offer a simulacrum of security to mask the exercise of venture capital and as such are nothing less than counterfeit money. Similarly, the entire idea of 'Disney's *The Little Mermaid*' is a form of counterfeit money which profits from the double deception that Disney is the origin of this story and that the Disney text bears a relation to 'classic' children's literature. The narrative itself as a simulacrum of a certain history of the collapse of communist regimes in Europe is also counterfeit money which issues itself as a false and misleading value. The New Disney which trades on its founder's name and imitates his sense of value and worth is similarly counterfeit. However, the debt of Disney to Disney, like Ariel's own debt, is a floating debt. Floating debt occurs when the state continues to print bills to cover debts without having treasury reserves to cover the value of the notes in circulation. *The Little Mermaid* as a film, and EuroDisney as a speculative enterprise, were issued at a time when the Disney corporation continued to peddle its goods based on a reputation which the previous 20 years of filmic production hardly merited. The financial, but by no means artistic disaster of *The Black Cauldron* nearly bankrupted the company in 1985. If *The Little Mermaid* is a film living on borrowed time and extended lines of credit then this is played out in the story of Ariel.

Estranged from her father after he destroys her collection of consumer items, Ariel is approached by two loan sharks (Flotsam and Jetsam, the queer-fish henchmen of Ursula the Sea Witch). Like trained tele-salesmen they tell Ariel, 'We represent someone who can help you ... make all your dreams come true.' Ursula is quick to explain the appropriative logic of Western capitalism to Ariel: 'The only way to get what you want is to become human yourself.' Unlike the flying fish in Valerio Adami's painting *Étude pour dessin d'après Glas* Ariel will not be allowed the quasi-transcendental role of being simultaneously in and out of the water, living in the duty-free space between the human and the mer worlds. She must choose between the Marxist social science which would permanently immerse her in the immanence of the social or the speculative discourse of Western philosophy that would pull her out of the water completely.[8] Ariel opts for the latter, preferring c.o.d. to her own liquid assets. Ursula makes debt the object of her own theatrical set-piece 'Poor Unfortunate Souls' (the first word of the title indicating the debt owed by the fishiness supposed by the last word). She tells Ariel that while in the past she may have merited the name 'Witch', she has now changed her ways and uses her magic to help the love-lorn and depressed. However, the small print comes in a later stanza when she sings, 'Now it's happened once or twice / Someone couldn't pay the price / And I'm afraid I had to rake them 'cross the coals.' The infrequency of such forfeited debts seems belied by the garden of souls at the mouth of Ursula's cavern. Rather than be alone, Ariel decides to take a loan from Ursula: 'have we got a deal?' the Sea Witch asks. Sure of her sea- and credit-worthiness Ursula presses Ariel to make a deposit at her sea bank: 'We haven't discussed the subject of payment ... I'm not asking much. Just a token, really, a trifle. What I want from you is ... your voice!' Like Cordelia, Ariel is told 'you can't get something for nothing' but, unlike Cordelia, by choosing not to speak she hopes to lay claim to a kingdom of her own denied to her by her father. Ursula's speculation on Ariel by contrast is precisely that which gets something for nothing because it profits by betting on the value of silence.

Offering the alternative of life with her father and sisters or with her 'man', Ursula tells Ariel to 'make your choice'. The melody itself owes a debt to Lionel Bart's 'Reviewing the Situation', Fagin's song in *Oliver* that is based on Yiddish dance rhythms. The figure of Ursula as an octopus also owes something to anti-Semitic cartoons of the usurious Jew whose tentacles ensnare the world economy. In early Cold War propaganda there is a direct relation between a supposed world Judaic conspiracy and communism. Ursula becomes a site for this history of representation, a representation which becomes obscured by her position as both the phallic mother and gay diva. However, here she takes the role of a lender of counterfeit money. Her contract with Ariel is based on a debt which can never be repaid. The odds are deliberately stacked against Ariel so that she will not be able to fulfil her obligations to Ursula, in order that the Sea Witch can then use the indebted Ariel as a bargaining chip in her ongoing struggle with King Triton. 'The deal' Ursula offers is that before sunset on the third day Eric must kiss Ariel with 'the kiss of true love'. If he does so, Ariel will remain human forever; if not she will turn back into a mermaid and 'belong' to Ursula. Without her voice, Ursula assumes that Ariel will not be able to make Eric fall in love with her. The deal is therefore funded by counterfeit money, a promise which offers a faked value in exchange for Ariel as her own liquid asset (liquid assets being the assets left over when all debts have been paid). After Ariel has paid her debt to Ursula, by losing her soul to her, she will then be of value to Ursula who can exchange her for Triton's throne.

Ariel as a human is also a form of counterfeit money, a fake put in circulation which passes unrecognised amongst the unsuspecting humans: from Ursula's fake value Ariel derives the value of being a fake. Ursula calls herself a 'busy woman' and her business presses Ariel into her consumer choice: 'It won't cost much / Just your voice!' This choice is also a choice for consummation, both in terms of her sexual desire for Eric and in terms of her death as a mermaid (the death of maidenhood here might amount to the same thing). In allegorical terms this wished-for death is also the desired death (or end) of history. A price will have to be paid for such totalization (the irremediable choice to become human and the cessation of historical development): Ursula sings in an apposite metaphor, 'If you want to cross a bridge, my sweet / You've got to pay the toll.' 'Toll' here equivocating between a lifetime of debt and the death Ariel desires; 'bridge' being the monument which both joins and separates two areas, mer and human, East and West. Ursula (an anagram of 'usur al' – everything is predicated on usury) offers Ariel a fate worse

than debt and urges her to 'sign the scroll'. The contract
which Ariel duly signs reads 'I hereby grant unto Ursula the
Witch of the Sea one voice in exchange for ...'; the rest is
obscured by seaweed. Ariel signs on the dotted line,
exchanging speech for writing, and forfeits the autonomy of
her signature by placing it as a mark of debt to Ursula.
Collapsing this founding speculative binary between the
sensible and the intelligible, Ariel's situation demonstrates the
ways in which all economy (the sensible) is based upon debt
(the intelligible).

By the end of the Cold War the Soviet economy had
collapsed as a result of the inefficient circulation of capital
and the poorly negotiated contest between command control
and market reforms. The subsequent history of the thawing of
the East is one in which the West sought to eliminate the
possibility of a return of the spectre of communism by
lending money to Eastern Europe to fund the development
of its nascent free market. Current turmoil in world markets
has shown these loans to have been offered without due
guarantees and with very little chance of their ever being paid
back. The settling of debts is of course not the point of
lending money; what is important is the interest gained on
repayments. However, the extent to which the market
economy in the new democracies of Eastern Europe is
predicated on debt is now proving to have severe repercussions for the global economy (which to all intents and
purposes means for the West). The fear in world markets is
that if the Russian economy were to collapse under the
pressure of unrepayable loans then this would result in a
general European recession and world economic crisis, based
on the realignment of interest rates and tightening of credit
facilities by banks and government treasuries affected by
Russian non-payment of debts. Faced with such spectacular
losses the banking system would be forced to call in debts
from other borrowers and to limit the amount of money it
was currently lending. Taking large quantities of capital out of
circulation in this way would inevitably lead to recession.
Therefore, in order to avoid such a scenario and to prevent a
return of communism in a bankrupt Russia, the West has
been compelled to make good Eastern debts regardless of

whether they can be repaid. Unlike Third World debt, Russian debts have been cancelled and/or even more money invested in a failing economy in which it is becoming increasingly difficult to tell the difference between commerce proper and organised crime. For this reason Baudrillard suggests that the East can be thought of has having won the Cold War, the West being compelled to pay limitless reparations to the East.[9] The economic crisis on the Eastern border of Europe, set free by the cancellation of the Cold War, demonstrates the question of debt which haunts the Western economy at its very centre. Like its metonym Disneyland, the entire Western economy is founded on debt. Ariel is merely the conductor of this message.

Derrida describes this situation succinctly in the essay 'To speculate – On Freud':

> Borrowing is the law ... without borrowing, nothing begins, there is no proper reserve [*fond propre*]. Everything begins with the transfer of funds, and there is interest in borrowing, it is even the primary interest. Borrowing gives you a return, it produces surplus value, it is the primary motor of all investment. One begins thus by speculating, betting on one value to produce as though from nothing. And all these metaphors confirm, as metaphors, the necessity of what they say.[10]

The restriction of economy, derived from the Greek words *oikos* meaning 'home' and *nomos* meaning 'law', depends upon a certain understanding of a logic of inside and outside which is regulated by fixed parameters of interpretation. What is foreign, unhomely, *unheimlich* is set outside of the economy which is regulated by statute, business laws and laws of commerce. Equally, to bring the outside into the sphere of the economic requires that foreignness to be made homely by its adherence to the law. If debt is the law then the foreigner, who by nature is uneconomic, can only enter into the economic when s/he puts themselves in debt. So Ariel becomes human by taking on the burden of debt and by dealing in counterfeit money; if a mermaid would be considered *unheimlich* by Eric then Ariel must be made homely by a transfer of funds and become human. The capitalist economy only ensures its own survival by placing each of its component parts in a relation of mutual dependence underwritten by reciprocal relations of debt. The fear of debt and the necessity of debt, as a prior condition of the economic, constitutes the law which polices the exchange of capital. The lenders are in turn also debtors to other lenders who are themselves debtors and so the simulacrum goes on *reductio ad absurdum* like a never-ending set of Russian dolls. Ariel borrows from Ursula, who in turn is determined to pay back King Triton, who in turn is indebted to Sebastian, who in turn 'owes' Ariel for saving him from Prince Eric's dinner table. Debt is the primary interest of this story: it determines all the relations in the film just as it produces the film and determines all that the film produces. Disney make a substantial return in Europe by borrowing from Europe (Hans Christian Andersen) just as the Eastern economies continue to 'profit' by their inability to pay back their debt to the West. The specular and speculative relations are inverted as the debtor profits from the lender's loss and the surplus value that borrowing brings becomes a value of surplus in which nothing succeeds like failure. Disney's counterfeit mermaid (which has little cultural capital in Europe) and Russian free-market incompetence are the foundations of a double investment, cultural and financial, by America in Europe. The offshore account of *The Little Mermaid* returns to the Disney Corporation (which takes its investments and the profits very seriously) the terms of its own economic and cultural imperialism and puts them in operation against that system by staging an all-singing, all-dancing rendition of the simulacrum of capitalism.

Ursula ensures the value of her investment by intervening in the libidinal economy between Ariel and Eric. Using Ariel's voice she hypnotises Eric into believing that she, disguised as the vampish Vanessa, rescued him from the shipwreck and so he should repay his debt by marrying her before the sunset of Ariel's third day on land – Eric's debt to Vanessa being a transfer of funds from two separate accounts, Eric's debt to Ariel and Ariel's debt to Ursula, tossed between currents and currency. All seems lost when the fateful sunset duly arrives and Ariel remains unkissed. Ariel belongs to Ursula and only her liquid assets remain to be speculated with against Triton's interest in his daughter. In Andersen's story the prince does in fact marry someone else (someone made more attractive by speech) and his little mermaid dies, reduced to a ball of foam dispersed by the waves.[11] Disney's mermaid seems to be in equal peril but rather than issue Andersen's salutary rebuke to young women tempted to leave home, the story of Ariel reassures us that if you get in over your head with your credit card, Daddy will be there to bail you out. The wanton punning which this film encourages is not merely the stylistic excess of two critics unwilling to recognise their own debt to a certain type of deconstruction, rather, to use Derrida's words 'all these metaphors confirm, as metaphors, the necessity of what they say' – the meaning of any pun confirming the debt of one word to another.

Triton arrives on the scene to find the stakes high and that Ursula has him by a hook. He is told by Ursula, 'She's mine now, we made a deal.' When Ursula produces the contract Triton attempts to destroy it with his magic gold trident, which along with his crown is the 'symbolic investiture' of all his power.[12] However, business law overrides national sovereignty and the gold standard no longer holds. Triton cannot break the bond; 'You see, the contract's legally binding and completely unbreakable, even for you.' By Ursula's final phrase here it is suggested that Triton has a history of bad debts; this exchange calls both Triton's credit and credibility into question. We know from an aside offered by Ursula at the start of the film that she once 'lived in the palace' and in contrast to Triton's 'celebrations' of paternity which open the story, Ursula 'had fantastical feasts' before she was 'banished and exiled'. The film is incapable of explaining this history of struggle between Triton and Ursula while its asks us to understand this contest as the premiss of its plot. It might be surmised from Ursula's later comments that Triton's rise to power and the accompanying ascendancy of the merpeople as the hegemonic group 'under the sea' was the result of some contractual duplicity or of a bargain reneged upon. This fishy past is sneaked into the story as a form of contraband, both in disguise and duty-free (it avoids

Triton having to pay the debt that must automatically be incurred with the assumption of the proper name of King). The love story of Ariel and Eric which has occupied the filmic narrative turns out to be only a subplot of the wider drama between Triton and Ursula. Ariel is now contractually obligated to Ursula, the result of and the motivation for the last 90 minutes of the film. Ursula tells Triton, 'The daughter of the great sea king is a very precious commodity. But I might be willing to make an exchange for someone even better.' The question of who is to pay now comes sharply into focus as Triton is faced with the stark choice of his daughter or his kingship. Like all such simulacra of choice this is a no-win situation in which each alternative involves paying the same price: either he retains his power and so loses his daughter, or takes Ariel's place in Ursula's garden of souls and is therefore permanently separated from the freed Ariel. Daddy has to pay. He picks up Ariel's bill and signs a contract (using his trident as a pen) which exchanges himself for Ariel by changing him into a sea-anemone in Ursula's dungeon. The price paid by the King of the Sea is his soul.

The price of the destabilisation of the benevolent paternalist ruler is the return of the spectre of a past despotism. The fear of the arrival of such a spectre in the future has no doubt helped Triton to retain power for some time. The moral of this story is that if there is no one there to help Triton meet his crippling debts (even though they are all of his own making) then there will be a return of dictatorship. The mer world would seem to follow the economics of a finely balanced psyche in which failure to maintain levels of expenditure to stabilise the exchange between id and ego will result in a return of the repressed. The repressed erupts in the giant bloated form of Ursula as Sea Queen who in an attempt to kill Ariel and Eric puffs up to the size of the giant squid in Disney's live-action *20,000 Leagues Under the Sea*. She comes between Eric and Ariel, when the middle point of her newly assumed and tumescent crown rises phallically from the sea to separate the lovers. The *fausse-amie* who offered *fausse-monnaie* has now become the source of all power in the sea-world: 'I command all the ocean, the waves obey my every whim, the sea and all its spoils bow to my power.'

Counterfeit money is finally the open currency which controls the currents from bank to bank and coast to cost. This is not a subversion of order but a restoration of the proper order in which Ursula reclaims her rightful throne denied her by Triton's duplicity. However, the truth of this account of forgery, and of forgery as the true form of accounting, is too monstrous to look at. Like the Real, it must be covered up. The cover-up is the conspiracy of illusion which legitimates Triton's rule as a bulwark against the illusion of Ursula's alleged conspiracy. Fortunately Eric is on hand to save the day, to cover up Ursula's naked power. The seaman impales her on the prow of a ship and with her death frees all the indebted souls from their bonds. There will be more to say about this Ur-text of Disney's representation of gender, but for the moment we will content ourselves by noting that the death of Ursula allows the freed Triton to reimpose an improper order by returning to his capital and offering Ariel to Eric in the symbolic exchange of marriage. He learns to accept the human way ('the spineless, savage' way) by compromising with the very interests which would consume him and his entire kingdom, when he grants Ariel's wish and exchanges her fins for legs. He no longer reprimands his daughter and so doubles his authority as an exchequer by which he both rules the mer-world and sets himself up as the regulatory value of its eco(nomy)-system: the gold fish. He pays his debt to Eric by offering him Ariel. However, the debt is paid by the counterfeit of a mermaid in human form and so Triton's rule (which depends on the illusion of his freedom from debt) remains as compromised as it was when Ursula acted as the fish supplement which both regulated the economy of his rule and interrupted that rule as an economy on the truth.

The Little Mermaid as a project seeks to make speculative gain in Europe; as a film it draws together all the discourses and concepts implied by such a hostile take-over and returns them against the system which puts them in play. The endless readability of this film (and we will return to it later) demonstrates the ways in which the Disney text carries within itself a radical ambivalence to the Disney narrative. In this film the simulacrum of European speculation (both philosophical and financial) is replayed as a speculation on the simulacrum which has installed itself, like a cuckoo in the nest, outside Paris. The rule of the Magic Kingdom is based upon the rule of debt and the position of EuroDisney as a supplement to the conurbation of Paris (the most 'European' sight on this most European of sites) reminds us of the fictions of capital which run to the very heart of Europe. However, this cuckoo may prove to be a bird of prey as well as the legitimate heir to the question of Europe.

Intermission

> The history of secrecy, the combined history of responsi-
> bility and of the gift, has the spiral form of these turns
> [*tours*], intricacies [*tournures*], versions, turning back, bends
> [*virages*], and conversions. One could compare it to a
> history of revolutions, even to history as revolution.
>
> Jacques Derrida, *The Gift of Death*[1]

If *The Little Mermaid* was intended to whet our appetites for
EuroDisney then *Beauty and The Beast* (1991) roars its
approval for the opening of the theme park. These films are
separated by the 1990 full-length animation *The Rescuers
Down Under*. We shall not deal at length with this film here on
the grounds that it seems to be the residual trace of a past
mode of thinking for Disney. It is a somewhat shabby attempt
to profit from the reputation of the 1977 Disney classic *The
Rescuers*. Every Disney film sooner or later becomes a 'Disney
classic', as if the force of the adjective compelled the epithet
of the noun. The term 'Disney classic' implies the weak
reading of itself (in which a particular film compared to others
in the *oeuvre* is a classic) but operates through an insistence on
the strong reading (in which the term is a double-barrelled
noun bestowing an honorific status on the film). The word
'classic' becomes part of the proper name of Disney and
implies not a restrictive qualification but a mark of excellence.
Just as the salient feature of The Mighty Joe Young is that he
is mighty, of the Great Mouse Detective that he is great, so
the defining characteristic of a Disney film is that it is a
classic. The classicism or otherwise of the film does not
depend on its cinematic qualities but on the fact that it is
inscribed in the Disney corpus *per se*.[2] However, we might
suggest that *The Rescuers Down Under* is more classic Disney
than Disney classic.

Like most sequels of this kind, which return to their source material several decades later in a grim attempt to recreate the success of the original for a failing film studio, *The Rescuers Down Under* cannot be saved. The film does not work because the eponymous heroes Bernard and Bianca are relics of the Cold War, their version of International Rescue having been the animated equivalent of other quasi-governmental organisations such as *Thunderbirds, The Man From U.N.C.L.E.* and James Bond. As the British security services are discovering in Northern Ireland, there is no proper place for structural espionage in a Europe no longer divided between competing forms of institutional secrecy. Phone-taps on road protesters seems little reward for the public money paid to retain MI5's overview of Millbank, particularly in a cultural space which now expects security to be as accountable as any other service industry. The film was in production before the end of the Cold War but attempts to place its secret agents in the caring new world of 1990s Australia (they are given the task of saving a golden eagle from an avaricious hunter). While Australia is finally given recognition as a dedicated out-reach of the Disney Empire there is no place for this film in the New Disney corpus which begins to develop after *The Little Mermaid*. The unexpected success of *The Little Mermaid* pointed towards a different way of 'doing Disney', one which did not rely on sloppy sequels gesturing towards Disney's past achievements as a valorisation of its present, but one which was caught up in the present political space emerging from a changing Europe. Such an argument might seem to repeat Disney's own mythology of 'the modern classics' in which this film has been erased from memory. It could be argued that *The Rescuers Down Under* is the hinge which connects New Disney to Old. This may be true but as a point of departure for analysis it fails to engage with the determinate political and social effects of a revitalised Disney corporation within the flux of a post-Soviet Europe.

Bernard and Bianca as cold war 'spooks' are spectres at the feast of this new Europe and the film dies a death because it appeals to its Disney heritage rather than its inheritance. Rendering the security services (account)able in narrative shows the diminishing returns available from pushing the secret world of MI5 further into the social fabric in order to find a use for its institutional apparatus, while at the same time suggests the ways in which the political space it attempts to account for is already structured by the question of the secret. Ariel and Eric, or Belle and the Beast, are more effective agents of secrecy than Bianca and Bernard whose understanding of the secret presupposes that a secret is in principle discoverable. This is why they belong to an organisation dedicated to their discovery. The entire conceit of this film, in which an alternative mouse world runs in miniature parallel to the human (messages are passed by mice from continent to continent using abandoned military technology left over from American entanglements all over the globe), presupposes the possible revelation of this world, as a secret, to the audience. As such the film presents the familiar mode of secrecy which at one and the same time justifies the existence of the security services and validates a hermeneutics of reading. However, a secret, if it is to remain a secret, is that which is absolutely unknowable. A secret presents itself but does not disclose itself.[3] Accordingly a 'true secret' does not involve any form of concealment but is that which is present and cryptic, remaining so as 'the unpresentable'. Therefore, secrecy (*le secret*) is that which is left in and of a text after revelation has taken place. In this way secrecy is linked to the political and to the question of responsibility.

Responsibility – let us deal with it here before pursuing Disney any further – presents a paradox. Following Bernard and Bianca's understanding of revelation it would be common sense to say that a responsible decision towards Disney can only be made on the basis of knowledge – only if we understand all that there is to know about Disney can we act responsibly towards it. However, this would be to limit the conditions of possibility of responsibility by suggesting that a decision can only be reached under certain circumstances with a determinate amount of knowledge. As such this would not be a decision but a programmed deployment of knowledge which presupposed that when we knew enough we could arrest thinking and make an 'informed choice' about Disney. The urgency demanded by the political requires us to do just that and so to act irresponsibly with regard to the formulation of our responsibility, which as a moment of decision must remain undecidable and thus unknowable and secret. As a secret, responsibility cannot respond and so fails to act responsibly. One can never be responsible enough with respect to Disney because in the process of formulating that responsibility one always fails to accede to the concept of responsibility.[4] If a reading of Disney films seems an irresponsible way of conducting a political analysis then this irresponsibility is related to the responsibility demanded of us by the political. Similarly, if we seem unduly responsible in our attitude towards the Disney text it is because we always fail to be responsible enough.[5]

Everyone in the new Disney canon has responsibilities and secrets (Ariel's collection, the Beast's past, Aladdin in disguise as Prince Ali, Simba's true identity, Pocahontas's dream, Quasimodo's help for Esmerelda, Hercules' godhood, Mulan's cross-dressing). These are secrets which each of the films reveals but what remains absolutely secret in every film is that text's irresponsibility to the Disney narrative. As a fiction each text remains irresponsible because it belongs to a space in which there is no absolute injunction to respond. The filmic text does not have to explain itself or answer for itself before the other regardless of the ideological motivation of its producers. As a speech act in the public domain the film says what it says, no more, no less, and so presents itself without revealing itself. There is something secret in each of these films but that something does not conceal itself, it *is* the film. The very superficiality (we should read this word both ways) of the Disney film means that it is irreducible to any hermeneutic endeavour or to any attempt to programme meaning by the authors of that text. Accordingly, it is the secrecy and absolute irresponsibility of these texts, as fictions, which enables them to re-immerse all the meanings which surround them back into the virtuality from whence they came and so to be read in a responsible way.

The secret world of Bernard and Bianca is indicative of Disney's own appreciation of itself during what is now euphemistically referred to in the company's publicity as 'the magic years'. The quality, detail and ambition of the Disney film seems to have diminished in direct proportion to its characters, demonstrated in Disney's lengthy fascination with the small world of mice in *The Rescuers*, *Cinderella*, and *The Adventures of the Great Mouse Detective*. Compared to the intricacy of *Pinocchio* or the grandeur of *The Lion King* these are 'Mickey Mouse' films. It is as if Disney saw itself as a diminutive companion to the classics of children's literature just as Basil of Baker Street is to Sherlock Holmes. With its new corpus of films Disney now imagines itself to be on a par with such literature and of equal cultural significance: the film is assuredly 'Disney's *The Little Mermaid*', not Hans Christian Andersen's. In new Disney even the first name 'Walt' has been dropped when naming its appropriations which extend the Disney dominion beyond Australia.

The generally sluggish and sexist nature of the *The Rescuers Down Under* (Miss Bianca looks like a relic of 1950s femininity compared to Ariel as an 1980s Action Woman) means that Disney publicity is now keen to leave the film in the outback where it rightly belongs. Such a sequel would now go straight to video. Disney have learned that it is a mistake to test the credulity of your audience by basing a sequel on a film which should have been flushed away first time round (clockwise or anti-clockwise).

2

Socialisme ou barbarie: **Welcoming Disney**

People have not the slightest idea of this, they have no need to know that they are paying (automatic withdrawal) nor whom they are paying ... when they do anything whatsoever, make war or love, speculate on the energy crisis, construct socialism, write novels, open concentration camps for poets or homosexuals, buy bread or hijack a plane, have themselves elected by secret ballot, bury their own, criticize the media without rhyme or reason, say absolutely anything about chador or the ayatollah, dream of a great safari, found reviews, teach, or piss against a tree.

Jacques Derrida, *The Post Card*, p. 100

'The intellectual and maybe even the communist, when they bring their children to EuroDisney, will have a good time.'

Michael Eisner[1]

The Legs of Freud

The Little Mermaid and *Beauty and the Beast* are joined by a pair of legs: Ariel's and the Beast's. In the 'Envois' section of *The Post Card* Derrida suggests that one day he will write a book called *The Legs of Freud*, but given the fictional context of 'Envois' we suspect that this is a book which will never be written. The title refers to a passage in *Civilisation and Its Discontents* in which Freud describes the '"cheap enjoyment" extolled in the anecdote – the enjoyment obtained by putting a bare leg from under the bedclothes on a cold winter night and drawing it in again'.[2] Disney itself is no 'cheap thrill'; it comes at a very high price but Freud's description is suggestive of an economy of enjoyment which might be worth pursuing with respect to these Disney films. The act of narrative itself ('the anecdote') is of this order of cheap enjoyment, cheap either because the price to be paid is minimal or because the value gained far outweighs the price paid. Disney's retelling of European folklore is cheap because it comes second-hand and without copyright. This economising on narrative also yields a considerable dividend for Disney because *The Little Mermaid* and *Beauty and the Beast* are the first salvos in the New Disney can(n)on which rescued the studio from artistic and financial mediocrity.

The economy of the cheap thrill Freud outlines here is invoked with specific reference to advancements of technology which bring benefits and increased pleasure but also involve an equal and opposite decrease in enjoyment:

> If there had been no railway to conquer distances, my child would never have left his native town and I should need no telephone to hear his voice ... What is the use of reducing infantile mortality when it is precisely that reduction which imposes the greatest restraint on us in the begetting of children, so that, taken all round, we nevertheless rear no more children than in the days before the reign of hygiene, while at the same time we have created difficult conditions for our sexual life in marriage, and have probably worked against the beneficial effects of natural selection? (*CD*, p. 89)

Why should humanity crawl out of the ocean onto the land if it only takes daughters away from their fathers and families? What good are the knives and forks Ariel collects from the humans if they only place limits on Triton's capacity to rear children? What is the value of modern technology's ability to compress the experience of time and space if the only testament to this 'small world' is the eponymous Disney ride outside Paris? What is the use of penicillin if it only means Freud has to tie a knot in it? The sight of Ariel's legs is the cheap thrill which offers comfort as the effect of the losses for which it stands.

Commenting on this passage Avital Ronell suggests that the extension of Freud's leg from under the cover is an attempt 'to test the threshold of exteriority'.[3] Ronell proposes that the pleasure is cheap because 'its discovery takes place in negativity, being reactively dependent upon a cold winter's night to know itself' (p. 90). The cheap thrill covers the cost of the realisation that the leg can be frozen and snapped off and so pays the price of 'anxiety's epistemological retreat ... in blindness from the memory of the castration complex' (p. 90). Similarly, the cheap thrill of Ariel's legs (which emerge suggestively from the water when she is first transformed into a human), together with the loss of her voice, mark her own castration. Entering into the human world she is symbolically castrated, no longer a princess but merely a possible love object for a prince. Only sharp camerawork and a modesty-saving sail spares us a glimpse of the other mark of the humanity which must accompany Ariel's legs (the 'nothing' she paid such a price for). This is a double absence since (we assume) that as a cartoon and not a live actor the animators never drew in the first place the female genitalia which they tease the spectator with.

However, to push Ronell's argument a little, but only a little, if the telephone extension is an inadequate substitute for the child which leaves home and the leg which Freud extends should never have left the cover, then Ariel's legs as a prosthetic mark of her humanity also identify her castrated position within the human order. Triton, like Freud (they share similar facial hair at least), is concerned with the irresoluble loss of a child. It is Triton who finally transforms Ariel into a human as a way of covering the cost of the *détente* between human and mer worlds. This second incarnation for Ariel is accompanied by a shimmering blue dress which also covers the cost of her own entrance into the human principality for which she will breed heirs. The problem for both Ariel and Triton is that, as Avital Ronell notes, 'technical advances multiply needs, hence their self-engendering character (the telephone to make up for the transfer of pain conducted through the railroad, etc.)' (p. 92). If Disney has made technical advances in animation with *The Little Mermaid* and made an advance on Europe through the technology of EuroDisney then it will also have multiplied its own needs. If the cause of capitalism was technically advanced by the collapse of communism then this was paid for by the creation of a new set of satellite states dependent on European credit. The happiness of the Disney corporation's shareholders being mortgaged to the fate of the new Europe requires that these new needs be identified and responded to in the next film, *Beauty and The Beast.*

Cosmopolitics

> There's a stake in your fat black heart
> And the villagers never liked you.
> They are dancing and stamping on you.
> They always *knew* it was you.
> Daddy, daddy, you bastard, I'm through.
>   Sylvia Plath, 'Daddy'

If *The Little Mermaid* is, roughly speaking, a film 'about' an economy of debt then *Beauty and the Beast* is a film 'about' an economy of hospitality and hospitality as an economy. Like Ariel, the Beast is estranged from the human world by his lack of legs; while Ariel has fins, the Beast crawls on all fours. The narrative follows the logic of Oedipus rather than Orwell in which four legs is considered a less advanced evolutionary stage (four legs bad, two legs good). By allowing Belle into his castle the Beast hopes that by reciprocating 'true love' she will prove to be the girl who breaks the Enchantress's spell placed upon him. Placing the question of what might constitute and ensure the rigorous purity of 'true love' to one side for a moment (but never forgetting that such metaphysical problems lie at the centre of the questions we are asking about Disney here), it may be productive to open ourselves onto the question of hospitality as it is encoded in this film.

One of the needs which are multiplied by the cheap thrill of 'the fall of the Berlin Wall' is the urgency of openness that resulted from the disintegration of the hermetically sealed borders of Eastern Europe. In part, the decline of the former Stalinist–Breshnevist dictatorships was a result of their inability to 'encondomize' their regimes from western penetration and from internal traditions of dissent.[4] However, having breached the prophylactic East the West is faced with the overspill of all that was held in check by communist repression: from economic migrants to ethnic conflicts. The fall of the Berlin Wall (and when using this slogan let us not forget all that it implies politically, ethically, economically and philosophically for a whole European and non-European history which dates long before the twentieth century) may have been an effect of globalisation but it is also an event which accelerated the effects of globalisation within the continent of Europe. The disputation in the West over the definition of itself, as exemplified by EuroDisney as a site of cultural and epistemological contest, is entirely related to this question of globalisation. As a term 'globalisation' is a cover for a number of political strategies and appropriations made in the name of a non-conceptual order, specifically 'the market' and its close allies 'liberal economics' and 'liberal democracy'. However, such appropriations screen out the event of globalisation, which has a long history and is at least as old as the nation-state itself. One might think of internationalism, cosmopolitanism and imperialism as modes of globalisation and these questions are as old as Europe itself.

If we are using the term 'globalisation' here, it is with due caution, given the way in which it is commonly employed as a synonym for the operation of the market. However, since the opening of the borders of Eastern Europe the issue of globalisation has taken on a certain urgency because the experience of this new Europe is an event which goes beyond the simple notion that the erasure of national boundaries is only made possible by the deregulation of capital and the concentration of extra-territorial telecommunications. Rather, events in Eastern Europe are a dramatic example of the ways in which the borders of the nation-state and the concepts of the border, state, authority, citizenship, immigration and democracy which attends them are undergoing a radical displacement. Globalisation is the space in which this violent deconstruction is taking place and is the name given to this deconstruction as a situation. Of course, the question of capital runs through this space like a red thread but the relation is not one of uncomplicated cause and effect. The principal problem which a company like Disney faces, and which is played out in these films, is that while 'the globalisation of capital' is on the one hand responsible for the consolidation of the traditional conceptual order of politics, democracy and the powers of the nation-state (and in so far as these concepts offer a definition of the category of the West or Europe this globalisation is an extension of Eurocentricism), on the other hand it also undermines that conceptual order. It is because of 'the globalisation of capital' that the deconstruction of the order around which capital is classically organised (the state, the nation, politics, democracy) is possible. Capitalism produces unintended effects that we might characterise as 'deconstructive' and which are returned against the traditional structures of politics which puts them in play.[5] The task for a company like Disney is to rein in these challenging effects so as to prevent the complete subversion of the political order upon which it depends for its share dividend. *Beauty and the Beast* as a paradigm of the multiplying needs of capitalism inscribes Disney within this deconstruction of Europe as a nominal effect of a classical conceptual order. This deconstruction is not confined to this book, or to the work of Jacques Derrida and others marked by the term 'deconstruction', but is what is more or less visible in the world today; Disney is just one of the minimal indices which make this event of deconstruction readable.

The Beast's castle, like the Magic Kingdom of EuroDisney, sits in the French countryside as a state within a state. This is a state of alterity: the very term 'magic kingdom' supposes the possibility of a delimited set of boundaries supervised by the exercise of state authority, as well as the fictional, illusionary and permeable (magical) nature of those boundaries. EuroDisney positions itself within Europe as a consumerist anti-capital to the spiritual capital Vatican City (also a state within a state). Both the Pope and Mickey Mouse urge the decondomising of Europe but Mickey's French letters have a potency which enables Disney to negotiate its way through the redefinition of Europe which this Polish pontiff may have helped initiate but has had difficulty keeping up with. Euro-Disney would like to present itself as a place of unconditional hospitality which welcomes visitors from all over the world, and offers them the cheap thrill of the *Star Wars* simulator regardless of age, race, gender, sexuality or creed – as long as they have the price of admission. Its unconditional hospitality, the 'Have a nice day' customer care which seems so out of sorts with Gallic manners, is offered by a workforce comprised of citizens of every European state. This is to ensure that no visitor is lost in translation, but is suggestive of the tower of Babel rather than the Holy Sea. Disney's hospitality comes at a price (220F for adults, 170F for children, per day) and can hardly be described as unconditional. The form of this hospitality is indebted to the North American model of consumerism and its delivery is dependent on a standard rate (in this sense, at least, it is democratic). Disney hospitality is only on offer to those who are prepared to pay the price of Disneyfication (which for King Triton was his soul) and to collaborate with the experience of the Magic Kingdom. Being accepted by Disney involves accepting Disney and all that it stands for: the French have been trying hard to resist; the Chinese are proving more willing partners.

If the Beast's castle is read as a substitution for EuroDisney (an enchanted space in the French countryside, inhabited by a cosmopolitan cast of animated figures, opening its doors in 1991) then the hospitality it offers is as limited as Disney's own. While the butler Lumière (one of the few 'French' voices in the castle) is happy to welcome Belle's father Maurice when he loses his way, the head steward Cogsworth (an English jobsworth) suggests that if they just 'keep quiet maybe he'll go away'. This is part of the comic tension between two minor characters indicative of these later Disney films (played out here as a contest between the French idealist and English empiricist traditions of thought) but Cogsworth's reticence is based on his knowledge of the Beast who, when he finds Maurice in the castle, imprisons him for trespassing, telling him categorically, 'You're not welcome here.' Cogsworth chastises Lumière's naïvety but the butler explains that 'I was trying to be hospitable.' For Lumière (his name implies both enlightenment and a cinematic self-referentiality) hospitality is an unconditional injunction: he has to welcome the Other because his relationship to the Other is already open even before he makes a decision about it.[6] As a butler it is his task to be hospitable to the Other unconditionally, opening the house to the Other whoever he or she is, without a name or a context. However, even Lumière's hospitality is founded on debt. As a servant he offers limitless hospitality to reflect the generosity of his master and bolster his master's reputation as a host: even the hot-dog sellers at EuroDisney are paid to offer hospitality. Lumière's gift of hospitality cannot approach the necessary conditions of a gift relation because he is rewarded for it in turn, even if Cogsworth upbraids him for it here.[7]

Samuel Weber reminds us that the German word, as used by Freud, for debt (*Schuld*) is the same as the German word for 'guilt' and that assuming a debt is also in an important sense also an acceptance of guilt.[8] In so far as we remain unaware of our debts we are also unaware of our guilt and vice versa. The Beast by contrast is reminded of his guilt by its daily embodiment in his unnatural form. The film opens with a sequence of still drawings voiced over by a narrator who tells the story of how a scornful young prince refused hospitality to an old crone, only to discover that she was a beautiful Enchantress who subsequently turned him into a Beast because he put a price on hospitality (only the beautiful people were welcome at his palace). The Prince is 'doomed to remain a beast for all time' unless by his twenty-first birthday he discovers the meaning of true love. He does indeed come of age by clearing his debts when Belle pays his bill; however, it is questionable whether the true love accounted for here is equivalent to unconditional hospitality. Like the Beast himself, unconditional hospitality is a frightening thing because allowing the Other to enter your space without conditions means that the Other is free to transform, undermine and destroy everything in that space. This is what the Enchantress does when the young Prince offers her hospitality too late: the Prince is then marked forever by the monstrosity of unconditional hospitality. Consequently, the Beast refuses hospitality to others, knowing the undesirable effects which openness to the Other can bring. The repartee between Lumière and Cogsworth represents the necessary conditioning of unconditionality, the need to negotiate and manage hospitality between the unconditional injunction and the necessary condition. The castle is doomed to remain frozen in this aporia until the intervention of Belle.

Belle herself has been an unwelcome immigrant to provincial France. The opening song tells us that for Belle even though 'Ev'ry morning [is] just the same / Since the morning that we came / To this poor provincial town' she is variously described by the townsfolk as 'strange', 'odd', 'peculiar' and 'different'. They opine in chorus 'It's a pity and a sin / She doesn't quite fit in / 'Cause she really is a funny girl ... That Belle.' Belle's difference is marked by her love of reading (not the texts of the Enlightenment but folklore and fairy tales) and by the eccentricity of her father the inventor ('My father is a genius'). Being ignorant provincial peasants the townsfolk are suspicious of these idiosyncrasies, preferring their own cultural pursuits, such as hunting, drinking and brass bands, to the advances of technology. Consequently, the film sets up a divide between the Americanised Belle who offers France a technologised entertainment complex and narrow-minded French culturalists who are blinded by their own prejudice to the benefits on offer. For Disney there can only be one winner in this contest and when eventually the townsfolk storm the enchanted castle they are soundly beaten, while Belle, the willing French collaborator, is fully assimilated into the Disney order and becomes mistress of the castle. The villagers attack the castle in Frankenstein formation with pitchforks and torches, singing, 'We don't like what we don't understand / In fact it scares us.' This image of provincial ignorance marching against progress is crossed with that of French revolutionaries: 'Raise the flag, sing the song / Here we come, we're fifty strong / And fifty Frenchmen can't be wrong.' Gaston, the mob leader, even uses the revolutionary slogan 'If you're not for us, you're against us.' In Disney's view those bolshy French intellectuals who criticise EuroDisney are more than just humourless *misérables* but rather like ignorant peasants defending a backward culture. Why advocate the Enlightenment when you can have cable television showing animated folklore?

Initially Belle is also an unwelcome guest in the castle. She rescues her father by taking his place in the Beast's dungeon (as with Triton the exchange of woman which resolves this film is as a payment of the father's debt). The Beast instantly recognises that Belle may be the girl who will fall in love with him and release his household from the Enchantress's spell. The conditional hospitality that he then shows Belle (she can never leave and can go anywhere in the castle except the west wing) throws into relief the question of hospitality as an economy. The Beast's hospitality towards Belle is a gesture of appropriation and misappropriation (he holds her prisoner with the avowed aim of using her to break the spell). In this way it is related to the question of economy in the narrow sense of exchange value (Belle for Maurice), capital (Belle is a more valuable prisoner), speculation (she may be the one to break the spell) and financial return (the Beast will return to being a Prince). It is also related to economy in the wider sense of propriety and the proper (the Prince will reclaim authority over the townsfolk and rebuild the castle). The question of hospitality here does not remain outside of the problem of what is proper to whom and the Beast-Prince's negotiation of hospitality is regulated by the principle that each person within the economy of hospitality (from Lumière to Belle) must recognise what is proper to them: the servants serve, Belle takes care of the Beast, and the peasants are excluded from the castle altogether. The same is true of the hospitality offered by EuroDisney: the profit gained by your visit is not of the same order as the one Disney makes by it.

However, hospitality is the name under which we arrange all our relations to the Other. The problem for the Beast (for Disney and for the West) is that any relation to the Other is open even before there is time to make a decision about it. Hospitality must be negotiated at every instant and the decision of hospitality (the rules for the management of the terror that unconditional hospitality can bring) must be constantly reviewed and reinvented with all the risks that this implies. Lumière takes a risk when he invites Maurice inside; this invitation eventually leads to the displacement of everything within the castle, including the way the master rules the house. He also takes a risk when he arranges dinner for Belle against his master's wishes. It is at this point of potential double jeopardy that Lumière provides the film with its thematic 'centre', his song 'Be Our Guest'. The routine which follows resembles the numbers in *The Little Mermaid* in which the Disney studio is only beginning to get to grips with the possibilities of computer animation. If songs in the *The Little Mermaid* were animated Busby Berkeley numbers then this song borrows from French cultural ambassadors such as the Folies Bergère and the Moulin Rouge. Like 'Under the Sea' or 'Kiss the Girl' there is nothing specifically 'computerised' about this song, there is nothing in it which could only be done by a computer and in which the possibilities of computer animation would dictate the nature of the cartoon (as is the case with the attack of the Hun army in *Mulan* or the Hydra in *Hercules*). Instead there is only the sense that it was less expensive to animate the song by computer than by human artists. Perhaps, this nascent teletechnology is suggestive of how Late Capitalism was only beginning to become aware of the ways in which its changing conditions would affect the conceptual possibilities of globalisation.

If the relationship with the Other is always open and it is necessary to remain in a permanent state of preparation for the arrival of the Other who will disrupt those preparations then there can never be closure to the question of hospitality. Lumière and his staff are always ready for the arrival of a stranger. One can imagine that the routine (both song and service) has been well rehearsed: 'We invite you to relax, let us pull up a chair as the dining room proudly presents – your dinner!' With Lumière as Maurice Chevalier the song runs through a range of national stereotypes and culturally received images of France – 'soup du jour' and 'hot hors d'oeuvres' to dishes which form the Eiffel Tower.[9] France is especially marked as a place of hospitality; 'After all, Miss, this is France / And a dinner here is never second best', and so EuroDisney as the most hospitable part of France becomes the hospitality capital of France, the chorus declaiming 'Be our guest / *Oui*, our guest / Be our guest'. Despite the 'culinary cabaret' and the dancing candlesticks the hospitality espoused by the lyrics is compromised by the constant reminders of the debts involved in offering this hospitality. Lumière calls attention to his status as a paid employee ('We only live to serve') before the tempo of the routine slows to Lumière speaking over tremulous strings with Cogsworth standing self-consciously in a spotlight offering actions to accompany Lumière's words:

> Life is so unnerving
> For a servant who's not serving
> He's not whole without a soul to wait upon.
> Ah, those good old days when we were useful
> Suddenly those good old days are gone.

This revelation stands out not only because it is presented *sotto voce* in contrast to the rest of the raucous number but also because it connects the castle's limited hospitality to economy by showing that what Lumière and his staff offer is a form of 'Hospitality Ltd' in which their openness to their guest is related to an ability to know themselves only through use-value. For the servants hospitality is a job of work and their excitement over Belle should be calibrated against the relative redundancy of their 'human' labour. As far as the servants are concerned this story could happily be abbreviated to B&B. In fact it would appear that the staff are ill-prepared for the arrival of the stranger and find that their well choreographed routine is disrupted by Belle, who flouts the conditions of her hospitality by visiting the west wing of the castle. This initially results in Belle leaving the castle after a confrontation with the Beast, showing that a programmed approach to hospitality will only result in misappropriation, misunderstanding and exclusion.

Belle returns after the Beast saves her from being savaged by a pack of wolves (the potentially complicated sexuality of the Beast being projected onto the wolves as beasts). Now that Belle is also in debt to the Beast she in turn opens herself to him by caring for him and eventually teaching him to love. While the encounter between the Beast and his Other (Beauty) results in unexpected changes on both sides and each character becomes imbricated in the needs of the other, there remains an attempt to programme hospitality. This is the focus of the Oscar-winning title song, accurately called 'Theme from *Beauty and the Beast*':

> Unexpectedly,
> Just a little change,
> Small to say the least,
> Both a little scared,
> Neither one prepared ...
> Finding you can change

The risks and constant revision required by an openness to the Other suggested in these lines is played off against an insistence on the inevitability of the narrative closure:

> Certain as the sun,
> Rising in the east.
> Tale as old as time,
> Song as old as rhyme,
> Beauty and the Beast.

While hospitality requires a moment of decision (which is also a moment of undecidability), with respect to the organisation of hospitality that moment can never be programmed in advance and, in order to retain the character of hospitality, is never as 'certain as the sun'. What Disney offers in this film, as the West offers to the new democracies 'rising in the East', is a simulacrum of hospitality in which a certain narrative of openness screens out a conditional hospitality in which the Other is assimilated in the interests of economy. Belle and her father move into the castle and join the *ancien régime*, while Western Europe welcomes those in the East who are able to bring wealth and investment with them and agrees to support only those governments which allow their markets to run along neo-liberal lines. Disney welcomes you in so that it can sell you T-shirts and cinema tickets.

However, despite this closure offered by Disney to its fiction of hospitality the seismic displacements of national boundaries and the conceptual orders which underpin them remain active. The Disney programme will have to constantly revise itself (and so lose the name of a programme) if it is to stay on top of these developments. The ways in which Disney is caught in this aporia of undecidability will be the subject of the rest of this book, which outlines Disney's management of geopolitical changes (from the New World Order to the opening of the Chinese market) in the form of its flagship productions, its annual feature-length animations (which are themselves extended adverts for all sections of the Disney Corporation). For the moment we will conclude by commenting on the ways in which the film *Beauty and the Beast* cannot be contained within the closure its narrative offers. The narrator whose recapitulation opens the film reminds us that the Enchantress warned the Prince that he should not be deceived by appearances 'for Beauty lies within'. If this is so then the Beast's pursuit of Belle (meaning beauty) has failed to pay heed to the advice he was given before the animated action ever began. He learns what it means to love when he releases Belle from her incarceration to attend to her sick father but he still requires the external agency of Belle to bestow a magic kiss on him before he can be turned back into David Ginola.[10] In other words, the Beast has still not negotiated the Otherness within himself. In order to pay his debt to the Enchantress the Beast should welcome the Otherness within himself, unconditionally. Certainly, he learns to love himself (he cleans up rather well) but an unconditional hospitality to his own beauty would involve an acceptance of his beastly form.

Nevertheless, freedom from this form remains the basic premiss of the film. The Prince gets to have his cake and eat it, just as the peasants are left to eat cake. This failed negotiation of beastliness might explain the two sequels (only available on video) in which the Beast makes a return. However, more importantly, once Disney has allowed its European Other to enter its home then it will be unable to control the effects produced in that space by Europe. While this Disneyfication of European literature on the one hand reinforces the traditional political order of Disney it also changes that order. This change is the force which produces the constant revisions of the subsequent Disney films, the French Other returning most noticeably in *The Hunchback of Notre Dame*. Whoever is at war with themselves cannot properly welcome the Other, and Disney's attempts to assimilate difference to its totalising world-view is complicated by the conflicts which bifurcate within its films, just as the West remains allergic to the Other so long as the contest between Disneyfication and Europeanism continues.

3

Domesticated Animus: Engendering Disney

A house that shines from the care it receives appears to have been rebuilt from the inside, it is as though it were new inside. In the intimate harmony of walls and furniture, it may be said that we become conscious of a house that is built by women, since men only know how to build a house from the outside, and they know little or nothing of the 'wax' of civilisation.

Gaston Bachelard, *The Poetics of Space*, p. 68[1]

I use antlers in all of my decorating.

Gaston, *Beauty and the Beast*

Raised the Disney Way

Before taking our arguments outlined in the previous chapters any further, let's rewind to the start of the tape and consider the beginnings of Disney. Before the main feature on recent Disney videos from *The Little Mermaid* onwards a trailer appears for other Disney videos and straight-to-video productions. This includes a range of publicity for other animated Disney films available on video and usually an invitation to visit EuroDisney. It also often features a self-referential advertisement simply for watching Disney videos themselves, allowing those who are about to watch the video to see themselves as interpellated by Disney, enjoying a quality family experience.

A mother and two children, a boy and a girl (no father), sit on a sofa in their lower-middle-class living room and open the video box, to reveal a video exuding magic Disney dust, *à la* Tinkerbell. The boy inserts the film and the family unit return to the sofa to cuddle and smile. The screen reveals a magical transformation scene from Cinderella in which the fairy godmother is turning various objects into Cinderella's appendages, and the magic from her wand spreads beyond the screen into the living room. It transforms the modern window of the ordinary house into an elaborate stained-glass pastiche and then the walls transform to stones that turn into a castle's ivy-strewn turrets. Then to the amazement of passers-by, a tower pierces the roof of the house and an entire enchanted castle grows up in place of the ordinary house. As the focus moves away, identical castles spring up across the housing estate, accompanied by the sparkle of fireworks. This house has quite literally been rebuilt from the inside into the ubiquitous Disney castle. Like Ariel, Disney is also a household name used for a domestic task. Rebuilding the house from the inside approximates the maternal role of transformation which Gaston Bachelard suggests the housewife must effect by constant cleaning, 'creating poetry' through the application of 'wax'. Disney waxes lyrical about doing the housework and whistles while it works.

For Disney there is much at stake in being a domesticated house-trained member of the family. Disney has both been domesticated and simultaneously contributed to the narratives that shape our understanding of this term itself. Disney's 'family values' privilege Disney's value to the family, and its elision of the proper name with the family. Watching a Disney movie *is* being a family, it's what families do, and the popularity in divorcee circles of the winning combination of a Disney film and McDonalds trip on a weekend is testimony to the performance of family life that Disney peddles. It may also account for Disney's use of straight-to-video releases for sequels to best selling films like *Beauty and the Beast* and *The Lion King*.[2] Parents allow these films straight into the home, not needing to accompany their children to the cinema (an expensive and potentially stressful experience) as the material is familiar and has 'already' been vetted through the experience of the original source film. For Disney being domesticated confirms its purchase on the obvious, everyday, the private realm of retreat from the outside world of politics, social conflict or a critical gaze.

Disney's success in becoming a familiar domestic icon impacts upon significantly wider apprehensions of the terms upon which it can be discussed, even for the cultural omnivores in academic circles. Raise the subject of Disney and even academics are more likely to talk about the superior expertise of their children or grandchildren on this subject; either that or they will offer an account of their ongoing battle to limit the consumption of treats on the sweet trolley of the Disney canon and their attempts to explain their own antipathy towards these films to their offspring. Hence the irony of a friend's (a professor of English Literature) comments, 'I tried to explain to my five-year-old about the problem with the mad mother elephant, but his response to my reasoning was "Dumbo, Dumbo, Dumbo".' This apprehension of the unworthiness of Disney for serious academic investigation, the sense of which even a child can unintentionally grasp, permeates even into the discourse of semioticians. Even those critics working on Disney appear to confirm this uncertainty about the legitimacy of using a 'critical sledgehammer' to crack a 'Disney nut'. This is the equivocation (which assumes the existence of determinate limits to both 'theory' and the Disney text, one being an innately more 'serious' concern than the other) set out by the editors of *From Mouse to Mermaid* in their introduction.[3] It would not be unreasonable to say that such thinking suits Disney very well.

Domesticity, the 'great discovery' of the bourgeois age, is 'discovered' in Disney's first animated film, *Snow White*, as a discourse that Disney is really at home with.[4] In this paean to all things domestic Disney rehearses the heterogeneous implications of domestication that will be and will have been synonymous with its name, that will constitute its self-proclaimed manner of (not) being-in-the-world. That is to say, not being worldly; outside of the realm of the political and inside the home. Having escaped from the chilly corridors of her old home the castle, now transformed into the inhospitable lair of her stepmother, Snow White finds herself lost in an equally inhospitable wood, but recovers herself when she awakens to find herself surrounded by an abundance of friendly animals. She comes to her senses, realising that she is unharmed and asks the animals for tourist information:

> Everything's going to be all right. But I do need a place to sleep at night, I can't sleep in the ground like you [rabbits shake their heads], or in a tree the way you do [squirrels shakes their heads], and I'm sure no nest could possibly be big enough for me [birds nod in agreement]. Maybe you know where I can stay ? In the woods somewhere, you do?! Will you take me there?

It is striking, Bachelard notes, that 'even in our homes where there is light, our consciousness of well-being should call for comparison with animals in their shelters' (*PS*, p. 91).

The significance of nests, burrows and shells lies precisely in their having been constructed from the inside out, through the actions of the body itself. For Bachelard, quoting Michelet, a bird is a worker without tools, its tool being its own body. 'The instrument that prescribes the circular form of the nest is nothing else but the body of the bird. It is by constantly turning round and round and pressing back the walls on every side that it succeeds in forming the circle' (p. 101). The nest, burrow and shell seem to offer evidence of the body, a house that 'grows in proportion to the body that inhabits it', as Bachelard says of the mollusc's shell (p. 118).[5] Such a pregnant metaphor underlines the peculiarly feminine jurisdiction of the domestic, offering a parallel that Bachelard is quick to embrace between interiors created and nurtured by women, and interior spaces within women. But by introducing a logic of en(gender)ing to the space of the house there may be repercussions, which complicate its cultural and political significance beyond any simple opposition to the gendering of domestic (feminine) and public (masculine) spheres that certain feminist criticism has offered. The suggestion of gestation is that domestication is always secondary; it comes after the original (lost origin).

In her discussion of domestication and deconstruction Rachel Bowlby notes,

In so far as domestication has to do with home it would seem to elide the starting point. Home is the place of origin, the place that has always been left; domestication, then, would be a return to or reinvention of the home that you left or lost.[6]

Vacation of the original maternal space can only be compensated for in Snow White's reinvention of home, which is achieved through this multiple use of her body in ways that explicitly embrace the maternal. Feminist critics have noted for some considerable time the high preponderance of lost mothers in the Disney canon. Here at the inception of its long history of animated films Disney's mother has already disappeared. At the origin of Disney's canon is a narrative of the loss of origins. The mother is erased in order for Disney to give birth to its narratives. Of course, Snow White has a stepmother, which might also be considered, following Derrida's use of the French word *'pas'* meaning both 'step' and 'not', as a not-mother.[7] *Pas* as 'step' also means 'pace', 'footprint', 'trace', suggesting that Snow White has both a step/not-mother and a trace of a mother.

The trace of the Mother haunts daughters in their own faces, whilst Snow White haunts her stepmother in the mirror, in which she asks, 'Who is the fairest of them all?' The stepmother, following Derrida's footsteps, is *belle-mère* in French, 'beautiful mother', meaning both stepmother and mother-in-law. Thus the beautiful step/not-Mother in Law haunts Disney's primal scene in a narrative of exile, from a space has already been left, the space of maternal gestation, a nest, shell, or burrow, that expands with the body that inhabits it. As *pas*/step/passage and *pas*/not/non-passage, a birth and a miscarriage, this logic offers a double bind which constitutes an aporia. In Disney's narratives which are founded upon the absence of a mother, she non-the-less will still continue to haunt her daughters, from the future, as the promise of the maternal (not the original origin, but a reinvented one).

This is a promise that is repeatedly sought by the daughters. Snow White is not alone in her loss. She assumes from the dwarves' neglected cottage that they too are orphans: 'Just look at that broom! You'd think their mother was ... [Pauses so as not to say 'dead'] maybe they have no mother! We'll clean the house and surprise them then maybe they'll let me stay.' Moments later, holding the broom, she sings Disney's labour movement anthem, 'Whistle While You Work': 'And as you sweep the room / Imagine that the broom is someone that you love / and soon you'll find you're dancing to the tune.' The broom both marks the absence of the mother and the reimagining of her, through a domestic action. In Bachelard's words, 'Through housewifely care a house recovers not so much its originality but its origin' (*PS*, p. 68). We might want to add that the origin is not recoverable but whistling while you work enables the figure of the maternal to be called up.

Snow White, like the rabbits, squirrels and birds, achieves her domestic transformations through her reliance on the body itself. She domesticates the wild animals in the woods through her singing, transforms the neglected cottage with the help of the newly domesticated animals, who use their bodies to perform household tasks in ways that labour-saving machines of 1950s America would achieve. She makes the dirty dwarves (whom she calls 'seven untidy little children') wash their hands with the help of the familiar maternal injunction before dinner. As they get the dirt from under their fingernails they utter what will become Disney's mantra for the next half-century, 'Ya douse an souse / ya rub an scrub / Ya sputter and splash all over the tub / You may be cold and wet when you're done / But ya gotta admit its good clean fun.' Snow White even manages to domesticate death itself with a kiss. The kiss enables her to leave the cottage immediately on the prince's horse and exchange it for a dream castle which appears in the pink clouds as they walk out of the woods. Snow White, like Disney, transforms the ordinary house into a castle through a concerted programme of domestication, which mirrors Disney's own techniques by training animals to be human and by teaching boys to keep their little men clean.

But Snow White's nesting instincts and her injunctions on personal hygiene are only one aspect of domestication as maternal haunting that Disney embraces. Walt Disney's penchant for nostalgic reconstructions of the main street of

his childhood town in theme parks in the early days of Walt
Disney World have frequently been criticised on similar
grounds as inventions of a fantasised sanitised past, or psy-
chologised as the yearnings of an adult for an idealised
childhood he never experienced.[8] But these criticisms fail to
grasp the uncanny logic of domestication that permeates
Disney's animated creations. If 'home is not the first place or
the natural place', then doing the laundry or washing the
dishes manifests an uncanniness at the heart of the domestic,
where the homely and familiar also reveals itself to be
profoundly unfamiliar.[9]

In *Peter Pan* (1953), and *Lady and the Tramp* which
succeeded it two years later, it is possible to trace the
development of a number of key domestic and domesticated
images to offer suggestions about the changing function of
domesticity in the Disney project which might be said to
follow the uncanny logic of *becoming* domestic. Before the last
battle between Hook and Peter all the action pauses to hear
Wendy sing a song in praise of mothers. She sings from inside
a hollow tree-trunk/burrow where Peter Pan and the Lost Boys
hide out. The boys are aptly all dressed in animal outfits –
rabbits, racoons, squirrels – that suit their neglected domestic
environment, but paradoxically point to Disney's hallmark
of creating domesticated animals. Outside this maternal
receptacle, the pirates surround their camp, waiting to attack,
but they pause to listen to the song, putting their ears to a
cavity in the tree. Wendy counters the boys' desire to remain
in Never-Never-Land, and 'grow up like savages' with the
retort, 'But you can't you need a mother, we all do'. Her
brother Michael asks, 'Aren't you our mother, Wendy?' as she
performs the maternal task of undressing him and putting
him to bed in a pink babygro. Despite her clear role as
substitute (following in the steps of the mother) she
nonetheless insists on the value of a real mother, in this film
not dead but forgotten. 'Why, Michael, of course not. Surely
you haven't forgotten our real mother?' But the Lost Boys
have no memory of their mothers. This, even during his short
stay with them, has now affected Michael too: 'Did she have
fluffy ears and wear a fur coat?' 'No, Michael, that was Nana
[the family dog/nanny].' If Nana's status as doggy mother is

ambiguous, the Lost Boys have similar problems distinguishing animal and maternal. One of the Lost Boys chips in, 'I
think I had a mother once', but when the uncanny twins ask,
'What was she like?' he confesses, 'I forgot.' A third boy adds
to the confusion: 'I had a white rat!', the first boy replies
angrily, 'That's no mother!' and a brawl ensues.

Wendy has privileged access to this subject, having consistently accepted a maternal role in the film, and having
previously rejected two invitations to participate in other
versions of gendered identities, refusing the bitchy mermaids'
invitations for a swim, and the forbidding Indian squaw's
commands to fetch firewood. 'I'll tell you what a mother is
[...] A mother, a real mother is the most wonderful person in
the world.' Her song unites the young boys in the burrow
hideout with the pirates listening above, who put their ears to
the hollow tree trunk. They hear the song through the
passages of the shell-like, nest-like burrow, through the
labyrinth of their (shell-like) ears as they silently listen to her
lullaby, 'What makes mothers all that they are, might as well
ask what makes a star.' Mr Smee lifts his shirt to reveal a
tattoo, 'MOTHER', on his stomach and bursts into tears on
Captain Hook's shoulder. The scene turns into a wake for an
absent mother, as Smee sobs like a child. Ultimately the
narrative pauses to reflect on the many lost mothers that have
faded into the background and enabled this narrative to
emerge. The death of the mother constitutes a mark of
exclusion which is a necessary condition of meaning, Derrida
suggests: 'The relation to the other (in itself outside myself in
myself) will never be indistinguishable from a bereaved apprehension.'[10] The lullaby/elegy, has the effect of both resigning
the boys to return home to domestication, leaving their
Indian warpaint behind and resigning Wendy to her biology.

Conversely the next film Disney produced, *Lady and the
Tramp*, very rarely leaves the confines of the house at all,
much of the action taking place inside Lady's owners' house
or in the adjoining garden and kennel. This is directly
opposed to the homeless state of the dogs in the pound, who
face execution if no owner claims them. Being claimed
involves being a domesticated pet, proudly bearing a collar,
the mark of a licence, which signifies belonging to a family.

If the question in *Peter Pan* is 'What's a mother?', *Lady and the Tramp* offers a parallel interrogation of the inscrutable maternal by approaching this delicate question from the opposite end, so to speak. The question Lady broods over is 'What's a baby?' In an uncanny moment in the film, Lady's question is finally answered through an image of a newly born baby after her owners bring home their first-born child and Lady attempts to look into the cradle. Here cartoon animation is eschewed for a moment and the film attempts to deny its own mediative role in the production of a 'lifelike' *still* image of a sleeping baby's head, revealed as the mother pulls back the covers of its cradle. The drawing technique is markedly different from the cartoon style in the rest of the film and evokes a painterly sensibility of verisimilitude.[11]

This disturbance of the medium of the cartoon through a reference to a 'real' outside its limits precipitates numerous experiences. It attempts to reach beyond the limits of the text of the film itself to something that precedes or pre-exists the narrative and which validates it. But here, through an insistence on the *heimlich* qualities of domestic life of belonging to the house and to the family, the text produces an unfamiliarity in that which was supposed to be familiar, an eerie scene, *unheimlich* and 'motionless like a stone image'.[12] This still life/*nature morte* disturbs Disney's positioning of itself in the role of the domesticator, both usurping the mother's place and deferring to it. The new-born baby appears as too sacred an image to be transformed, to be animated by Disney's magic, and is hence rendered inanimate. Animation, the bringing to life of inanimate objects, is also resonant with the sense of animus as spirit. The *unheimlich* is also spectral, it enacts a kind of haunting of the *heimlich*.

Disney stops being animated at the moment of return to origins, in the face of the 'miracle of life', of reproduction. Animation, which bestows life where there was none before, finds itself spooked when it gets too close to procreation and defers to it. The uncanny, as Freud points out, 'is nothing new or foreign, but something familiar and old – established in the mind that has been estranged only by the process of repression [...] Something which ought to have been kept concealed but which has nevertheless come to light.' Disney's uncanny 'cot-death' signals a repression of the maternal which has enabled its narrative to emerge, and its own form of conjuring spirits has concealed its murder of the Mother.

However, if the repression of the maternal has been a pre-condition for the Disney canon, it has nonetheless succeeded in its description of itself as the ambassador of the family. But, if narrative cannot be contained in such a way, how might these texts be understood in a deconstructive sense, how might they be seen to return these conditions of their existence against the patriarchal, logocentric, androcentric logic of Disney? Derrida's comments on the academy seem peculiarly appropriate here.

> No woman or trace of woman, if I have read correctly – save the mother, that's understood. But this is part of the system. The mother is the faceless figure of a figurant, an extra. She gives rise to all figures by losing herself in the background of the scene like an anonymous persona. Everything comes back to her, beginning with life; everything addresses and destines itself to her. She survives on the condition of remaining at the bottom.[13]

Disney's renaissance in the 1980s was marked by the birth of a new breed of newly born women. The first two films in the second wave of the Disney canon, *The little Mermaid* and *Beauty and the Beast*, signal a change in the kinds of experiences of gender that Disney has felt it necessary to address following the transformation of women's roles in postwar America and Europe. Female heroines are now teenagers, who have desires to escape the prisons of domesticity in Ariel's case and 'this provincial life' in Belle's. Ariel and Belle are both young women who don't immediately adopt a maternal function in the narrative, and have a physical sexual identity which is lacking in *Snow White*, and which is not appropriate for Wendy or dogs like Lady. However, their mothers are still absent. Ariel's mother is never mentioned, neither is Belle's; in subsequent films, Princess Jasmine is motherless in *Aladdin*, Pocahontas bonds with her father by grieving for her dead mother and Quasimodo's mother dies on the steps of Notre-Dame in the opening sequence of *The Hunchback of Notre Dame*. Only Hercules, Simba and Mulan have mothers who survive to the end of the film, although Hercules' mother is merely a shimmering pink haze in her brief appearances. Arguably there are specific cultural and political reasons why Simba and Mulan have mothers, which will be addressed in a later chapter.

Ariel is a teenager and her parental relationship is with her father, just as Belle's is also with her eccentric inventor father, whose 'madness' places him ambivalently as a paternal figure, allowing him to be infantilised, both by the villagers and by Belle when she puts herself in his place as the Beast's prisoner in a classic piece of maternal self-sacrifice. Princes Jasmine's father in *Aladdin* is also infantilised, a soft-hearted trusting simpleton, who is a cross between a dwarf and a baby, rounder and smaller than Jasmine herself, completely ineffectual at protecting her from Jafar and who gets hypnotised into ordering Jasmine to marry him. All of these men appear as flawed and endearing potential law-givers who will ultimately be proven wrong about key paternal decisions by their strong-headed daughters and will sanction their choices, having initially opposed them.

This preoccupation with father/daughter relationships appears to be a way of sidestepping the significant transformation of women's roles in the West, and is also suggestive of the crisis in masculinity that these shifts contribute towards. The films no longer appear to ask 'What's a mother? What's a Baby?', but focus on teenagers who even as rebellious daughters remain loving and dutiful in the final analysis. It is tempting then to view the impact of heterogeneous feminisms as only approachable for Disney as a 1960s teenager's act of defiance in putting on a wonderbra and lip gloss, in which sexual freedoms are no longer explicitly linked to the expected biological destiny of mothering, to which slightly anxious but doting fathers concede. Yet the wholesale approval for these very young teenage marriages appears to militate against the wholesome family values of Disney. The hasty romance, the quick marrying-off, has the sniff of a shotgun wedding. Jasmine has three days left to choose a husband; Ariel, the youngest of all her sisters, must repay her loan to Ursula after the same three days with the kiss of true love; and Belle makes an instant decision to live in the castle forever with the Beast. It is significant that after *The Little Mermaid* none of these films actually ends in a wedding scene for hero and heroine, underlining Disney's problem in reconciling family values and good clean fun with precocious teenage marriages.

Belle appears to buck the trend in the opening section of *Beauty and the Beast*. She is immune to the attractions of the great advocate of married life, Gaston, whose offer of marriage holds little appeal – 'Picture this, a rustic hunting lodge, my latest kill roasting on the fire, my little wife massaging my feet, while the little ones play on the floor with the dogs, we'll have six or seven.' Knowing her value, she concedes, 'I'm very sorry, Gaston, but I just don't deserve you.' Once he has left she repeats indignantly the laughable image of herself as his 'little wife'. Gaston is boorish, brainless and provincial, that is to say, a Frenchman who has not realised that time has moved on in the West. Disney derives a lot of humour from its ridiculing of Gaston's cleft chin, his 'built like a barge' stature and his penchant for covering walls with hunting trophies. But Gaston's interest in decorating marks the actual difference between him and the Beast. Gaston's ontological interior design, marked by preoccupations with remains, faces the hauntological conditions in the Beast's house. Gaston's attempt to ontologise remains, to localise them and to ensure that they stay put (on his living room wall), contrasts with the hauntological properties of the rather lively décor in the Beast's castle, a kind of haunted house.

However, the domestic realm has not disappeared. Both Gaston and the Beast offer a domestic role for Belle; she doesn't escape 'provincial life', but does avoid being a provincial wife (as lady of the manor). Rather, the underlying uncanny doubleness of domestic logic, which operates simultaneously as a kind of 'animation' of the domestic interior and a maternal haunting, is realised in different ways, suggesting the indispensability of the kind of domesticating logic that we have outlined in earlier films in Disney's animation history. The paradox of this logic is to be found in the etymology, the 'search for the origins', of 'animation' itself. To animate is to give life, or to inspirit; to be animated can variously mean to be full of life or its opposite, to move as if alive. To be animated is also to be full of spirit, or, put another way, in possession of animus, spirit, possessed by spirits. That which is animated may be inanimate but made to appear to be alive, as *Pinocchio* and 'The Sorcerer's Apprentice' in *Fantasia* show. Animation, animism, anthropomorphism, automatism of every variety constitute Disney's entire cartoon *oeuvre*. Every animated Disney film is a version of a becoming domestic, moulding Bachelard's 'wax' of civilisation into living things. Bachelard is not a domesticator in the way that Disney is, but Disney's films seems to haunt Bachelard's writings: 'How wonderful it is to really become once more, the inventor of a mechanical action! (*PS*, p. 67).' Specifically *Snow White* and *Beauty and the Beast* suggest an ironic answer to Bachelard's inquiry 'How can housework be made into a creative activity? (p. 67).'

The logic of the B&B

> From one object in a room to another, housewifely care weaves the ties that unite a very ancient past to the new epoch. The housewife awakens furniture that was asleep.
>
> Gaston Bachelard, *A Poetics of Space*, p. 68

> Ten years we've been rusting
> Needing so much more than dusting
> Needing exercise, a chance to use our skills,
> Most days we just lay around the castle,
> Flabby fat and lazy
> You walked in and oops-a-daisy.
>
> Lumière, *Beauty and the Beast*.

When Belle resigns herself to living in the castle indefinitely, she finds herself held hostage to the laws of the boarding house. Having refused to eat supper with the Beast at a time of his convenience, she finds the kitchen is closed for the night. Snow White's cottage, which opened its doors to her maternal care, has been transformed into a vast 'Bed and

Breakfast', a simulacrum of home where the private quarters of the host are forbidden to guests and one is not invited into the kitchen. However, as Belle emerges for a late night snack she conjures domestic spirits at a seance around the dining room table.

As Lumière sings, the contents of the house which have been waiting for ten years to be awoken from their slumbers emerge from the cupboards like Snow White herself. Snow White's transparent glass coffin in which she lies in state is a close relation of the display cabinet in which the best tea-set is kept and brought out only for guests. Belle resurrects this ghostly image of Disney's origins as she animates the crockery. The plates, knives, forks, spoons and glasses, soup tureens, tankards, and platters of hors d'oeuvres appear on the table before her, in a performance in which the table is a stage. Lumière sings under a spotlight and the forks dance the can-can.

When household objects dance, it is because they are spectral. As Belle comments to Cogsworth after the show, his fear that Lumière has revealed the ingredients to 'mama's secret recipe' (the mother as secret) is unfounded; she had worked out for herself that the castle was enchanted. If the objects are considered to be animated in the sense of being re-animated, brought back from the dead, then the 'return' to the domestic in *Beauty and the Beast* is the revenant of a domestic ghost – a haunted house. Marx understands the household object, as a commodity, in terms of a spectral dance:

> The form of wood, for instance, is altered if a table is made out of it. Nevertheless the table continues to be wood, an ordinary, sensuous thing. But as soon as it emerges as a commodity, it changes into a thing which transcends sen-suousness. It not only stands with its feet on the ground, but, in relation to all other commodities, it stands on its head, and evolves out of its wooden brain grotesque ideas, far more wonderful than if it were to begin dancing of its own free will.[14]

Marx uses animation here to describe the ways in which com-modification installs the haunting of use-value within a domestic object, just as the use-value of the servants installs itself within the animated haberdashery. A wooden table as an 'ordinary sensuous thing' is transformed, in Derrida's words reading this passage from Marx, 'when it becomes a commodity, when the curtain goes up on the market and the table plays actor and character at the same time'.[15] The household object becomes a supernatural thing, 'a sensuous but non-sensuous, sensuously supersensible' thing, haunted by the uncanny effects of commodification, which at one and the same time are related to performance and parthenogenesis.[16] The table is said to evolve 'out of its wooden brain grotesque ideas, far more wonderful than if it were to begin dancing of its own free will', suggesting that, as an animated figure, the table (*tisch* is a masculine noun in German) develops the commodity relations it engenders through a parthenogenic generation from out of its head; the head or brain being the traditional image of the male sublimated womb in the patriarchal fantasy which replaces the Mother with the figure of the parthenogenic Mother–Father.[17]

The spectro-domestic object which appears to 'imag-ineer' itself, to borrow a word from Disney's own construction programme, is the ultimate consumer item of the second half of the twentieth century. Increasingly technologised household commodities in the West signal a house increasingly filled with ghosts. When the inanimate object 'comes alive' and is filled with spirits, it is also a sort of automaton, which is neither dead nor alive, like the puppet Pinocchio or the mechanical doll in *The Adventures of the Great Mouse Detective*. This spectral logic of the commodity can also be found in the spell which Belle must break (she must banish the ghosts of the past) and which constitutes the inversion of the important ideological space of home. If Disney wishes to present the home as a space which exists outside of the economic (even when Disney as 'home entertainment' works to undo this image of non-commodification) then the Beast's castle as a B&B bears the marks of a commercial enterprise, all the trappings of home without any of its familiar qualities, which must be exorcised of its ghosts. Belle may not be afraid of ghosts, but Disney certainly is. Disney turns the talking teapot Mrs Potts back into a real woman, ontologising in order to banish the disruptive effects of the hauntological. Disney is haunted by the ghosts of the European stories which it has *reproduced,* by a dead little mermaid who has been resurrected in a Disney rewrite of the fairy tale's gruesome ending, and by the spectral apparition of the Mother who continually returns to threaten the phallogocentrism of each film, only to be ex(or)cised once again.

If ghosts have a singular relation to the literature which Disney appropriates, then the spectral also makes an appearance in the tele-technologies of film and television which Disney has made its own. Derrida has commented, 'These technologies inhabit as it were a phantom structure ... when the very first perception of an image is linked to a reproduction, then we are dealing with the realm of phantoms.'[18] In film all representation is a form of reproduction and thus all film is caught up in a set of ghostly relation. If the commodity is spectral then the commodity which is the film *Beauty and the Beast* is doubly haunted. Like Ebenezer Scrooge, this film is visited by at least three different (but related) ghosts: animation, commodification and reproduction. The enchanted castle in this film is of course a haunted house, one of the favourite 'rides' in any Disney theme park. It is, logically, the simulacrum, that which enables the rest of Disneyworld to keep its skeletons in the closet.

4
Spectographies: Conjuring Disney

The greatest symptomatic or metonymic concentration of what remains irreducible in the worldwide conjuncture in which the question of 'whither marxism' is inscribed today has its place, its figure, or the figure of its place in the Middle East.

Jacques Derrida, *Specters of Marx*, p. 58.

Call me Al

While constructing his argument that there is 'a coherent and directional history of mankind that will lead the greater part of humanity to liberal democracy', Francis Fukuyama calls 'the creation of a universal consumer culture based on liberal economic principles' the 'ultimate victory of the VCR'.[1] Disney's 1992 film *Aladdin* currently holds the record of all-time best-selling video cassette ever in North America (exceeding 21 million copies sold) and might be thought of as the ultimate victor in this victory of the VCR.[2] Fukuyama suggests that 'the enormously productive and dynamic world created by advancing technology and rational organisation of labour has a tremendous homogenising power' and 'the attractive power of this world creates a very strong *predisposition* for all human societies to participate in it, while success in this participation requires the adoption of the principles of economic liberalism' (p. 108). In other words, it is the irresistible metonymic attractiveness of home video entertainment which ensures the inevitability of global capitalist hegemony. Such a crude rendition of the conditions of postmodernity takes some believing. However, it is in this record-breaking video/film that Disney keeps faith with the structure of Fukuyama's messianism.

Released in the year after the Gulf War and following more than a decade of hostility in the region, *Aladdin* on a superficial level is the story of an evil Islamic dictator who aspires to rule the world but is brought low by an American-ised youth, his Western-friendly allies, and advanced military technology. General Schwarzkopf, Commander-in-Chief of Allied forces during the Gulf War, chose an apt location when he celebrated his victory party at Disney World in Florida.[3] However, there is something more significant about this film (and its successor *The Lion King*) which goes beyond its unashamed affront to the Arab world. Like *The Lion King* this film responds to the changing circumstances of and helps consolidate the political appropriations which take place under the now largely neglected name of the New World Order.[4] Back to back, post-Cold War films set in the Middle East and Africa have an important relation to the fate of that Marxism from the supposed death of which the New World Order takes its name. As Derrida notes, the term 'New World Order' reminds us that the global political 'order' which emerged after the dispersal of the Soviet Union is one which takes place under the hegemony of the New World, meaning America.[5]

The acquiescence of a critical mass of Arab states with Israel and the Anglo-American expeditionary force during the Gulf War undoubtedly raised the possibility of a future compromise over the Palestinian question (even though the PLO itself offered open support to Baghdad during the conflict). However, the question raised by a possible resolution to the Arab–Israeli conflict was a matter of how might America and its allies accommodate the just claims of a national struggle waged in the name of socialism? Recognising and supporting the rights and demands of the people represented by Yassar Arafat (and so working towards regional stability in this area of strategic and economic interest) means giving tacit encouragement to a form of rev-olutionary and 'terroristic' socialism which it was the avowed aim of US foreign policy to destabilise. In order to negotiate its way through this political aporia it was necessary for the art of diplomacy to 'domesticate' the PLO and make Arafat a household name. Similarly, as American economic and strategic interests required stability in South Africa there was a concerted effort to work a similar mediatic magic on the

Marxist ANC and its imprisoned 'terrorist' leader Nelson Mandela. What is at stake in this process is the conjuration, both the calling forth and the exorcising, of spectres of Marxism. In so far as *Aladdin* and *The Lion King* (released in 1994, the same year as the first democratic election in South Africa) might be read as embodiments of this political theatre, these films are an attempt to ontologize the ghost of Marxism which haunts the Disney castle.

Aladdin opens with a recognition of the geographical ambiguity implied in the occidental term Middle East. The song over the opening credits notes that Disney's desert is a place where 'winds from the East' meet 'sands from the West'. This desert song calls attention to the spatial relativity of the Middle East (East of where? In the middle of what? What lies east of the east?) and points out that the nominal effects of this location are the result of the historical forces of imperialism. Caught in the middle between the capitalist West and the communist East, the Persian Gulf is marked as a site of contest between the ideological forces of old Europe. With the imperialist construction of Israel bordered on every side by socialist Arab states (and containing within its borders a socialist *intifada*) this geographical space was not only a location of 'indirect conflict' during the Cold War but also represents an important site of contest for the New World Order. If the wind of change is blowing from the East and the sands of time are running out for Western hegemony then this might explain a cultural intervention in the form of one of Disney's 1001 tales. Such animated discourse may also be a symptom of the frantic desire of capitalism to impose the fiction of a New World Order on a global situation which suggests that the privileged position of capitalism and of the West has never been so unstable.

The task for Disney is to manage geopolitical change in order to keep up with the game at a time when the traditional order of politics and economics which underpin the corporation are undergoing radical revision as a result of that change.[6] The moment of decision (the representation of change as non-change in the full-length animations) is also a moment of undecidability in which a proactive response to transformation pulls against a cartoon version of the dialectic in which the geopolitical is appropriated in the name of Disney. It is this undecidability which makes the Disney film readable and enables its signifying effects to deconstruct the Disney system which puts them in play. *Aladdin* involves just such a contest. On the one hand, it offers us Aladdin as a Palestinian 'street rat' whose antics in the marketplace and ongoing feud with the palace guards call to mind the teenage revolutionaries who raised an *intifada* against Israeli troops in the West Bank and Gaza Strip. Aladdin's life of street crime is ethical (he sings, 'I steal only what I can't afford'), and the viewer is reassured of his virtue when he gives away his stolen bread to doe-eyed Arab urchins. There is a romantic appeal in such political pantomime but Disney makes it clear that it will not win Aladdin the girl and the kingdom. He is able to woo Princess Jasmine by renouncing subversion and becoming a statesman in the form of his pseudonym Prince Ali. He is equipped and trained for government (by marrying Jasmine he is invited to become Sultan) by his (American) advisor (voiced by Robin Williams the genie).

On the other hand, the film distinguishes between Jafar as a threat to regional stability and Aladdin as an American interest (rather than a friend). The genie ultimately wants Aladdin to free him to do whatever he wants. Jafar, 'a dark man with a dark purpose', is a cross between the Ayatollah and Saddam Hussein. He is encoded by the familiar marks of Western racism, wearing black clerical robes and a 'sinister' Islamic moustache and goatee. When the film opens Jafar is already manipulating the sultan and dictating policy in the kingdom (he is particularly noted for his repressive police force, the one which chases Aladdin) and dreams of regional hegemony. To this end he is searching for the cave of wonders and the genie of the lamp to be found inside. The genie's powers will help him 'rule on high': like a phantomatic weapon of mass destruction the lamp is figuratively a super gun. However, as the old story goes, Aladdin (tricked by Jafar) finds the lamp only to be locked in the cave with it. Importantly, there is a marked difference between Aladdin's encounter with the supernatural (the genie as wise-cracking Robin Williams, the domesticated animus of the magic carpet) and Jafar as an evil sorcerer.

Much of the action and setting of *Aladdin* calls to mind the Indiana Jones films (from the soundtrack and special effects which accompany the disappearance of the cave of wonders to borrowed humour – 'He's got a sword! Idiot, we've all got swords'). Disney uses the visual vocabulary of these chronicles of contemporary orientalism to place the viewer within a familiar version of the Middle East (as the opening song notes, 'It's flat, it's intense, it's immense, it's barbaric, but hey, it's home'). More interestingly, the references to Indiana Jones and *Raiders of the Lost Ark* call to mind the absence of Israel from the Disney film. In the Spielberg–Lucas film the question of the relation between Israel and its Arab neighbours is portrayed in spectral terms. The Ark of the Covenant as representative of an Israel 'yet to come' (the action takes place in the late 1930s) contains the spirits of the historical Judaic nation. It is the return of these ghosts at the end of the film which destroys the Nazis who seek to harness the ark's power. For the Nazis these are ghosts which, like the spectre of communism conjured in the opening line of *The Communist Manifesto*, arrive from the future: the postwar (re)foundation of Israel bearing testament to the history of Nazi genocide.[7] By contrast, Israel is a ghostly absence from *Aladdin* as a film which responds to the specific historical conjunction of the Gulf War. There is a sense in which such an absence was the strategy that enabled the US to hold together the multinational coalition during the Gulf conflict. By giving guarantees of its safety and persuading Israel not to respond to SCUD missile attacks it was possible for Israel to adopt a simulacrum of neutrality which in turn enabled Arab states to reconcile themselves with American attacks on Iraq. For the brief and specific purposes of defeating Saddam Hussein the interests of Israel and the interests of America were one and the same and by agreeing to this equivalence Israel allowed America to act in its name.

Aladdin is the figure in which this simulacrum of the name (implied by the anagrammatic potential of Israel) has its place. Aladdin, as a hero, relies on the genie to act in his name and achieve his desired goals. The genie makes him a prince, saves him from drowning and sings to Aladdin that now, 'You've got some power in your corner / Some heavy ammunition in your can.' When separated from the genie Aladdin uses the magic carpet as a technical prosthesis to ensure his success. The only occasion on which Aladdin has to act unaided is when he tricks Jafar with the same rhetorical duplicity with which he cons the genie into granting him an extra wish. The all-powerful genie sings a song entitled 'You've never had a friend like me' and is an encoding of American support. Therefore, Aladdin's reliance on his American ally could position him as Israel as well as acting as a metonym for the Palestinian struggle. Like Israel Aladdin has no history, a bastard child of Western imperialism, at the same time as having an ancient historical provenance. Aladdin's independence being marked by a defining duplicity, his 'double-facedness' and 'con-artistry' allow him to represent both Israel and its other.[8] Aladdin is characterised by doubleness, 'Aladdin' with a double 'd', a-lad-in-disguise; Jafar calls him 'a two-faced son of a jackal'. He spends most of the film posing as his alter ego Prince Ali and this ambivalent identity might also explain the curious vacuum at the 'centre' of his character. Like the ill-fated *Rescuers Down Under*, *Aladdin* is one of the few films in the new Disney *oeuvre* with a male lead (Princess Jasmine is 'spirited and independent' but Aladdin is the eponymous hero). The impotence of Aladdin as a hero without prosthetic supports may be a reflection of the crisis in Western masculinity which these films negotiate but Aladdin's vapidity may also be a result of the impossible demands of representation made upon his character. American hegemony in the Middle East relies upon the dependency of both Israel and the Arab states on aid from the US; the Disneyfication of the world depends upon the colonial expropriation of all otherness in the name of a certain Western consumerism. Disney as a form of imperialism involves the incorporation of all heterogeneous and non-synchronous histories and cultures into one homogenising cultural and historical schema, namely the wonderful world of Disney. Here Aladdin is asked to represent the interests of both Israel and the Palestinians as they are both appropriated as American spheres of influence and made over into Disney characters. At the end of the film Aladdin tells Princess Jasmine that rather than refer to him by his full

name she should 'call [me] Al'. Aladdin as both Arab and
Israel is indeed all: everything which is distinct and heterogeneous in the region can be reduced to the banal and
homogenising Aladdin. This would represent the ultimate
victory of the VCR.

However, such 'ontological imperialism' (to use Robert
Young's phrase, after Emmanuel Levinas) does not reckon
with the rewind and play-back facilities of the VCR.[9] Disney's
fast-forward to the end of history can be paused and the
distorted image produced by such an interruption may seem
to have a ghostly quality. Disney's animation is obsessed by
ghosts. From the magic mirror in *Snow White* to Angel
Lansbury's phantom army in *Bedknobs and Broomsticks* the
Disney corpus is haunted by spectres. However, like Marx,
Disney is interested in exorcising the hauntological in the
name of ontology.[10] *Bedknobs and Broomsticks* concludes with
the loss of Eglantine Price's powers of 'substantiary-
locomotion' and the dispersal of her ghostly soldiers; *Aladdin*
ends with the freedom of the genie in which he turns from a
spirit to an embodied person (significantly this involves
giving him legs) and the expulsion of Jafar and his magic
powers. The new Disney *oeuvre* always involves ontologisation as a form of closure (the death of the Sea Witch and
Ariel's being-in-the-world, the transformation of the Beast
and his servants, Pocahontas replacing the spirit of her dead
mother as a guide to her people, Hercules' decision to remain
human). Disney wants to domesticate its ghosts by giving
them bodies and so removing their defining characteristic as
ghosts, that which troubles, haunts, or 'spooks' the Disney
corporation. If Aladdin embodies on one level the Palestinian
struggle then that struggle is domesticated not only through
American diplomacy but also through Disneyfication.

Despite Disney's genius for ontology, Jafar the magician
survives the attempt to expel him just as Saddam Hussein has
resisted all American attempts to exorcise him. Jafar is tricked
by Aladdin into asking the genie to make him into the most
powerful genie in the universe.[11] Such dizzying supplemen-
tary logic, in which the genie produces from nothing powers
more powerful than his own, leads to the collapse of Jafar as
he finds that the price of his 'phenomenal cosmic powers' is

the 'itty bitty living space' of a genie's lamp. Trapped inside the lamp, Jafar is imprisoned in a cave of wonders for a thousand years. However, as Lyotard points out in his apocalyptic essay 'The wall, the Gulf, and the sun: a fable', a thousand years is a relatively short time for someone with a cosmic overview which extends beyond universal histories.[12] Jafar returns in the straight-to-video sequel, imaginatively entitled *The Return of Jafar*. His reappearance would suggest that not only will the spectral always return to haunt but that justification for the continued intervention of America (the genie) in the region requires the threat of the return of this ghost at some point in the future. When Jafar does return it will be in the form of an all-powerful genie having been produced as such by the genie which armed him, just as Saddam Hussein's (the genie calls Jafar 'Xeno Psychopath') perceived threat lies in his possession of weapons of mass destruction given to him by the West during the war with Iran.

The curious hollowness of Aladdin as a character might also be explained by his contrasting relation to the genie. The success of this film depends upon Robin Williams's reprise of his DJ role in *Good Morning, Vietnam* and his character overshadows the entire proceedings. In this respect the genie's freedom which concludes the film represents not only an exorcism of America's role in the conflicts of the Middle East but also the exorcism of the ghosts of Vietnam. The myth of a clean war and decisive victory in the Gulf offered by CNN is a similar attempt to exorcise the ghosts of Vietnam from the national psyche. However, what makes the genie such an impressive character is his postmodern condition. What separates *Aladdin* from its predecessors is Williams's knowing irony and self-referential pastiche (he makes intertextual references to American game shows and Jerry and June's coverage of televised parades and offers impersonations of Groucho Marx, Peter Lorre, Robert De Niro, Jackie Mason and Jack Nicholson). The genie first appears as a game show host with Aladdin as a competitor. Aladdin's name is projected in neon lines and then punned upon. His subsequent high-speed delivery and polymorphous identity lead one to suspect that he is the very spirit of American television. This *genius loci* of the Middle East is a haunting of that region by the tele-technology of satellite television, CNN, and the victorious VCR rented out by Fukuyama. In other words, the genie is both postmodern *Zeitgeist* and the spirit of American cultural imperialism, the genie is Disney itself. The genie is on hand to ensure Aladdin wins and to police the ontologisation of Disney's ghosts.

The non-bodily presence of television channels, beamed in from a satellite which doubles as a global surveillance camera, makes this tele-technology a spectral force. It is employed in the Middle East in an attempt to Disneyfy the region and so takes part in what Derrida calls the 'appropriation of Jerusalem'.[13] He suggests that metonymically:

The war for the 'appropriation of Jerusalem' is today the world war ... Messianic eschatologies mobilize there all the forces of the world and the whole 'world order' in the ruthless war they are waging against each other, directly or indirectly; they mobilize simultaneously, in order to put them to work or to the test, the old concepts of State and nation-State, of international law, of tele-techno-medio-economic and scientifico-military forces, in other words, the most archaic and most modern spectral forces. (p. 58)

Aladdin is a representation of the Gulf War (one might think here of the elision between 'magic carpet' and the magic carpet bombing of the allies which supposedly produced no 'collateral damage') and as such takes its place as a representative figure in this 'world war' which contests the status of the strategic site of the Middle East. Disney polices the region with its own surveillance cameras, appropriating otherness and interpellating postcolonial subjects into objects of cultural imperialism – giving a suggestive twist to the term 'satellite state'. Disney follows Jafar's 'golden rule ... whoever has the gold makes the rules' and so endeavours to support American economic interests in the region's liquid gold (oil) by offering *Aladdin* as a cultural prosthesis to strategic intervention.[14] However, the problem for Disney is that such policing requires constant surveillance and a constant (re)negotiation of the continual transformation of the geopolitical. To ensure the success of Disneyfication *qua* ontologisation there must be a permanent proactive vigilance which monitors and responds to the violent deconstructions which disrupt the Disney world order.[15] Even if Disney were capable of such a domineering presence the 'phenomenal cosmic powers' required to institute it, like the massive military mobilisation of the Gulf War, would be an explicit acknowledgement that the order which Disney was defending had never before been in such serious danger.

Aladdin won the Oscar for best song with its hymn to victory in the Gulf 'A Whole New World' in which Prince Ali and Jasmine survey the New World Order from the vantage point of a 'magic carpet ride'. The journey takes them over Egypt, across Arabia, into Europe, and finally (although, in geographical terms, inexplicably) coming to rest on the imperial palace which over looks Tiananmen Square in Beijing. Sitting on the roof of the palace, Jasmine recognises Prince Ali for who he really is. This covert reference to the other spectres of Marxism who died struggling for democratisation in Tiananmen Square (the denouement of *Mulan* takes place in this same square) might also help us to recognise 'the attractive power' of Disney for what it really is. *Contra* Fukuyama, there is no 'very strong *predisposition* for all human societies to participate in' the wonderful world of Disney (the balance sheet at EuroDisney is testament to this) but the continued success of that world as the New World Order does require the forceful 'adoption of the principles of economic liberalism'. Even if in this context 'liberalism' hardly seems an appropriate term.

An African Hamlet

'Our country has not been lucky. Indeed, it was decided to carry out this Marxist experiment on us – fate pushed us in precisely this direction. Instead of some country in Africa, they began this experiment with us.'

Boris Yeltsin, speech to a meeting of
Democratic Russia, June 1 1991[16]

'Everyone reads, acts, writes with *his or her* ghosts', says Derrida in *Specters of Marx*.[17] *The Lion King* was released in the same year as the English translation of *Specters* and deals with the same source material, Shakespeare's *Hamlet*. Like Shakespeare, Disney finds its characters and plots in the work of others and makes them over in distinctive ways. It is apt then that at the same time as Derrida was formulating his reading of *Hamlet* as a ghost story about Old Europe, New Disney was 'copying' the oldest 'copyist' in Old Europe. By resurrecting *Hamlet* Disney comes face to face with the 'nursery tale of the Spectre of communism' which is haunting the West wing of its castle.[18] Marx and Engels claim that 'all the Powers of old Europe have entered into a holy alliance to exorcise this spectre' (p. 2). From the members of the 'holy alliance' listed by Marx and Engels we would like to substitute the iterable term 'French Radicals', who might now be 'decried as Communistic by [their] opponents in power' (p. 2), for that defender of old European orders the Walt Disney Company. *The Lion King* is haunted by the ghost of *Hamlet* because the film attempts to protect the boundaries of a European order which by its own actions it is helping to unravel. Night is falling on old Europe and Mickey and Donald patrol the ramparts of their castle just as their vigilance brings in a new dawn.

In 1994 South Africa went to the polls in its first democratic election (Derrida's dedication of *Specters* to the ANC-leader-turned-communist Chris Hani is timely in its untimeliness). The release of Mandela in 1990 was like the return of a ghost which the Pretoria government had long tried to exorcise, keeping him locked away like a genie in a bottle on Robin Island. He was a ghost which had refused to go away and who had in fact never stopped being 'conjured up' by his supporters who had campaigned for the metonymic power of his release since the start of his imprisonment. However, as Aladdin knows, letting the genie out of the bottle can bring with it unexpected effects and 'phenomenal cosmic' change. The undoubted moral authority of Mandela was tempered for Western governments by his unrenounced socialism and the unreconstructed Marxism of the ANC. Here were spectres of Marxism which threatened to return at the very moment when the holy alliance of old Europe was congratulating itself on their final demise. The New World Order is an order without ghosts, the term 'order' being suggestive of an absence of the disruptive effects of mischievous spirits. The return of the spectral would challenge the 'newness' of that order which grounds itself in the distinctly ontological 'world'. The genie allowed out of its bottle in South Africa had to be conjured, it had to be spoken to and asked to return to whence it came. Mandela would become a household name and the ANC would be domesticated, South African politics (an overdetermined site for the contest between a postcolonial socialism and what Derrida calls 'racism's last word', the ultimate logic of Western logomachy) had to be Disneyfied.[19] To this end Disney offers us a rewriting of *Hamlet* ('What, has this thing appear'd again tonight?').

The Lion King opens with an inscription to a ghost. Before the opening credits the film acknowledges a debt 'In Remembrance of Frank Wells, President of the Walt Disney Company, 1984–1994', Frank Wells having presided over the financial and artistic resurgence of Disney, turning the disaster of *The Black Cauldron* into the later pot of gold. *The Lion King* is then a testament to new Disney's own success dedicated to its own ideological values and share dividend. This opening injunction to remember is a memorial to the Disney project, lest we forget why this film is being made ('Remember me ... I am thy father's spirit'). There then follows the Disney trademark castle, this time not accompanied by the 'When You Wish Upon a Star' jingle but the sounds of the African bush. Like good European colonialists Disney has set its castle in the heart of Africa and only the uncanny sounds of the African night remind us that there is a profound otherness beyond the walls of the encampment. The film then opens with a cartoon Africa (the Serengeti, Kilimanjaro, the Victoria Falls, *Tarzan*, *Jurassic Park*) in which the whole of the animal kingdom is making its way to Pride Rock for 'the presentation of Simba', the newly born Lion King. Disney simultaneously signals its geopolitical ambitions and the futility of their totalising project in the song which accompanies this great trek: 'From the day we arrive on the planet and blinking step into the sun / There's more to see than can ever be seen, more to do than can ever be done.' These early scenes in which zebras, elephants, rhinos, meerkats, storks, giraffes and all God's creatures make their way to bow down to sovereignty is repeated in the advertisement for the straight-to-video sequel *The Lion King II: Simba's Pride* in which all the children of the world converge on the video shop. In the original film this universal congregation is explained as 'The Circle of Life' (the title of this opening song) which 'moves us all through faith and hope / Through faith and love'. These lyrics remind us again of the ghosts of Disney, written by Tim Rice who was brought into the Disney fold to replace Howard Ashmen (*The Little Mermaid, Beauty and the Beast*) who died during the making of *Aladdin*. Rice's Pauline sentiments remind us of the history of the colonial mission and missionaries in Africa. 'We are all connected in the circle of life', Simba is told by his father, just as Fukuyama suggests that we are all connected by our predisposition towards home video entertainment.

The Circle of Life seems removed from the teleological end of history proposed in *Aladdin*'s inscription of the Promised Land. However, what goes around comes around and there is a touch of *déjà vu* about the Circle of Life. In one of the film's early scenes Simba wakes his father King Mufasa before daybreak so that he can be instructed in his princely duties. Mufasa, voiced by James Earl Jones who also gave a voice to Darth Vader, would prefer to be the lie-in king but reluctantly takes his son to the edge of Pride Rock. As the sun begins to rise, Mufasa tells Simba, 'Look, son, everything the light touches is our kingdom. A king's time as ruler rises and falls like the sun. One day, Simba, the sun will set on my time here and will rise with you as the new king.' Disney has always preferred autocracy to democracy, from the regal worlds of *Snow White, Cinderella* and *Sleeping Beauty* to contemporary despots like King Triton, the Beast-Prince, Prince Ali, and the Emperor of China. It is significant that this 1994 film apologises for monarchy ('The play's the thing / Wherein I'll catch the conscience of the king') not so much because at this time the monarchies of old Europe had never before been so threatened but because supporting kingship in Africa was the political strategy of the West during the apartheid era. Chief

Bhutalazi and his Inkata party were the wrong horses on which Reagan and Thatcher bet their diplomatic shirts against Nelson Mandela and the ANC. However, support for local despotism as a bulwark against the return of the spectre of communism through the spirit of democracy seems to be standard foreign policy for the West: Noriega, Marcos, Duvalia, Pinochet.[20] The locus of these films is the difficulty Disney has in holding together the conceptual order of politics and economy which ensure its global dominance while extending its world market and so simultaneously compromising all of the terms which predicate the order it seeks to defend. In a global economy there ought to be no room for kings who seek to defend their Pride Lands from outside speculators.

Simba asks Mufasa if they own 'the shadowy place' which the sun does not touch. 'That's beyond our borders', says the king, who finds himself explaining the apartheid logic of segregation. The hyenas ('slobbery, mangy, stupid poachers', voiced by Whoopi Goldberg and other black actors) live in the elephant's graveyard in this 'shadowy place' and the border is strictly policed. Despite rigorous pass-laws the hyenas ('at the bottom of the food chain') still stray onto the Pride Lands to steal food; Mufasa has a secret police force of underground moles who let him know whenever the hyenas step beyond their segregated space. Mufasa justifies this exclusion to his son: 'Everything exists together in a delicate balance; as king you need to understand that balance and respect all the creatures from the crawling ant to the leaping antelope.' The suggestion being that hyenas disturb that balance by poaching, just as migrant labourers 'poach' jobs from local workers. However, Simba is from the deep end of the gene pool and questions his father, 'Dad, but don't we eat the antelope?' 'Yes, Simba, but let me explain. When we die our bodies become the grass and the antelope eat the grass and so we are all connected in the great Circle of Life.' This seems a thin argument even by Disney's philosophical standards; it is Hamlet's advice to Claudius that 'a king may go a progress through the guts of a beggar'. It is also faintly reminiscent of the 'trickle-down' effect of wealth creation much loved by neo-liberal economists in which the inequalities of capital are justified as the best way to achieve social justice. Such an argument is precisely like putting a lion in charge of a safari park. What Mufasa's circle of consumption neglects to mention is the role of excrement in maintaining the Lion's dominant position. Lions eat the antelopes, lions excrete the antelopes, excreta fertilises the grass, antelopes eat the grass, lions eat the antelopes, 'a certain convocation of politic worms are e'en at him'. The lions manage to square the circle even if they do not acknowledge that they are talking shit.

Fukuyama suggests that apartheid collapsed because of 'the impossibility of defying the laws of modern economics' and that 'the apartheid system's loss of legitimacy among whites was thus ultimately based on its ineffectiveness' (p. 21) as a system of capital. He says:

> Apartheid in South Africa ultimately broke down because it was built on the belief that black industrial labour could somehow be kept permanently in the countryside. For labour markets to function efficiently, labour has to become increasingly mobile: workers cannot remain permanently tied to a particular job, locale or set of social relationships, but must become free to move about, learn new tasks and technologies, and sell their labour to the highest bidder. This has a powerful effect in undermining traditional social groups like tribes, clans, extended families, religious sects, and so on. The latter may in certain respects be more humanly satisfying to live in, but since they are not organised according to the rational principles of economic efficiency, they tend to lose out to those that are. (p. 77)

The Disney family should beware! We might quibble over the notion that the liberation of black South Africans came about as a result of 'the apartheid system's loss of legitimacy among whites' and the claim that democratisation will produce more profit from an increasingly exploited labour force. We could also be suspicious about the very idea of 'the rational principles of economic efficiency' which would consider the care of the elderly irrational and sale of Mickey Mouse ears rational. However, there is a sense in which the globalisation of capital, of which Disney is a symptomatic or metonymic concentration, produced deconstructive effects within South Africa which precipitated the end of apartheid. These effects were not the supposed flexibility of labour but the questioning of the boundaries from which the apartheid regime takes its name (Fukuyama calls it a 'system' but we prefer the doubleness implied by 'regime'). If apartheid was the 'last word' in logocentrism, the ultimate logic of the logos and the last place on earth where it took the form of state-sponsored racism, then the disturbance of the conceptual orders of old Europe brought about by the deconstructive effects of the capital which attempted to shore up those same orders (what we are calling here 'Disneyfication') must take some credit for undoing the apartheid logic of inside-outside that this film attempts to justify. Ironic inversion or cynical manipulation, it is striking that *The Lion King* offers monarchy and the tribe as a figure for African government while the film's own commercial work undoes the very possibility of such a model. 'The body is with the king, but the king is not with the body.'

In the Circle of Life history happens twice, once as tragedy and once as a Disney cartoon. The Disneyfication (the complex collapse of the ontological into the hauntological and vice versa) of South Africa replays democratisation as rewriting of *Hamlet* in which dark subversive forces murder the good king and replace him with a communistic regime that destroys the economy and lays waste to the country. Africa is saved from Marxism by the intervention of the rightful heir to the throne, the voice of American youth Matthew Broderick. After Scar (Mufasa's brother voiced by Jeremy Irons) kills Mufasa and convinces the young Simba that he is to blame, Scar claims the throne.[21] With a bad back and laconic wit Scar is more Richard III than Claudius and more George Sanders's Shere Khan than Peter Ustinov's King John, 'No more like my father / Than I to Hercules'. He has been planning the death of Mufasa since the birth of Simba displaced him from the royal lineage and he makes an alliance with the hyenas who are also excluded by Mufasa's rule.

Scar makes his intentions known in a song named after the motto of the Scouting movement, 'Be Prepared'.[22] The song warns the hyenas to expect the unexpected ('We're talking kings and successions / Even you can't be caught unawares'), because the consequences of disrupting Mufasa's phallogo-centric order will be far-reaching and unforeseen. The hyenas expect the death of the king to mean the end of autocracy ('Yeah, who needs a king, no king, no king, la la la') but Scar tells them, 'Idiots! There will be a king ... I will be king!' Scar gives his troops the empty promise of all revolutionaries: 'Stick with me and you'll never go hungry again', as he stands on a rock promintory and his shadow casts the shape of a fascistic eagle onto the cliff face. This image is quite explicit as the cartoon collapses all socialisms with National Socialism, which has displaced 'Red Indians' as Hollywood's favourite metonym for absolute evil. As Scar finishes his speech the camera pans out to reveal that the cave is full of saluting hyenas, tiered on either side, proclaiming, 'Long Live the King'. They raise their heads rather than their paws to give the '*Sieg Heil*'. A group of hyenas march past Scar's podium and sing that their column 'will soon be connected to the king that we all time adore'. This column becomes an army goose-stepping in time to Scar's song and the camera swings round to offer the aerial view of such regimentation familiar from news footage of Mayday parades ('Here's fine revolution, and we had the trick to see't'). Scar warns his all-black army against subversion because 'you won't get a sniff without me'. At this point the ground gives way under Scar's feet and unexplained volcanic activity (the inexplicable sort you only get in pop videos) turns the set from the yellows and golds associated with the fascistic eagle into a deep Soviet red.[23] Scar skips around the rearranged terrain telling the hyenas to 'prepare for the coup of the century / Be prepared for the murkiest scam' which will come about through 'meticulous planning, tenacity scanning' and 'the wonder I am'. Regicide is never about policies; its always about personalities, 'foul and most unnatural murder'. It is at the mention of a possible 'coup' (the 'coup of the century', the coup which did most to define the twentieth century, being the Russian Revolution) that the animation begins to make full use of the setting in the elephant's graveyard. Skeletons begin to dance, held up by hyenas laughing behind skull masks. At the news of the appearance of this spectre of Marxism a rib-cage is transposed into a xylophone on the soundtrack. Scar reaches his high note with the concluding exordium 'My teeth and ambitions are paired / Be prepared!' and the volcanic rock on which he stands ascends skywards so that the figure of Scar crosses over the bottom arc of the crescent moon and a passing cloud comes to rest in line with his head. The camera pans out from this scene to reveal that this configuration creates a silhouette of a hammer and sickle. The hyenas sit on various outcrops of the rising rock formation to suggest the image of Tatlin's monument to the Third International. Finally, as Scar repeats his Boy Scout challenge, the camera pulls out to view this *danse macabre* through a skeleton lying in the foreground ('As if 'twere Cain's jaw-bone, that did the first murder! This might be the pate of a politician, which this ass now o'erreaches') before fading to black and silence.

Disney animation may have improved since Dorfman and Mattelart analysed Farmer Donald's attempts to shoot two pesky crows called Marx and Engels but the sentiments exorcised here seem remarkably similar. After Scar kills Mufasa he uses his inaugural speech as king to declare, 'We shall rise to greet the dawning of a new era in which lion and hyena come together in a great and glorious future.' This reappearance of the spectre of marxist dictatorship in Africa is the nightmare Other of the New World Order and its appearance in the richest and most industrialised African nation is a cause for concern. Scar takes his name from the cut across his left eye and his distorted vision on the left reminds us of the Claudius who has 'one smiling and one drooping eye'. However, Simba runs away to another regional homeland where he befriends the wart-hog Pumbaa and the meerkat Timon. Pumbaa is a Shakespearean ham actor offered to us as Falstaff in *Henry IV Part I*. Along with Timon of Africa he teaches Simba the 'problem-free philosophy' of *Hacuna Matata* 'it means "no worries"'.[24] The rest of the film is a haunting of one Shakespeare play by the other in which Simba must be taught to reclaim the responsibilities of kingship and be reminded by his dead father to challenge

Scar: 'Yet I / A dull and muddy-mettled rascal, peak / Like John-a-dreams, unpregnant of my cause.'[25]

Despite Simba's attempts to forget the past – 'Bad things happen and you can't do anything about it' – Nala (Ophelia to his Hamlet) finds him and encourages the by now adult Simba to return to Pride Rock. She tells Simba on seeing him again, 'It's like you're back from the dead', and with this ghost comes the possibility of good kingship: 'You're alive, that means you are the king.' Mufasa's witch-doctor, Rafiki the baboon, sniffs Simba's scent on the wind and, realising that the spirit of Mufasa is still alive, declares 'It is time.' 'The time is out of joint' and Simba's reluctance to give up his tavern life with Pumba and Timon reflects Hamlet's annoyance: 'Oh cursed spite / That ever I was borne to set it right.' Nala uses her feminine wiles to bring Simba round, their courtship being a sign of a 'world for once in perfect harmony', as Tim Rice states in his panegyric to the virtue of the New World Order. However, Simba only chooses to return to the Pride Lands after the ghost of his father appears. The scholar monkey Rafiki tells Simba that Mufasa is 'alive and I'll show him to you'. He leads Simba to a pool of water. Simba says, 'That's not my father, it's just my reflection.' 'Look harder', replies Rafiki, as Simba's image is transformed into that of his father. A voice comes from gathering thunderclouds which metamorphose into the ghost of Mufasa: 'Son, son, you have forgotten me, you have forgotten who you are and so have forgotten me. Look inside yourself, you are more than you have become. You must take your place in the Circle of Life.' Mufasa has previously told Simba that the constellations are the great kings of the past who look down on everything they do and Mufasa's appearance here calls to mind Hamlet's words to Laertes that his 'phrase of sorrow / Conjures the wand'ring stars'. Simba is still unsure whether to go home and take over the family business but Mufasa insists: 'Remember who you are, you are my son and the one true king. Remember who you are, remember, remember, remember.' This direct reference to *Hamlet* tells Simba that he is Mufasa's son and true king, in that order. The ghost places an injunction on the son who has no choice but to act in his father's name. When he returns to Pride Rock for the inevitable happy ending, in which *Hamlet* is 'de-tragefied', both Scar and Sarabi (Simba's mother) initially mistake the adult Simba for the ghost of Mufasa. The spectre of filial duty shows through in biology regardless of the son's intentions.

An inheritance, says Derrida, 'is never gathered together, it is never one with itself. Its presumed unity, if there is one, can consist only in the *injunction* to *reaffirm by choosing.*'[26] Simba's inheritance, like the inheritance of the Disney corporation (which openly declares its own eponymous spectral debt), is a matter of choosing to reaffirm the injunctions of the Law of the Father. However, the injunction to choose (and the injunction cannot be more than this) asks the son to decide and distinguish from among what he inherits. The injunction of the father can only operate through its own division and distinction into several parts and several voices. Simba chooses Kingship and Disney chooses the New World Order but that moment of decision is also torn apart by the contingencies and eventualities which give rise to the cut of a decision and which render its moment as undecidable. Simba banishes Scar, the land is renewed, he mates with Nala, produces an heir, and continues the Circle of Life. However, Scar remains a threat to his rule, the hyenas remain poised to revolt, and no one will ever forget the time of the hyenas and everyone will always fear the return of that spectre: 'If it be now, 'tis not to come; if it be not to come, it will be now; if it be not now, yet it will come – the readiness is all.' Simba reaffirms the phallogocentric injunction of inheritance, against the resounding thump of drums which accompanies the red on black logo 'THE LION KING' that appears at the end of the film (as it did at the start), with the presentation of Simba's son ('The rest is silence'). However, at the end of the film Pumbaa and Timon also stand on Pride Rock along with the parents and Rafiki. The rule of the lions has been adulterated (perhaps even slightly 'democratized') and never before has their privileged position been so in question. With the election of a democratic majority government in South Africa the financial backers and apologists of apartheid in the West (that is to say the British and American governments) had never before been shown to be the unholy alliance of old European interests that they are.

This film's desperate attempt to offer monarchy as an alternative political future for Africa is a demonstration of the terrible conjuration of ghosts which is taking place in the castles of old Europe, including Disney's own haunted house.

Derrida suggests that 'Hamlet curses the destiny that would have destined him to be the man of right, precisely [*justement*] as if he were cursing the right or the law itself that has made of him a righter of wrongs, the one who, like the right, can only come after the crime, or simply *after*: that is, in a necessarily second generation, originarily late and therefore destined to *inherit*' (p. 21). There is an untimeliness about the injunction placed upon Hamlet to right the wrongs of Denmark because Hamlet cannot help but inherit that wrong just as he cannot help coming after his father: 'Your father lost a father / That father lost, lost his, and the survivor bound / In filial obligation for some term.' Similarly, Simba as a righter of wrongs (and as an absolute monarch challenging a marxist regime he is certainly of the Right) is 'originarily late' and is destined to inherit his father's debts. Such lateness is like the 'late' in Late Capitalism: it is always too late, it must inherit the debts of capitalism as a precondition of its own operation. It comes after capitalism but it is constitutionally and ceaselessly haunted by the aporias of 'classic' capitalism and capitalism's desire to transform itself, through growth, into a state other than itself.[27] Capitalism, as Fukuyama's dream of the 'rational principles of economic efficiency' shows, always wants to become Late Capitalism even if that process of change leads to the violent deconstruction of the political and economic order on which capitalism is predicated. Just as Late Capitalism is always already implied in capitalism, the destabilising effects of deconstruction are always already present in capitalism. If deconstruction is the situation which we are describing and the strategy (it is strategic in the sense that it is provisional) we are adopting to respond to the aporias of Late Capitalism, might we also call deconstruction 'Late Marxism' with all that this lateness implies for both Marxism and deconstruction?

5

'You Can't Lionise the Lion': Racing Disney[1]

It is sometimes advantageous to be unseen, although it is most often rather wearing on the nerves.

Ralph Ellison, *Invisible Man*, 1952[2]

Look, a Negro ... Mamma, see the Negro! I'm frightened.

Frantz Fanon, *Black Skins, White Masks*[3]

An ape like me-e-e
Can learn to be hu-u-uman too

King Louie, *The Jungle Book*

Not since James Baskett played Uncle Remus in the semi-animated film *Song of the South* in 1946 has a black man, that is, an African-American male, been portrayed by Disney in an animated film in human form, and only in *Hercules* (1997) have African-American women appeared *as* black women. In fact the hybrid form of the semi-animated film cut with live action actually means that Disney has *never* figured an African-American man as an animated human in its entire history of feature-length films. Early American films produced from the 1920s until the Second World War frequently featured black singers such as Louis Armstrong and Cab Calloway in non-animated form singing alongside cartoon characters such as Betty Boop, a rash of such short films occurring in the 1930s.[4] As with *Song of the South* this formula appears to perform what for Disney is the necessary domestication of black representations that infantilise and emasculate the image of a black man through his elision with children, animals and entertaining cartoon capers, what James Snead calls 'a rhetoric of *harmlessness*'.[5] Yet this also suggests something of the ambivalence of the stereotype, which anxiously repeats that which should already be known. The black man does not enter the cartoon as an animated man but exists on its threshold, in another medium, where his tantalising and frightening actuality can be experienced simultaneously with the confirmation of his domestication. Disney was apparently singularly oblivious of the racial tensions articulated within the Uncle Remus tales, and they are translated into entertaining animal fables through which a young white boy learns the black art of signifyin'.[6] Uncle Remus, like an early incarnation of Sidney Poitier, exists in an unquestionably white world with, 'no wife, no sweetheart, no woman to love or kiss, helping the white man to solve the white man's problem'.[7]

The political nature of such an enterprise as *Song of the South* was certainly not overlooked by black groups in America. At the New York première in Times Square pickets carried placards stating, 'We fought for Uncle Sam not Uncle Tom'. The NAACP called for a total boycott of the film and the National Negro Congress called for black people to 'run the picture out of every town'.[8] Disney's difficulty with black characters in the animated films started in 1940 with *Fanstasia*. A short scene featuring a very young black centaur, figured as a little girl with four pigtails standing vertically off her head, large hooped earrings and a huge white grin, eagerly shining the hoofs of an elegant white centaur who is coolly filing her nails, was censored for its racist content.[9] *Fanstasia*'s reliance on the iconic pairing of black with evil and white with goodness is far more pervasive than a singe image, however, and the final episode, 'Night on a Bare Mountain', indulges in the infinite codings of race with terror, where a fantasised black devil unleashes terrible retributions which are only resolved through the intervention of Christianity. In the calm that follows the storm small figures process through an immense natural landscape, singing a Disneyfied version of Schubert's 'Ave Maria'.

Dumbo (1949) has usually been perceived as Disney's first major use of characters which are racially marked as black. The crows who find it hard to believe Dumbo can fly inhabit a set of codes that are readily recognisable as performances of blackness which conform to white audience expectations in the 1940s, drawing on the codes current in music hall and short cartoons for supposedly 'obvious' character traits. Disney's borrowing of the Uncle Remus tales point to a potential, perhaps unconscious source for this rather strange tale of a flying elephant, which might be read as a version of the African-American myth of the flying African ancestor who leaps into the air and so escapes slavery by flying back to Africa, this time staged with chained-up (African?) elephants. Without pushing such a reading, it is possible to see how Dumbo's blackness may not stop at the crow scene, for perhaps in this all-animal film we can detect the beginnings of what will become Disney's major strategy for negotiating the tricky issue of representing race: exclusive anthropomorphism.

Ev'rybody Wants To Be a Cat

This anthropomorphism is resented by some people – they say we are putting people into animal suits.
Disney writer, *National Geographic*, August 1963

We are Siamese if you ple-ease
We are Siamese if you don't please.
Siamese cats, *Lady and the Tramp*

Here Kitty, Kitty Kitty!
Hyenas, *The Lion King*

Ev'rybody wants to be a cat.[10] Except of course a dog. Having cornered Nala and Simba, the hyenas in *The Lion King* indulge their apparently inexhaustible sense of humour, punning on Simba's feline status. 'What'll we have for lunch? I know! Anything that's *lion* around!' 'I got one a *cub* sandwich!' The genetic propensity for the hyena to laugh is matched by the sworn enmity of dog for cat, an opposition supposedly marked by absolute difference, one which has existed for all time. The lion and hyena are supposed to be at the opposite ends of the food chain, one killing bravely and ruling wisely and the other sneakily scavenging and poaching, but here the hyena threatens to eat the lion, enjoying the time-honoured privilege of the dog to pursue the cat. The logic of absolute and eternal difference finds itself marked by the necessity of acknowledging the uncanny similarity of hyena and lion and the potential intervention of history (the possibility of revolution) which might disturb this relation. This is a predicament which the film attempts to deny, but cannot avoid communicating, as the hyenas join with the lions temporarily under Scar's rule. *The Lion King* resolves this inadmissible presence of sameness in difference by purging the pride of the hyenas at the end of the film.

However, every dog must have his day, as Hamlet remarks, and nearly forty years earlier *Lady and the Tramp* trounced the scheming Siamese cats who (again temporarily) invaded the domestic territory of 'man's best friend', masquerading in Lady's role, putting her in the dog-house. Here too, though, the logic of sameness and difference is also under duress, for both cat and dog must compete to fulfil the same role in the domestic human arena despite their mutual aversion. However, this difference is anxiously underlined in the film by the insistence on the cats being 'a race apart'. The Siamese element is overdetermined, marked by the facial features, voice and accompanying music of the feline 'Siamese twins'.

Disney's early films are notorious for their clumsy depictions of racial stereotypes: for the crows in *Dumbo*, the travesty of plantation life in *Song of the South*, for King Louie in *The Jungle Book*. *Lady and the Tramp*, however, is not usually regarded as one of these 'racially suspect' films despite this depiction of wily, duplicitous, troublemaking, freeloading, Asian illegal immigrants (they are brought in under the covers of a basket) into the American domestic arena who threaten to destabilise domestic politics by permanently estranging Lady from her owners and who endanger the life of their baby by encouraging other aliens, rats, to enter the usually policed boundaries of the house, while Lady is chained up outside.[11] It is not our intention, however, to merely add *Lady and the Tramp* to the ever-growing list of Disney films in which race is '*mis*-represented', and to offer a corrective to the racial stereotype by deconstructing it to reveal the truth of experience that has been betrayed by it. Rather, following

Homi Bhabha's intervention into critical analyses of the role of the stereotype in colonial discourse, we wish to discuss the terms upon which such images operate and the kinds of identities and positions they enable.[12] This will suggest the ways in which the Disney corpus is embroiled in the changing historical and discursive productions of race, difference and otherness which operate in both America's domestic and international affairs.

Lady and the Tramp's racial problems are not confined however to the felicitous coincidence of the name of a breed of cat with the fantasised threat of the 'Yellow Peril'. Rather this scene provides the signpost to the preoccupation of this film with immigration. The Siamese cats have accompanied their owner Aunt Jane for a short stay but they immediately threaten to move in: they sing, 'Now we looking over our new domicile / If we like we stay for maybe quite a while.' The film was released in 1955 but is set at the turn of the century with horse-drawn carriages and women in floor-length skirts. As such it negotiates between two historical moments of immigration concern, the campaigns for Chinese exclusion in the 1870s and 1880s which resulted in the Chinese Exclusion Act, and the campaign to repeal the act in the 1940s following the American and Chinese alliance against Japan in the Second World War. The widespread vilification of the Chinese, which also spread to the Japanese in the 1890s, signalled the failure of an immigration policy in the States based upon a 'melting pot' principle. Whilst quotas were agreed for immigrants throughout Europe this blanket exclusion sanctioned an expression of ethnic intolerance that was supposed to be very 'unAmerican' but became enshrined in American law. Disney polices this boundary of the nation against these unacceptable immigrants and unashamedly introduces race into its depiction of American family life and translates this into an examination of the dangers represented by unlicensed breeding.

Lady and the Tramp is concerned with every dog's desire to acquire a licence and its signifier, a collar. Like Kafka's philosophical dog, Lady and friends find it hard to imagine life outside these parameters; when Tramp shows Lady the big outdoors she stares at the landscape in confusion.[13] Tramp watches from a hole in a fence as a dog warden pastes a notice stating that any dog without a licence will be rounded up and put in the city pound. When Lady pays the pound a short eye-opening visit after running away from home she finds herself in a state-run immigrant reception centre where all the dogs are howling the tune of 'No Place like Home'. These homeless mutts inhabit very particular national and ethnic identities. Amongst the motley crew are Boris, a Russian wolf-hound who quotes Gorky (marked by the animators as Jewish by his pale blue eyelids, long eyelashes, and long nose), Pedro, a Mexican chihuahua, a German dachshund and a Cockney bulldog, who all live in hope of attaining a licence and gaze at Lady's collar jealously. As the shih-tzu Peg, the pound's regular female 'tramp', explains to Lady, 'It's your passport to freedom, honey.' They watch from their cages as a demented dog is led away to be destroyed. These candidates for a residency permit, some hopeful, some unsuitable, figure as 'other' to the naturalised Americans, of the 'leash and collar set' as Tramp refers to them – Jock the Scottie Dog (with a dubious accent), Trusty the Southern Bloodhound, and Lady the Spaniel, who is referred to at one point as Tramp's 'Spanish girl', by an Italian waiter.[14] Tramp escapes the fate of the pound dogs by virtue of his multiple identities, which embrace a range of approved national identities that are acceptable immigrant blood. He is Fritz on Monday and eats schnitzel with the Schulzes, Mike on Tuesday with the O'Briens, because 'Begorrah, that's when they're after havin' that darlin' corned beef', and Butch on a Wednesday when he has pasta at Tony's Italian restaurant. Melting pot is translated into cooking pot; Tramp may change national affiliations every time he eats his next meal, but his seal of approval on legitimate citizens confirms that Disney films have always been something of a dog's breakfast when it comes to questions of race.

Disney's all-cat film , *The Aristocats* (1970) returns to this theme to tread over the same ground with racially differentiated cats instead of dogs. Duchess (Lady), a sophisticated French feline of bourgeois origins, is pursued by O'Malley the alley cat (Tramp). Here the engagement with race takes place on the margins of the main narrative, in one key song relegating race to a spectacle which acts as an interval delaying the resolution of the plot, as film-makers frequently did in the 1930s and 1940s. In the song 'Evr'y body wants to be a cat' Scat-cat the black trumpet player has a multinational jazz band, and their speech is coded as that of 'hip cats'. O'Malley greets Scat-cat with, 'Blow some of that sweet stuff my way', and 'Lay some skin on me.' The blackness of jazz is enjoyed by all the cats: 'It isn't Beethoven, mamma, but it sure bounces.' This song also sees a return of the Siamese cat, his contribution to the song, 'Shanghai, Hong Kong, egg fu yung / Fortune cookie always wrong', continuing where *Lady and the Tramp* left off. The Siamese cat plays the piano with chopsticks, wears a cymbal as a 'coolie' hat, is cross-eyed and has a maniacal laugh. Disney's concession to the fact that this film is set in Paris (although set back in time some distance from current politics, in 1910) and not America is to include a 'beatnik' cat in the racially variegated musicians: 'Everyone digs a swinging cat.' As Disney's post-May 1968 film, though, it simply incorporates the politics of Paris into an established format for both repudiating and appropriating the other and lumps them all together, in the alley with the rest of the trash.

Turning from *Lady and the Tramp* to *The Lion King* involves a kind of Orwellian symmetry, reversing 1949 and Tramp's cosmopolitan palette to 1994 and Simba's chances of becoming a hyena's snack. The demented and dangerous hyenas, whose leader is voiced by Whoopi Goldberg, reproduce stereotypes about black Americans that should be out of place in the revisionist Disney corpus of the mid-1990s. The stereotype returns despite a culture-changing civil rights movement, some major soul-searching about racial discrimination in America, the birth of PC agendas and the arrival of numerous high-profile black stars on screen from the 1980s. *The Lion King* appears both to signal its participation in the new political agendas around race and yet to continue to produce racial signifiers first used in *Dumbo*, despite the presence of Goldberg's voice.

This is particularly incongruous given that some of the most recent Disney films have appeared to be actively engaging with questions of race, racism, ethnic cleansing and tolerance of cultural difference, marked by the climate of liberal social politics ushered in by the Clinton era. In the period immediately following his inauguration as President in 1993, from 1994 to 1996 Disney produced three films which signalled that bad old Disney would be purged and a new agenda for approaching race and national identity might emerge: *The Lion King* (which despite previous remarks can still be fruitfully considered in this light), *Pocahontas* and *The Hunchback of Notre Dame*. These three films clearly signal their interest in three major strands of liberal concern about racial issues in the United States: African-American identity and politics, a revisiting of the history of Native American genocide by white settlers and fears over ethnic cleansing and persecution of religious minorities in Europe from the Second World War to the present. The latter two of these three films are notable for the fact that both feature almost exclusively human characters with minor, mute animal companions. Both are focused around 'non-white' women, the eponymous Native American heroine, and the sensual, intelligent gypsy Esmerelda. Both women have political interests and intervene in the homosocial political sphere singlehandedly in order to challenge injustice and ignorance. Disney makes much of its worthy portrayal of 'authentic' Native American life in *Pocahontas*, and represents the gypsies of Paris in *Hunchback* in terms of present-day concerns with refugees, whereas *The Lion King*, which, despite its problems with hyenas, could conceivably be viewed as Disney's 'black' film, operates in an exclusively animal kingdom. Like *Lady and the Tramp*, this film is significantly preoccupied with race but is also in a keen state of denial about the politics of representation. The opening scene of the 'Circle of Life' song affirms a hermetically sealed animal world, but also an Africa which is always in excess of what can be represented. 'From the day we arrive on the planet / And blinking step in to the sun / There's more to see than can ever be seen / More to do than can ever be done.' This rhetoric of excess continues with a shot of myriad exotic birds and animals accompanied by the line 'There's far too much to take in here / Or to find than can ever be found.' This self-confessed inability to represent Africa masks the less loudly proclaimed reluctance to represent black people as people at all, African or otherwise.

The Lion King is set in a part of Africa that both is and is not locatable. The opening scene pans from the Victoria Falls, to Mount Kilimanjaro, to what may be the Niger Delta. These dispersed landmarks offer a shorthand for 'Africa the continent' whilst deferring any realisation of an actual place. Yet its release with that of South African democracy continually haunts the film. We may be nowhere in particular but a strict racial segregation operates here. Apartheid South Africa, Derrida suggests, might be viewed as 'a giant tableau or painting, the screen for some geopolitical computer' onto which Europe (and America) seemed to project 'the silhouette of its internal wars'.[15] 'Apartheid would be an *American problem*',[16] which needed to be objectified in order to prevent the recognition of too great a resemblance between South African and American segregations. In Disney's widescreen Africa the West's ambivalent relationship with the ANC is screened out by a plethora of fictional references, to the evil Empire in the *Star Wars* trilogy which return to haunt the story of Simba. The use of James Earl Jones to voice Mufasa as Simba's father creates an uncanny chain of deferral where numerous scenes draw on moments from *The Empire Strikes Back*, restaging them in Africa, whose own colonial past might have once been read as embedded in the *Star Wars* films themselves.[17] Here however the tension between the coloniser and colonised has been resolved, and Simba looks up at the stars to see not a battle between the Imperial army and the rebels but all the great kings of the past, including Mufasa, looking down on him. This theme continues with Rafiki the African witch doctor doubling as Yoda, Jedi master.[18]

We have however suggested that this film can still be viewed as Disney's conscious attempt to engage with the new political and cultural agendas of race in America such that the recovery of African cultural origins by black Americans is tentatively addressed here. In rather less reverent terms than *Pocahontas, The Lion King* signals its understanding of 'cultural difference'. Rafiki's sayings are sprinkled with Swahili, and as the wise monkey mediator between the animals and the gods he could be seen to represent, in Disneyfied form, the figure of Esu in African mythologies, which has become an important reference point in African-American cultural criticism.[19] Other supposed customs, which draw more on the production of Africa, by the West, as underdeveloped and backward, such as betrothal in early childhood, meet with less approval in the film: 'When I'm king that'll be the first law to go', the young Simba retorts, having been informed that his betrothal to Nala is tribal custom. These references represent a minor concession to a new African-American politics in this film, but the film is complicated by the fact that both hyena *and* lion are figured as black. Simba owes a debt to Michael Jackson in his Jackson Five years for his song, 'I Just Can't Wait To Be King', making him African-American rather than African along with Nala, but otherwise the lion/hyena divide coincides with an African/African-American divide, with African-American criminals menacing an endearing and caring African culture. Complaints were made about the racist implications of the hyenas and certainly Disney drops them completely for the straight-to-video sequel *The Lion King II Samba's Pride*. However, we would argue that this only serves to confirm Disney's ongoing problem with race.

Disney's Africa is the Africa of the zoo or safari park, something which is confirmed by the opening of Disney's own Animal Kingdom in 1998, taking some people and a small range of African species and transplanting them in America, in a kind of virtual Noah's Ark. In a bizarre reversal of the colonial model of Disney's ever-expanding grip on global culture (usually involving Disney's 'variations on a theme park' in other nations – France, China, Tokyo) Disney realises there is no money in Africa and incorporates Africa into its American theme parks. However, one should not be too swift to see Disney's venture into the safari business as marking a shift from the 'virtual reality arcades' of Disneyworld.[20] Disney has been synonymous with the imitation of animal life, of sweaty young actors in oversized suits hugging small children. But Animal Kingdom is involved in a seemingly endless logic of the simulacrum. Animal Kingdom, is a simulacrum of a simulacrum, in that it purports to be a safari park (which is itself a simulacrum of an uninhabited wilderness) whilst it is actually a simulacrum of a safari park joined by a cruise ship (another simulacrum of a holiday resort) to Disneyworld, and hence is just one of many 'rides' available for consumption. It is also a simulacrum of *The Lion King* (itself also a simulacrum of Africa), and it contains within it numerous automated animals and a huge Tree of Life with hundreds of mechanical creatures inhabiting it, providing a technical prosthesis to the non-originary originary animals in the safari park.

That is to say that Disney persistently sets up a false opposition between simulacra and representation when portraying Africa. These layers of simulacra screen out Disney's inability to represent African-Americans in its films which as such are themselves nothing more than representations. A film as representation is itself a ghostly simulacrum which produces the real in a constructed form. This however is precisely what is missing from Animal Kingdom, suggesting that the simulacra of Disney's theme parks therefore exclude 'representation as simulacrum' from the logic of simulacrum itself. African-Americans are thus unrepresentable because the representation of African-Americans lies outside the remit of an animal kingdom. We would argue that the representation of representation of African-Americans as such is the decisive indice which deconstructs the logic of inside-outside which seals Disney's Magic–Animal Kingdom from a black presence. Disney's filmic anthropomorphism, as a representation of a representation of blackness, constitutes a supplement to Disney's world of race. The supplement being that which cannot be understood in terms of the origin but which also defines the possibility of the origin as non-originary. These 'black characters' demonstrate both the absence of African-Americans as people from Disney films and the racially motivated ideological structure of the Disney Kingdom. The Animal Kingdom provides a massive readability of the explicit ways in which Disney's racial ideology is related to capital.

The strategy of using well-known black actors to voice cartoon animals in Disney's more recent films confirms this logic. Whoopi Goldberg as the hyena Shenzi, James Earl Jones as Simba's father Mufasa in *The Lion King* and Eddie Murphy as Mushu, the dragon in *Mulan*, along with Sebastian the singing hermit crab in *The Little Mermaid* represent the classic

Disney formula for racial representations in 'Disney Classics'. Sebastian the hermit crab is clearly of Caribbean origin, a fishy sidekick to the (white) mer world, Mufasa is African-American playing African, whereas Shenzi and Mushu are streetwise black Americans. The most 'endearing' of these characters, Mushu and Sebsatian, reproduce the early elisions of blackness with children, humour and harmlessness, being notable for their tiny stature in relation to the rest of the characters in these two films. Mushu is a minute red dragon, prompting Mulan to call him 'a lizard', and Sebastian, a red hermit crab, is served up on Ariel's plate as the main meal when she arrives on land. These minuscule appendages to the heroines, who provide light relief to the earnest journeys of self-discovery of the female characters, appear to satisfy the dual imperatives to both represent black characters on screen and to simultaneously render their racial identities invisible (both Mushu and Sebastian are bright red). Their pairing with two female leads also points to the domestication of their potential for sexual relations; whatever the myths about black masculinity, these boys are definitely tiny. Sebastian and Mushu clown around in films that draw their sources from two 'classical' tales, one European, one Chinese. The addition of these characters to supplement the original narrative means that they are signature characters, peculiarly Disney creations, confirming the specific interest Disney has in introducing them to its source stories and disarming the destabilising potential of America's racial fantasies and fears.

Red Men Tell No Tales

What made the red man red?
Peter Pan

Whether we are white or copper-skinned we need to sing with all the voices of the mountain, we need to paint with all the colours of the wind.

Pocahontas

The journey from *Peter Pan*'s Red Men in 1953 to *Pocahontas*'s, copper-skinned Native Americans in 1995 would appear to constitute a singular shift in the intricacies of racial terminology which signal the re-accommodation of the Native-American into the revisionary narrative of America's origins so solemnly portrayed in *Pocahontas*. *Peter Pan*'s monosyllabic, grotesquely bright red, misshapen, savage 'injuns' become a tribe of bronzed, articulate, civilised, beautiful people. The playmates for the Lost Boys transform into defenders of the eco-system and guardians of its 'spiritual forces'. This rapprochement with the original enemy of white America stands starkly in contrast with the representations of African-Americans which we outlined above. If white Americans have learned to love the 'Indian', it is precisely because the extent of Native American genocide has left little that constitutes a serious threat to white American hegemony. This is not for a moment to suggest that Native American cultures in the present day do not offer powerful critiques of late capitalist America's ambitions, nor that these cultures are not actively resisting the continued threats they face from the dominant order to their families, land, traditions and languages. Rather, a growing interest in Native American culture among non-Native Americans, associated with the increasing interest in New Age 'philosophies', has been accompanied by a translation of a range of beliefs and practices into forms that are readable and consumable in mainstream white America and elsewhere.

As red turns to copper, the role of 'Indians' changes in relation to the demands made on Native American cultures by white consumers and the debts they owe. For the Lost Boys these demands take the form of three questions about origins: 'What made the red man red?', 'Why did he first say How?' and 'When did he first say UG?' Here then are exemplary questions about origins, where the 'Indian' must provide explanations for his own difference *and* the origins of difference as it is understood and defined by the white coloniser. The 'Indian' is complicit with the manifestly overdrawn stereotyping in the representation of these heavily caricatured natives, yet also needs to be explained in order for the already known inferiority of the Indian to be explained yet again. Here, as with the other stereotypes discussed, the anxious desire for this knowledge to be affirmed points to the ambivalence which structures such images. The 'red men' set about a song-and-dance routine in which they offer answers to the three questions. However, as each question has at its heart a fantasised proposition about Native American origins the answers can only ever be a series of primal scenes for white Americans in which difference and desire are rehearsed through a prism of race. Accordingly the Red Man is red because he blushed with embarrassment when kissed by a young squaw. This of course cannot be represented by the 'red men' themselves as the are already absolutely lurid bright red, so Peter Pan demonstrates this logic, wearing a feather head-dress as a small squaw rubs noses with him. As he begins to blush with embarrassment, his face slowly turns from white to red. This provides a logic of origins in which the Red Man must have at one time been white in order for this blushing to take place at all, collapsing difference into sameness. It also produces the 'red men' (and, by association, 'red women'), as in a permanent state of sexual excitement. 'Red men' are that colour because they are *constantly* blushing. This explicit introduction of sexual excitement is continued in the explanation for UG, which is uttered by a newly married brave when he sees the formidable mother of his lovely young wife.

The 'red men's' song demonstrates the fictions of racial cat-egorisations with its improbable parables of origin. The Indians are simultaneously readable and unreadable, through the logic of sexualised otherness and a rehearsal of European cultural preoccupations. They have their unreadability signalled as the attributes of racial difference are revealed to be inexplicable in any other terms than these patently fictional ones which construct our make-beliefs. The boys and Indians happily enter a contract of 'make believe'. The Indians are playmates for the boys, enabling them to 'make believe' in safety – they always let the boys go if they catch them. This play in the imaginary place Never-Never Land, too fortunate ever to exist in reality, reveals that *Peter Pan*'s colonial logic and its racial fantasies are obtained 'on the never-never'.[21] Never-Never Land is a place in which all kinds of credit can be obtained, but where ultimately something cannot be had for nothing. Eternal childhood is gained at the expense of losing a mother; once the island has been left it can never again be returned to; Native Americans can live in harmony with the white boys if they consent to play their games, and keep to their allotted roles in those games. Peter Pan as an American who goes to London to invite Europeans to Never-Never Land reminds us that the origins of America have unpaid debts both to the Old World, and to the Native American population. White America is founded upon a loan, a bad debt that it can never repay. *Pocahontas* attempts to pay off some of the late instalments of this debt as it accrues interest.

Going Into the Red

> WIGGINS: Do you think we'll meet some savages?
> RATCLIFFE: If we do we'll give them a proper English greeting.
> WIGGINS: Gift baskets!
>
> *Pocahontas*

Wiggins's, Ratcliffe's camp manservant, confirms his unsuitability as first assistant to the mercenary prospective governor of Jamestown, when he fails to understand the man's aim of getting something for nothing from the natives – by discovering gold and claiming land for the King; not, as Wiggins suggests, distributing goods and goodwill to the indigenous population. In acknowledging the economic motivations of the early Jamestown settlers, *Pocahontas* attempts to face up to the debt that founded modern America. It does this both through the depiction of greed that motivates the white settlers, but also through its new-found 'respect' for cultural and racial difference. It does this by adopting what Derrida has recently called 'the expression worn enough to give up the ghost', namely, an attitude of 'openness to the other'.[22] The phrase may be overused in some circles but for Disney it constitutes a newly discovered country. Disney cannot give up the ghost because the ghost has only just begun to walk. 'The ghost walked' is theatrical slang for when salaries were about to be paid, an allusion to

Hamlet when Horatio asks the ghost if it 'walks' because 'thou hast hoarded up in thy life / Extorted treasure in the womb of the earth.' This film of dead men walking attempts to pay off its actors, who walk because they have secrets they have taken to the grave about America's debts.

The openness to the other takes the form of an acknowledgement of cultural difference, with a strong emphasis on 'positive representation' which recognises Native American life *as* a culture. It does however point to the limitations of the demand for positive images of groups that have been widely stereotyped to be replaced with a 'real' that was misrepresented. Like *The Lion King*, *Pocahontas* contains a sprinkling of language other than English, signalling Disney's disavowal of its own collapsing of linguistic difference and the hegemony of American accents in Disney movies. When Pocahontas and John Smith meet for the first time, despite Native Americans having spoken continuously in English in the previous scenes, Pocahontas and Smith find they have a language barrier. Pocahontas momentarily speaks her native tongue and neither its English-language audience, nor Smith understand her. Grandmother Willow, however, urges her, 'Listen with your heart and you will understand.' She does this momentarily and then begins falteringly, and miraculously, to speak American English. As the film signals its desire to respect difference and be open to the other it simultaneously demonstrates the impracticalities of any such attempt to agree about difference. It cannot avoid reminding us that Native Americans all speak English anyway in the late twentieth century, whatever other languages they speak. This linguistic slip of the tongue mirrors the numerous other incorporations of Native Americans into a readable familiar context. Pocahontas's young female friend has the facial expressions and haircut of a knowing High School deb, and speaks the language of an American teenager, at one point telling Pocahontas to 'quit fooling around' (they also exchange girl-talk about Kocoum's muscles). The project to erase historical specificity whilst claiming to represent it is most clearly outlined though in the songs sung by Ratcliffe and Powhatan as their respective sides prepare for battle. Disney turns a highly uneven history of colonial genocide into a lesson about the stupidity of war based on mutual tribal or ethnic ignorance. Ratcliffe's and Powhatan's sides repeat almost identical accusations against one another. Ratcliffe sings, 'Here's what you get when races are diverse / Their skins are hellish red, they're only good when dead'; while Powhatan sings, 'This is what we feared, the paleface is a demon / The only thing they feel at all is greed.' Both songs unite to repeat the same refrain, so that opposing sides sing in unison, 'They're savages, savages, barely even human, [...] we must sound the drums of war.'

In returning the term 'savage' to the settlers who have applied it to the 'Indians', the song underlines the desire to atone for the disrespect shown to native customs, but equally the insistence on equivalence of antagonism in each group resists any notion of colonial history and universalises prejudice and hostility irrespective of cultural, political and economic concerns. Far from paying back a debt *Pocahontas* demands that Native Americans share responsibility equally, insisting on an 'evenness' in the massacres that would follow the arrival of the Jamestown settlement. Such a demand, that the Indians 'go Dutch', is of course at odds with the proclaimed interest in, and respect for, cultural difference. Instead the film posits a universal suspicion of strangers, independent of the uneven nature of their interaction.

6

It's the Economy, Stupid: Bill 'n' Disney

THOMAS: What do you suppose the New World will look like?

JOHN SMITH: Like all the others I suppose. I've seen hundreds of New Worlds, what could possibly be different about this one?

Pocahontas

Each of you, a bordered country,
Delicate and strangely made proud,
Yet thrusting perpetually under siege.
Your armed struggles for profit
Have left collars of waste upon
My shore, currents of debris upon my breast.
Yet today I call you to my riverside,
If you will study war no more.

Maya Angelou, 'On the Pulse of Morning',
read by the poet at the Inauguration of
William Jefferson Clinton, 20 January 1993

It Takes a Village

With a new Democrat President in the White House and the promise of a new order of politics (the arithmetically friendly 'Third Way') Disney's flagship animations changed tack once more. Following the phenomenal financial success of *Aladdin* and *The Lion King* (the fifth highest grossing film of all time), the new dawn offered by the Clintons, after the long dark night of Late Capitalism, inspired the studio to turn its attentions to the founding myths of America. A new politics always requires a new myth of foundation (reading that possessive both ways). *Pocahontas* (1995) constitutes a risk for

Disney: it is the only film in the entire *oeuvre* to be based on a historical event. In the racially sensitive climate of 1990s America the claim on the Disney press release for the film that 'at various stages of the production, the creative team consulted with Native American historians and storytellers to incorporate authentic aspects of the Powhatan culture into the film' is not surprising.[1] However, the press release offers as one of 'The Facts' about the film that it combines 'historical fact with popular folklore and legend' to construct 'a compelling and romanticised tale of' Pocahontas. Chiding Disney for a lack of historical accuracy may seem a bit like 'feeling let down' by President Clinton's confession that he lied, but given our commentary in the previous chapter concerning the financial rewards to be gained by 'blacking up' Disney and this claim to the factuality of this fiction, then we might seek independent counsel.

It is a 'Fact' (the press release enunciates it in bold with bullet points) that the film combines 'historical fact' (which is a variety of fact with a supposedly privileged distinction from any other kind of fact) with 'popular folklore and legend' (which, although also based on 'historical fact', are not themselves factual). It is a fact that this film is a fiction. The fiction which results from this reconstruction of fact (but when do the facts stop being facts and become fiction?) is re-merged back into the facts (presumably 'historical facts') provided by 'Native American historians' (even though the film's credits do not acknowledge the help of any historians, Native American or otherwise). In fact, there is very little which might be described as 'factual' in *Pocahontas*.[2] What is more interesting as a 'historical fact' is the fact of the film itself. Firstly, the fact that Disney have made a film based on the story of Pocahontas which offers itself as a 'faithful' representation of Powhatan culture; secondly, the fact of *Pocahontas* as Disney's first fully elaborated encounter with Bill Clinton. Having touched on the first of these facts in the previous chapter we will now attempt to elaborate the second fact through a discussion of the factual content of *Pocahontas*.

Neither the unmediated racism of *Peter Pan*, nor the revisionism of *Dances With Wolves*, *Pocahontas* is the third way. The Disney version of the Pocahontas story goes something like this. Greedy British colonists arrive in Virginia to dig for gold in the New World (although not all of the British are greedy, just the effeminate ones who are in charge, and certainly not the Aryan hero John Smith, voiced by the Australian Mel Gibson, who is a cross between Errol Flynn and Riggs in *Lethal Weapon*). Thus the British are singularly to blame for the history of genocide which is the later history of the Native American people. When the British arrive the Algonquian tribe are immediately suspicious of them and hope they will go away. Tension arises between the two groups through mutual misunderstanding and irrational hatred. John Smith is taken captive and war between the Amerindians and British seems inevitable. Pocahontas saves the day by intervening in Smith's execution and everyone sees the error of their ways. The injured Smith sails back to Britain and the remaining colonists live in peace with the Powhatan tribe. If, as Disney claim, Native American historians were consulted during production then the final film seems to be suffering from amnesia. The particular sticking point here being the 'Peggy Lee effect' at work in the film which, like Lee's song 'Fever', compares Smith and Pocahontas to Romeo and Juliet (perhaps what the press release had in mind when it described the film as 'romanticised'). In other words, what is wrong here is the entire story of two warring factions driven by *mutual* suspicion. The Disney film would seem to have more in common with the presentation by CNN and the State Department of the late 1990s conflicts in the former Yugoslavia than with the history of the 1607 expedition. In this way the film, as a simulacrum of neo-colonialism, presents the idea that the colonial process involves an equity between two sides and not the violent appropriation of one by the other.

In fact, the historical Powhatan tribe offered a welcome to the European colonists based on their indigenous traditions of reciprocity. In keeping with the exchange systems analysed by the philosophical-anthropologists Mauss and Bataille, the Powhatan tribe sought to make an alliance with the Europeans through a ritualised gift of hospitality. In *A True Relation of such occurrences and accidents of noate as hath hapned in Virginia since the first planting of the Collony* John Smith recounts the way in which he was the guest of honour at an elaborate and bountiful feast which lasted several days during which the chiefs of the Powhatan confederacy decided whether an alliance should be made or not.[3] During the period of hospitality Smith occupied the position of 'the stranger' and was offered unconditional hospitality as any such alien would be. There was no Third Way in Powhatan culture and after a decision had been reached Smith would cease to be 'the stranger' (so, the elaborate hospitality would stop) and would either be offered an alliance or killed. Historical consensus (not necessarily the same as historical fact) suggests that Chief Powhatan decided that the British were too dangerous to be left to their own devices and an alliance should be offered with a view to absorbing them into the confederacy of tribes. The disappearance of the 1587 colony of Roanoke might be explained in this way, as having 'gone native'. In this respect Roanoke is erased from the Disney story as providing a too ambiguous point of departure for 'American' history and so the 1607 colony becomes the non-originary origin of America. Like Pocahontas's dream of the spinning arrow which guides her destiny in the Disney film, the elision of Roanoke in favour of Jamestown stages an insufficiently primal scene for the founding of America. As part of the ritualised alliance-making a ceremony was prepared in which Smith was laid out on the *pawcornoce* and clubs held over his head. In accordance with the ceremony Pocahontas threw herself on Smith and pleaded for his life. Her request was then granted and an alliance offered, Smith having passed through the ritual of mock execution.

Smith's own journals show that he had only the dimmest of understandings of what was going on during this ritual. The presence of Pocahontas at the ceremony is itself in doubt given that Smith neglects to mention her salient intervention in his 1608 account, only to inscribe her into history in his 1624 *The Generall Historie of Virginia, New England, and the Summer Isles* with the single sentence '*Pocahontas*, the king's dearest daughter, when no entreaty could prevaile, got his head in her arms, and laid her owne upon his to saue him from death.'[4] This appearance of Pocahontas in Smith's narrative seven years after her visit to London and subsequent death suggests that Smith's *True Relation* and *Generall Histoire* might have as much credence as Disney's 'Facts'. The facts which follow Smith's mock execution, as the history of European colonialism, is a history of the European misunderstanding of the gift relation and the Amerindian simulacrum of hospitality. Chief Powhatan exchanged his daughter Pocahontas for an English boy named Thomas Savage (no doubt the Thomas in *Pocahontas* who befriends Smith) who he believed to be Governor Newport's son. Pocahontas was christened Rebecca (the mother of Esau who sold his birthright to his brother Jacob for 'a mess of pottage') and married another colonist, John Rolfe.[5] It was not until the introduction of land grants in 1619 by colonial policy-makers in London and the growing success of tobacco imports brought an unprecedented increase in colonists to Virginia, all demanding land, that the Algonquian Indians decided that the laws of reciprocity had been irrevocably flouted by the Europeans who, because they now intended to stay permanently, must be repelled at all costs. This led to the 1622 massacre of the Virginia settlers (Disney's basis for Powhatan's hostility to the British) which 'justified' whole-scale annexation of Virginia by the British and provides what Peter Hulme calls 'the authoritative organising principle' (p. 172) for the history of America *qua* the history of white colonialism.

The Disneyfication of Pocahontas systematically undoes 'The Facts' as any Native American historian worth his or her tenure would know them. Under the cover of a politically correct revisionism (ostensibly turning Peter Pan's island into 'Never Again' Land) Disney manage to reinscribe all the erasures and elisions of white American history (while adding a few more of their own) back into this myth of foundation. However, *Pocahontas* is not *Peter Pan* and its questionable New Age ballads are not 'What Made the Red Man Red?' What, then, marks *Pocahontas* with this same-but-different logic which separates it from (and connects it to) previous accounts of Pocahontas and previous films in the Disney *oeuvre*? Having spent some time relating the 'historical facts' of Pocahontas it may now be profitable to examine the fiction of *Pocahontas* and the 'historical facts' of its own production, which are inscribed within the filmic text and which work to undo Disney's own undoing of the gift relation.

Undoing an undoing, in a sense, implies a 'doing'. *Pocahontas* 'does' Disney in the by-now-familiar fashion, with a 'feisty' heroine, sound-alike songs, a central love story, nasty villains, comic sidekicks, a doting father, no mother and a happy ending. However, it also does Disney differently because it makes a more or less explicit attempt to respond to the political agenda of a Democratic President, not in terms of American national interests abroad but in terms of internal, as well as external, affairs. There is something missing from this film which makes a virtue of recording the minutiae of seventeenth-century Native American agricultural practice. The opening song, 'Steady as the Beating Drum', provides a catalogue of agrarian technique ('Seasons go and seasons come / Bring the corn and bear the fruit / By the waters sweet and clean / Where the mighty sturgeon lives / Plant the squash and reap the bean') to accompany text-book representations of fishing, husbandry, harvesting, milling, village life, care for the elderly and lacrosse. However, in keeping with 1990s sensitivities the Powhatan confederacy neither grows nor uses tobacco. Even Wendy had been offered the 'pipe of peace' in 1955. This would seem a peculiar absence given that tobacco was the crop which persuaded the Virginia company to take up permanent residence in Jamestown. Disney suggests that Governor Ratcliffe (piped on board his ship along with a subliminal rat) is disappointed by not discovering gold in the New World, but Golden Virginia proved extremely profitable for so-called 'tobacco lords' in Britain. When Smith describes gold to Pocahontas, 'It's yellow, it comes out of the ground, it's really valuable', she produces a head of corn on the cob. Smith consumes the corn and takes some back to share with the other sailors. It is not hard to see what the corn is a substitution for in this 1990s family film.

Bill Clinton's presidency has been marked by its relation to tobacco in one form or another. His election was dogged by allegations over whether he inhaled or not; the intent of the early, failed healthcare reforms was displaced into anti-smoking legislation, education and taxation; simultaneously,

American insistence on the implementation of global free-
trade agreements is a recognised attempt to open new markets
for the tobacco companies whose domestic market is going
up in smoke; Kenneth Starr is the lawyer defending the
tobacco industry against civil law-suits; and Monica
Lewinsky's testimony demonstrated that there is no smoke
without fire. Even before his impeachment Clinton was
famous for secretly enjoying a drag on a cigar in the Oval
Office after Hillary had gone to bed. Like Freud, Bill Clinton
could say of his cigar that it was 'the only and best
companion of his life'.[6] Cultivating such personal habits as a
public persona, Clinton managed to appear neither pro- nor
anti-smoking in a skilful 'deconstruction' of a binary
opposition which runs to the heart and lungs of the American
body politic. Tobacco (and the exclusion of tobacco) cannot
help but re-emerge in *Pocahontas* as that which marks its
historical and social context as Disney's first Clinton movie.
Tobacco in this film, as when it is smoked, like the spirit
world of *Pocahontas*, disappears in its appearance and appears
in its disappearance. It is also intimately linked to possibility
of the gift as such.

Pocahontas is linked to belief and credit and thus to capital,
economy, and finally to the presidency, by the *authority* with
which it wishes to speak about its subject. The case for the
film's authority having been questioned above, there remains
the fact of accreditation by Disney as an author, in which
some subject is touched by the name of Disney and is both
legitimised as an effect of belief or credulity, and of bank
credit. The story of Pocahontas becomes a matter of
capitalised interest (in both senses of this term) by becoming
'Disney's *Pocahontas*'. This accreditation is a form of
counterfeit money in which *Pocahontas* as a title (a heading or
a capital) is multiple in its reference, referring to Pocahontas
(The Fact), Pocahontas (the cultural narrative), and *Pocahontas*
(the Disney film itself). In this sense the film presents itself as
both fact and fiction at the same time. Counterfeit money, as
Derrida notes 'is never *as such*, counterfeit money. As soon as
it is what it is, recognised *as such*, it ceases to act as and to be
worth counterfeit money.'[7] Counterfeit money is a fiction
which passes itself off as true using the established structures

of true money, namely, contract and alliance between individuals in an exchange. The exchange of true money is authorised by the signature of the symbolic figure on the bank note who makes a promise ('I promise to pay the bearer on demand') which as a promise is open to the possibility of being broken. In so far as *Pocahontas* makes a payment on demand (it repays the debt of *Peter Pan*) it is impossible to distinguish between the film as counterfeit true money or truly counterfeit money (it does pay a debt but it is also not true). The exchange (*Peter Pan* for *Pocahontas*) and the contract between film and audience is authorised by the Disney signature (one proper name underwriting another) which inscribes the narrative in an incredible network of accreditation. With Disney's signature we know we are getting a fiction but we also expect this fiction on some symbolic level to be true; at least, it should be true to itself.

Pocahontas as counterfeit money (it cannot even be said to be a 'real' Disney film since it was the first film since *The Rescuers Down Under* not to be drawn by the studio's lead animators) is linked to the tobacco it excludes by the question of contract and alliance, gift and counter-gift. On one level because tobacco is an unproductive expenditure (money going up in smoke) it is not surprising that the multinational Disney corporation has no room for it in its text. However, tobacco also operates in exactly the same way as attendance at the cinema to view *Pocahontas*. It is a pure and luxurious moment of excess and the pleasure it authorises exists only for the moment of consumption. Both Disney and tobacco offer the consumer expenditure at a loss in the form of a pleasure which does not extend beyond the limits of the act of consumption, dissipating its excessive self in smoke or in the spectral projection of the cinema. And yet, tobacco never achieves its own aspirations to excess but rather always leaves a trace in the ashes it produces. There is a remainder left behind which undoes the excess of the moment of consumption. Being what is left behind, ashes are a symbol of remembrance, sacrifice and offering in both the Western Judaeo-Christian and Native American traditions. Tobacco also leaves a trace in the Disney text. *Pocahontas* is a film predicated on the ashes of remembrance: the 'revisionist' premiss of the text asks us to recall the history of sacrifice of the Amerindians and also to remember the new political landscape in Washington. There is no doubt a generous helping of amnesia here as well, but the film as counterfeit-true could not have been made without the emergence of Clinton's rainbow politics and the place occupied by race in American political and intellectual life at this historical conjuncture.

For Disney, history is spectral. The history of the Native Americans, the history of America as a history of cultural imperialism, the history of America as a history of the economics of tobacco, and the history of Disney as the history of the misrepresentation of race are what return in this film. Like all ghosts these spectres of Disney have a history, they have a context in Disney itself, and are history. These ghosts are historical because they are not the same ghosts which haunt *Snow White* nor are these *Zeitgeists* of the Clinton presidency necessarily the same ghosts which appear in *Aladdin* and *The Lion King*. Much is made in *Pocahontas* of the spirit world and of Native American mysticism in its form as a New Age appropriation. The chorus of the title song calls out 'Oh great spirit hear our song' while important moments in the narrative are signposted by the appearance of multi-coloured confetti blown on the breeze to represent the 'presence' of spirits. Pocahontas is advised by Grandmother Willow, the spirit of ancient wisdom embodied in a thousand-year-old tree. She tells Pocahontas, 'All around you are spirits ... they live in the earth, water, sky. If you listen they will guide you', while in the song Pocahontas sings to John Smith she tells him that, 'every tree and rock and creature / has a life, Has a spirit.' Smith in return later tells Pocahontas that conflict is inevitable because 'everything about this land has them [the colonists] spooked'. The spectral thematics of *Pocahontas* call attention to the structure of reproduction which places the film as a film in the realm of the phantomatic. As a film, or a home video, *Pocahontas* is a series of reproduced images which return without ever having been properly present in the first place and so is itself a ghost. This spectrality is connected to the question of the gift through the mediation of tobacco.

Tobacco haunts *Pocahontas*, its sublime smoke appearing in the film without being fully present.[8] If the suggestion that conflict arose between colonists and Indians due to suspicion and hatred on *both* sides (the Disney text, like John Smith's narrative, singularly fails to appreciate the reciprocity operated by the Powhatan confederacy) is the point at which the film might be taken to be truly counterfeit then this is also the moment at which the absence of tobacco is most present. After a Native American is shot Chief Powhatan summons the chiefs from the surrounding villages to plan for war. Mauss's essay gives as an example of the gift the ceremony which accompanies just such a meeting. In the Disney film scant attention is paid to the council of the chiefs beyond the fact that Pocahontas as a woman is excluded from it. However, Mauss notes that the spirits which are said to be 'all around' Pocahontas are the first guests at the council and have an active part in the meeting:

> In the tribe of the Winnebago (the Sioux tribe), the chiefs of the clans very typically give speeches to their fellow chiefs from other tribes; these speeches are very character-istic, models of the etiquette widespread in all the Indian civilisations of North America. Each clan cooks food and prepares tobacco for the representatives of the other tribes during the clan's festival. Here, for example, are excerpts from the speech made by the chief of the Serpant clan: 'I greet you. It is good. How could I say otherwise? I am poor, worthless man and you have remembered me. It is good ... You have thought of the spirits and you have come to sit down with me ... Soon your dishes will be filled. So I greet you once again, you humans who take the place of the spirits, etc.' And when each chief has eaten, and has put offerings of tobacco into the fire, the closing formula points to the moral effect of the festival and of all the presen-tations: 'I thank you for having come to sit down in this seat, I am grateful to you. You have encouraged me ... The blessings of your grandfathers who have enjoyed relations (and who incarnate in you) are equal to those of the spirits. It is good that you have taken part in my festival.'[9]

Such a meeting between chiefs of a Native American confederacy is the proper place of reciprocity and of tobacco as a symbol of this exchange of gifts in the presence of spectres. The alternative meeting in Disney is a fiction (as is the conflict which follows) and chooses to ignore the ritual reciprocity involved in the historical meeting. The ceremony presents tobacco as a gift to the spirits, placing the spectre and tobacco on the same symbolic level of excess. However, this excess as a *pure* gift is counterfeit because each 'gift' is repaid with reciprocal hospitality and the possibility of the gift is reduced to an exchange which places each of the recipients in a relation of debt. Nevertheless, this ceremony leaves us ashes to remember it by and will return, in its absence, to haunt Disney's attempt to repay an excessive debt in *Pocahontas*. If the excesses of Disney's film are intended as a gift to those it has offended in the past, then the absence of this ceremonial reciprocity signals the ways in which 'the gift of Disney' is drawn back into a restricted exchange by which the company profits. The same is of course true of any 'gift of representation' which proposed an 'authentic' and unmediated portrait of historical actuality. However, in an economy of representation some portraits are more accurate than others.

During a previous meeting of the village elders the shaman, on Powhatan's request, had conjured from the smoke of the fire images of the colonists as 'ravenous wolves' who 'prowl the earth ... consuming everything in their path'. However, there is no such conjuration at the later gathering; ghosts and tobacco are swept under the carpet as the Native Americans prepare for war. The film turns the ceremony of the gift into a council of war and presents it in period detail as a true relation of Powhatan culture. What then follows is an escalation of tension between the two sides, leading inevitably to war. 'Sometimes our paths are chosen for us', Powhatan tells his daughter. This figuring of the conflict between colonists and Indians as the result of tribalism is symptomatic of the meshing of 'political correctness' with the bourgeois liberal ideology which frames it. The film's denouement presents an all-too-familiar, reductive and deeply reassuring view of political violence which rewards a 'sophisticated' form of viewing that spectates on the atavistic residue of pre-modern and irrational social formations. This is the 'evening news' version of Ulster, Bosnia, Kosovo, Palestine and so on. What this view of political violence fails to engage with is a critique of the state and the systems of capital which produce and depend upon such social formations.[10]

Pocahontas erases the economic specificities in the colonisation of Virginia, which are explicitly linked to the question of tobacco. The occupation and later annexation of the region by European settlers was a direct result of the profits to be made through the exportation of tobacco to European markets. The perceived threat of hostile natives was a threat to lines of trade between Britain and its new colony and the massacre at Jamestown gave colonial policy-makers in London a mandate to secure the lines of 'free trade' by force. The exclusion of tobacco from this film provides a double marking of its status as a Clinton cartoon. On the one hand it flags up the health fascism, enabled by promiscuous litigation, of 1990s America; on the other hand, the presentation of a threat to global markets as a residue of pre-modern and irrational social formations offers us a paradigm of Clinton's foreign policy, from the Persian Gulf to Kosovo. Tobacco is an insignia of modernity and its absence from the film marks this early modern tableau as distinctly pre-modern. The Powhatan confederacy demonstrates its configuration as a military entity when in the title sequence of the film the warriors return from their victory over the Massowomekes; Powhatan and Kocoum (who wants to marry Pocahontas) as the only examples of Native American masculinity we have access to are characterised by their warrior identity. Despite the carefully sketched drawings of Amerindian children playing lacrosse, this film's understanding of Native American culture still depends on the essentially bellicose nature of 'Red Indian' identity familiar to us from Hollywood westerns and films like *Peter Pan*.

Pocahontas offers an aesthetic resolution to a real conflict constituted at a quite specific historical juncture through the recapitulation of the myth of Pocahontas and John Smith. This ghost returns in the opening years of Clinton's presidency, haunting America without ever having been truly present in the first place. The Disneyfication of what was always an Americanisation of Shakespeare's *Romeo and Juliet* (itself taken at several removes from an Italian source) involves putting a specifically contemporary spin on the narrative as the negotiation of a 'peace process'. The film reaches a climax with the song 'Savages' in which both camps demonstrate their mutual loathing and ignorance. Governor Ratcliffe sings, 'They're not like you and me which means they must be evil', while Powhatan sings, 'They're different from us which means they can't be trusted.' A plague on both their houses. The song is accompanied by images of glowing fires and smoke as a substitute for the excluded tobacco and both sides unite to sing the chorus: 'We must sound the drums of war / They're savages, savages, barely even human.'

Guided by 'the spirits of the earth' Pocahontas intervenes to save Smith from execution and part the warring factions. As if standing on the White House lawn in front of the assembled world media, she declares, 'Look around you! This is where the path of hatred has brought us, this [holding Smith's head to her panting bosom] is the path I choose, Father. What will yours be?' Powhatan is moved to spontaneous generosity (for seemingly that is what the Bosnian, Palestinian and Ulster peace accords depend upon, not the months of detailed negotiations and the economic incentives which underpin them) to say, 'My daughter speaks with a wisdom beyond her years. We have all come here with anger in our hearts but she comes with courage and under-standing. From this day forward if there is to be more killing, it will not start with me.' His daughter speaks with the measured civil servant's vocabulary of the Dayton peace accord. As with all such 'peace processes' ideological difference is put aside in the interests of the greater good of free trade.

The reconciliation press conference at the White House has become the expected norm in the 'peace process' narrative. As a ceremony of reciprocity (in which Yassar Arafat shakes hands with Yitzak Rabin) it replaces the Algonquian ritual effaced by this film. However, like tobacco it comes at a price and while it aspires to the condition of the gift always remains caught in a system of exchange. The symbolic handshake has been paid for with US dollars in the form of aid and security. The reciprocity is unequal: the warring factions have their infrastructures rebuilt but America furthers its global interests and legitimates its legislative presence around the globe. Bill Clinton is presented ceremonially as the figure of the giver. Being recognised as such immediately annuls the possibility of the gift and of this apparently spontaneous and excessive gesture of goodwill, but Clinton must be present at an event of this kind to give it his symbolic blessing. He stands between the two leaders and facilitates the handshake, as a metonym of state department diplomacy and the healing effects of a Senate-approved development grant. In fact, Clinton's political career as a world leader has been built upon a series of such ceremonies in which he gives 'the gift of peace' to those nations who have expressed a desire for America to intervene in their internal affairs. As a simulacratic 'pope of peace' Clinton is passed in a chain of exchanges from ceremony to ceremony in a rhythmic restriction of the gift which reduces the excess of non-violence to the surplus value and profit of a violent economic appropriation.

The film ends with the wounded John Smith invalided home along with other 'cargo' from the New World, while Pocahontas stays to guide her people through the market reforms effected by the colonisation of Virginia. Any remaining threat to liberal economy resides in the film, as it does in state department mythology, with the malevolent agency of evil individuals. Governor Ratcliffe breaks the ceasefire (accidentally shooting Smith while trying to kill Powhatan) but is overpowered by his crew and shipped back to England. For Ratcliffe, read Scar, Jafar, Gaston and Ursula, but also read Noriega, Saddam and Milosevic.

Cosmospolitics

'[It's] time for the human race to enter the solar system.'
Vice-President Dan Quayle, 1989

Warning: Use only the projectile provided with this toy. Do not fire at people or animals.
Instructions on Buzz Lightyear doll, The Disney Store

Like the Carter years (*The Many Adventures of Winnie the Pooh* to *The Rescuers*) Clinton's presidency has been characterised by aspirations towards an ethical foreign policy the net results of which have involved US military intervention on a scale baulked at by most Republicans. One of the prevailing myths of the New World Order has been the notion that the combined military power of the West (meaning America with the enthusiastic support of alternative British governments and the tacit diplomatic, and sometimes token military support of countries from the European Union), no longer having a defensive role against the Eastern bloc, should be directed towards humanitarian interventions. These interventions, from the liberation of Kuwait to policing the Balkans, have been unequal in their implementation and always coincide with Western economic interests. The pretext for the exercise of Western military power is usually the destabilising actions of an autocratic individual (head of state or terrorist leader), always figured as a psychopath who threatens to undermine world peace by his adherence to extreme ideological dogma. This is not new. It is the same pretext offered by the British and French to invade Suez when their own superpower status was on the wane.

However, what is undoubtedly new about the computer-generated wars of the Gulf and beyond is the ways in which they redefine the conceptual as well as non-conceptual orders of war itself. No longer is war a contest between equal sides fought in a mutually occupied space in which political decisions are willed by force through the defeat of one of the two sides. Instead, 'war', if this term is still applicable, involves a radical inequality between the West and its perceived enemy (figured as an individual and 'his' army rather than a people in general), the techno-scientific military apparatus of the West meaning that war can be waged from another continent in order to police international law, which whenever it is selectively applied is itself a Western concept of the law. War is now waged, and occasionally put on hold, in the name of the humanitarian. This humanitarianism has an international scope and its interventions are multiplying as the New World Order becomes increasingly unstuck; unstuck in the sense that such a vast techno-scientific military complex requires an identifiable enemy to sustain itself, and when it does not exist it has to be invented. The humanitarian justification for Western military might involves a complex relation between governmental, non-governmental and pan-governmental institutions and is multifaceted in its medical, economic, technical and military dimensions. It also involves an understanding of human rights which presupposes the right to intervene in the affairs of sovereign states by alliances of other states and relies upon a practical and conceptual reformulation of the orders of the nation-state and state-nation.

Such a consideration is the subject of the 1995 full-length computer animation *Toy Story*. Technically this film is not within the remit of our book but it would be churlish to ignore it on the grounds that it was constituted entirely by the technique which enables the formal adventurousness of all of the films which concern us here. The eponymous event involves two competing myths of American militarism (the cowboy/sheriff Woody, voiced by Tom Hanks, and the astronaut/Space Ranger Buzz Lightyear, voiced by Tim Allen) coming to terms with their place in the New World Order. Woody has long recognised that he occupies a position. He knows he is a toy, but maintains a privileged role in relation to the rest of the toys: he is 'Andy's favourite' and toy shop steward. The comic potential of the plot is derived from Buzz Lightyear's belief that he is a real Space Ranger who has crash-landed in Andy's bedroom and whose function it is to protect the universe with the phrase 'to infinity and beyond'. While Woody's task of expanding the frontiers of the West ended with genocide of the Native Americans, the 'final frontier' of space offers Buzz no such liminal boundary. There is a moment of terrible realisation when Buzz watches television and sees an advert for the Buzz Lightyear toy as a merchandised spin-off from the fictive television show of the same name. He opens a flap on his space-suit to find the words 'Made in Taiwan' embossed onto its plastic coating. As a once proud cold warrior Buzz must come to terms with his place in the mediatic space of a global economy. He has a nervous breakdown and loses an arm while coming to terms with such knowledge.

The action of the film is based upon a rescue mission in which Woody attempts to save Buzz from the psychotic child next door, Eric, who tortures toys. This is also a mission to rescue Buzz from his own psychosis. Woody and Buzz become trapped in Eric's bedroom, surrounded by the monstrous hybrids he has created (a pterodactyl head on a doll's body, a doll's head on spider's legs made from Meccano, an Action Man's head on a skateboard). It would be too disturbing for the film to allow these uncanny automata to speak, so the all-American Woody must speak for them. Led by Woody, the hybrid toys rescue Buzz and teach Eric the lesson that he should respect his toys and 'play good' by breaking the unwritten rule that toys should never be animated in the presence of humans. The toys which Eric has tortured turn on him, some of them rising from their graves in the garden, while Woody pronounces on Eric's psychotic ways, forcing him to retreat in horror. This moment, in a film whose action takes place primarily in neighbouring houses, demonstrates the *heimlich/unheimlich* nature of the toy and the construction of childhood in general. However, it is also suggestive of a double engagement with post-Gulf geopolitics.

Eric is taught the lesson that he should respect the commodity. Any interference with the commodity and its use value is a challenge to the chain of production and is figured as a psychosis. The injunction against Eric's 'experiments' is an injunction against imagination and against play as a space of non-productive expenditure. For Disney play is fundamental to the construction of childhood but also to the construction of the consumer. Eric's disrespect for brand labels and the singularity of merchandising is an affront to the global entertainment complex which underpins Western economic and military hegemony through cultural imperialism. Obviously the child is disturbed and his victims must be the object of a humanitarian intervention on the part of the US. Buzz's breakdown during the rescue also points towards the simulacrum of commodification undertaken by this film. Buzz Lightyear was the 'must have' toy of Christmas 1996, the film having triggered a merchandising frenzy. However, the recognition of the chain of exploitation involved in producing Buzz as a commodity leads to temporary insanity and cross-dressing. Woody saves the hysterical Buzz from a doll's tea-party at which he has been dressed by Eric's little sister as 'Mrs Tompkinson'; Woody has to slap Buzz to bring him back to reality. Contained, explained, and naturalised within the film the uncanny and monstrous nature of the toy as commodity is free to operate in an extra-textual realm carefully prepared by the desiring apparatus of the film.

Buzz is a desirable toy in the film because he has techno-logical embellishments (he has a flashing red light which he thinks is a laser). However, as a toy Buzz is as obsolete as all the others in the film. What is absent here is the tele-technological revolution in play which has marked youth culture in the 1990s, namely, Nintendo Game Boys and latterly Play Stations. In a film entirely produced by computer technology the absence of such tele-technological toys seems like a disavowal, even though *Toy Story* computer games and CD-ROMS were released along with the film. The plot of *Toy Story*, like so much of Disney, is based on a denial of the death drive (we might think here of the aneconomy of the Circle of Life or the (person)ification of Ariel). Eric is told not to 'kill' toys, objects which the audience know to be inanimate, smashed toys rise from the grave to confront Eric, and none of the toys take seriously the prospect of Andy's impending puberty which will mean their exile from the bedroom. If, as Freud suggests, children's play can be characterised by the paradigm of *fort/da* in which the child learns to negotiate the competing influences of *eros* and *thanatos* and to develop the primary motor of repression, there is an assumption by the film that Game Boys and Play Stations represent a more immediate experience of the death drive than Andy's Etch-a-Sketch or Mr Potato Head. In a computer game it is possible to kill and be killed endlessly with impunity.[11] In accordance with its own liberal bourgeois ideology the film makes the suggestion that Woody and Buzz are a more pure form of toy and that, given a choice as to their educational merits, Woody is a better toy than Buzz. However, if all play represents an economy of *fort/da* then no single toy is more deathly than any other: one can be killed and be brought back to life in a computer game but one can also draw, erase and draw again on an Etch-a-Sketch. In fact, because a violent computer game involves the arti-factual and instantaneous representation of death, as opposed to the sublimated construction and reconstruction of Mr Potato Head, such play involves a certain avoidance of repression. Thus, the action of a computer game might in fact be said to be less of a denial of the death drive, just as that denial is predicated, like *Toy Story*, on the spectral tele-technology of the computer.

This is precisely the situation we find in the computer-generated wars of the 1990s in which television audiences at home expect a bloodless war in which operational targets are specifically military with little or no 'collateral damage'. Most important of all is the necessity to ensure that there are no Western casualties, and for this reason war is waged from hundreds of miles away by computer-guided missiles. War is no longer about killing soldiers or inflicting damage but about 'degrading' the capacity of an enemy to wage war in the first place. In *Toy Story* Eric is not defeated but his encounter with the animated toys 'degrades' his capacity to mutilate and torture. Andy has a Bucket-of-Soldiers who have no clear enemy but who are called upon to undertake humanitarian missions to investigate what presents Andy receives for his birthday and Christmas. They report back to the other toys via a baby monitor so that they can have a live report from the theatre of operations. Given such a profoundly contemporary insignia the film's insistence on the purity of the cowboy and the space cadet as suitable toys for boys demonstrates both a deep insecurity about American masculinity and the difficulty experienced by bourgeois liberal ideology to maintain its priviliged space in the flux of globalisation.

Buzz Lightyear's catchphrase 'to infinity and beyond' would seem to offer an alternative understanding of the geopolitical circumstances of Disney than the Circle of Life or Pocahontas's insistence that 'we are all connected to each other in a circle, in a hoop that never ends'. This appearance needs to be questioned. The drawing of the borders of the Pride Lands or of the frontier of the West policed by Woody presupposes a 'beyond' of those frontiers (and therefore the immediate transgression of those frontiers). This 'beyond' cannot be understood in terms of the area on the inside of the border; the Jamestown colonists erect a wooden fence in the belief that it will 'keep everything out'. Buzz Lightyear's military-policing mission assumes both an 'absolute exteriority' and a limitless responsibility to protect and serve.[12] In the context of the New World Order as global policeman there can be no limit to the frontiers it sets because the world is round and the beyond of a limit will lead back in a circle to the liminal point. War, according to Kant, occurs when groups encounter a limit drawn by another group.[13] A contest at a limit leads to the dispersal of groups over the globe. Such dispersion ends when those moving south reappear in the north, for example, and because the globe has a finite and continuous surface dispersion cannot go on forever. Therefore, suggests Kant, war must at some point cease and humanity reach a state of perpetual peace through negotiation. The Circle of Life and Pocahontas's hoop suggest that all creatures should live in harmony and therefore border conflicts should not happen and perpetual peace ensue. In *The Lion King* the liminal conflict is resolved by a dispersal of the hyenas while in *Pocahontas* the border is removed to allow the colonists and Indians to live in peace (for the film this is a permanent peace, for the Algonquian it was a contingent peace premissed on the belief that the colonists would leave), while the press releases of the US State Department insist that the perpetual peace of universal liberal democracy is inevitable.

Kant, like Buzz Lightyear, is aware of the possibility of other planets being inhabitable but he thinks of them only in terms of a native population and not as a site for infinite dispersal from wars on Earth:

> We do not know how it is with the inhabitants of other planets and with their nature, but if we ourselves execute this commission of nature well [dispersal to avoid war], we may surely flatter ourselves that we occupy no mean status among our neighbours in the cosmos. Perhaps their position is such that each individual can fulfil his destiny completely within his own lifetime. With us it is otherwise; only the species as a whole can hope for this.[14]

Accordingly, Kant's argument concerning the shape of the earth (and Disney's closed-surface logic) provides a transcendental argument in which there is no 'beyond' to the Earth. There is no *a priori* reason as to why a human diaspora should not extend into space and Kant's argument concerning new encounters as a result of dispersal and the peace negotiations which follow ought to be expanded into this final frontier. However, to do so and still arrive at a perpetual peace policed by Buzz Lightyear would involve assuming, as Buzz's paradoxical mission statement does, that the universe is finite like the Earth. The phrase 'to infinity and beyond' suggests a 'beyond of infinity' which must therefore be finite. Accordingly, the universe for Buzz is finite and within that restriction the Federation of Planets is sovereign. This is also the case for Mufasa and Powhatan just as it is for the permanent members of the United Nations Security Council. The expansion of Disney's interests over the globe will inevitably result not in an economy of excessive consumption but in a restricted economy which has gone right round the world and come back again. When Buzz reads 'Made in Taiwan' on his arm he realises that he is the product of economic growth which has gone from west to east and returned through the other side. Buzz is a commodity within a restricted economy and there will be neither infinity nor beyond.

The attempt by Disney to expand its economic activity beyond the bounds of its restricted markets is part of the economy of restriction itself and a demonstration of economy as a form of restriction. With each new 'modern classic' that Disney produces the company is confronted by a law of diminishing return in which it cannot hope to repeat the spectacular successes of *The Little Mermaid*, *Aladdin* and *The Lion King* because these films have altered the mediatic circumstances under which such success would be possible. These films were successful because they followed years of failure. To repeat their success, as 'successes', Disney would have to experience a similar period of failure. As long as Disney continues to produce films like *The Little Mermaid* it cannot produce another *The Little Mermaid* and the growth of the company will be restricted by its own success.

In his political writings Kant came to realise that the perpetual peace he envisaged as a result of the geopolitical frontier conflicts produced by the sphericity of the globe would be the perpetual peace of the graveyard.[15] Kant's cosmopolitanism in its early stages also associated this deathly peace with universal democracry. Since this eternal rest is as undesirable and impossible as perpetual war, because they both depend upon fictional limits, we are left constantly in the middle with 'perpetual frontiers and therefore [with] violence, without end, but always within limits. This violence cannot, without resolving into the death of perpetual peace, be absolute or finite, but is never-ending.'[16] This is the other possible reading of Buzz Lightyear's phrase, that beyond infinity is an equally infinite space and in this sense to be at the limit of infinity is to be in the middle of infinity. For Disney this means that its constant attempts to expand its economic sphere of influence involve a permanent collapse back into a restricted economy struggling to maintain its own limits. What this cosmopolitics means for the New World Order is not the perpetual peace of universal democracy but an engagement in a never-ending state of war. For Simba this means *The Lion King II* (in which the outsiders declare war on Simba, and at the end of the film the absent hyenas retain their potential for border conflict), for Pocahontas it means *Pocahontas II: The Journey to a New World* (coming soon on video), and for Buzz and Woody a sequel is as inevitable as the rewind button on a VCR, which installs them in a constant state of finite but never-ending war. *Toy Story* is a tale of the gift (each of the toys is a present). The action of the film suggests, despite its ideological enframing, that the gift is always in the middle without limits. There is no gift as such, only the restricted *fort/da* of exchange which reduces excess to surplus value and to profit. There is no 'beyond' for Buzz, only infinity and the marker of profit and exchange, 'Made in Taiwan'. Rescuing Buzz from such knowledge means rescuing Disney as a metonym for cultural imperialism from the devastating knowledge of its own limited potential to inflict its value on the universe.

7

King of the Swingers: Queering Disney

'We are talking to Ira Gershwin about a musical version of *The Hunchback of Notre Dame*, Quasimodo Jones.'
Woody Allen, *Bullets over Broadway*

Schwinger? Vot is a schwinger?
Duchess, *The Aristocats*

Forever Friends

The Hunchback of Notre Dame (1996) continues Disney's troubled negotiation of America's status as humanitarian policeman and its failure to act effectively in the then ongoing war in Bosnia-Herzogovina. The question of 'ethnic cleansing' is as much a background to the film as the computer-animated cathedral. Minister Frollo recalls 'the gallant Captain Phoebus home from the wars' to help him liquidate the gypsy population of Paris. Frollo and Phoebus meet on the balcony of the *Palais de Justice*, which is opposite Notre-Dame and similarly overlooks the whole of Paris, providing a hellish counter to Quasimodo's humanitarian bird sanctuary and bell tower. Frollo tells Phoebus, 'You've come to Paris in her darkest hour, Captain. It will take a firm hand to stop the weak-minded being so easily led.' Frollo surveys Paris and declares, 'Look! Gypsies, they live outside the normal order. Their heathen ways inflame the people's lowest instincts and they must be stopped.' Frollo clutches his fist, relishing its crushing action, as the sceptical Phoebus objects, 'I was summoned from the wars to capture fortune-tellers and palm readers?' Frollo is more certain: 'The real war is what you see before you. For 20 years I have been taking care of the gypsies one by one [he kills three ants on the balcony with individual fingers] and yet for all my success they have thrived [he lifts a slab from the balcony to reveal a colony of metaphorical ants]. I believe they have a safe haven within the walls of this very city. A nest, if you will.' As an American soldier gunning for the wrong side Phoebus, voiced by Kevin Kline, is familiar with the contemporary jargon of 'safe havens' but, unsure as to their purpose, he asks, 'What are we going to do about it, sir?' Frollo inverts the slab and grinds it on top of the ants. 'You make your point quite vividly, sir', responds an alarmed Phoebus.

Like Native Americans the Romany present a suitable object for humanitarian intervention because their lack of numbers after genocidal onslaught means that their otherness can be negotiated with relative ease. Frollo's hatred of the gypsies also associates him with Hitler, the comparison of choice for State Department briefings about evil dictators, rather than the more complicated mapping suggested by ethnic cleansing of Frollo with the Serbs, who were equal victims of the Nazi-sponsored Croat–Muslim Ustace. This nazification of Frollo allows Disney to make the same complacent gesture as Steven Spielberg in the Indiana Jones films in which the Nazis represent the absolutely Other of an enmity without compromise.[1] Frollo demonstrates his Serbian credentials however when he burns 'down the whole of Paris' in his search for Esmerelda. He personally leads his soldiers in a series of atrocities, removing any possible ambiguity over his role as a public official. Acting on his own initiative, for the king never makes an appearance to take sovereign responsibility for this genocide, Frollo performs the familiar televisual vocabulary of ethnic cleansing: rounding up families hiding in cellars, driving an occupied gypsy caravan into a river, arresting innocent Parisians for possessing gypsy talismans, offering pieces of silver for information about Esmerelda, and setting fire to a house with a family – including young children – still inside. Phoebus cannot stand idly by and protests, 'Sir, I was not trained to murder the innocent.' Frollo tells him that he was 'trained to follow orders' and laments the fact that Phoebus throws 'away a promising career' when he intervenes to save the family burning in the house.

Paris burns with the metaphorical intensity of Atlanta in *Gone With the Wind* as, in a reprise of *Beauty and the Beast*, a Disneyfied alliance of Phoebus and Quasimodo save Esmerelda and Europe from its own *ancien régime*. Again, this film attempts to explain ethnic cleansing as a residual trace of pre-modern social formations rather than the mechanised production line of death disseminated by European colonial powers, the US cavalry, and later the Nazis. As a story of the triumph of good over evil (and no previous Disney villain had ever set fire to occupied buildings, an image which can be tolerated in a 'family film' since the family has become so inured to such depictions on the nightly news) the film comes unstuck on a seemingly marginal point – friendship.[2] Frollo's ethnic divisions depend upon the same concept of 'friendship' as the bond which unites Phoebus and Quasimodo (brothers-in-arms), the same concept of friendship which structures ethnic separation in the former Yugoslavia as well as the experience of democracy in the West (including Victor Hugo's appreciation of the term) and the alliance of nations in Nato or the UN. The values which uphold this understanding of friendship can be identified as the familial and phallocentric inscription of fraternity and the homo-virile schema of virtue.

At stake in this friendly parallel between Phoebus and Frollo (who were one-time allies) is the double exclusion of the feminine and the homosexual, both of which this film takes great pains to present as central to its concerns. Esmerelda is another of Disney's cloned heroines whose presence screens out many of the ideologically conservative manoeuvres of these later films. While the gargoyles Victor, Hugo and Laverne camp it up in the bell tower during Quasimodo's song-and-dance routines: there are citations here from *The Wizard of Oz*, Shirley Temple films, and torch song. One of their numbers runs, 'We've all gaped at some Adonis / Then we've craved something more nourishing to chew / [But] you're shaped like a croissant-is.' However, despite this increasingly open recognition of its gay and lesbian audience the gargoyles know that they are just 'spectators' on the family dramas of Paris. They are only 'out' as animated characters in the presence of Quasimodo whose own difference could also mark an ambiguous sexuality (his opening song is entitled 'Out There'). When confronted by other humans they are straightlaced and stony-faced and when animated they are voyeurs rather than participants. Their own friendship as blood-from-stone brothers excludes the possibility of a homosexual relation between them. Ultimately, they are more peripheral than the Sea Witch Ursula (allegedly modelled on the actor Divine) and might be said to work on the level of tokenism. In this way Disney repays a considerable debt to its queer audience by 'shoving the queer' to one side.[3]

In the full-length animations the exclusion of homosexuality is based on an understanding of the primacy of homosocial relations, which as Eve Kosofsky Sedgwick notes with respect to the nineteenth-century novel, are:

> Tightly, often casually bound up with ... other more visible changes; that the emerging pattern of male friendship, mentorship, entitlement, rivalry, and hetero- and homosexuality [is] in an intimate and shifting relation to class; and that no element of that pattern can be understood outside of its relation to women and the gender system as a whole.[4]

While the new Disney *oeuvre* provides a collection of look-alike simulacras of femininity it also presents a familiar model of libidinal economy in which the centrality of the heroine screens out the shared desires of the men who pursue her as a means of 'maintaining and transmitting patriarchal power'.[5] We might think of Hercules and Hades, whose competition is focused by their desire to possess Meg; Kocoum and Smith provide an example of the potentially lethal erotic dynamic which exists between men in these films, as it does between the Beast and Gaston; Jafar and Aladdin come to blows over Princess Jasmine; while Simba, Timon and Pumbaa enjoy an exclusively male friendship similar to Eric and Grimsby. Despite the pretensions of these films to present themselves as feminist texts (undoubtedly their commercial viability and their seeming novelty depends upon a successful presentation of themselves as such), there is a distinct resemblance between these circuits of desire, which exclude women from desire, and the libidinal patterns of past Disney films. It might be useful to consider here Basil and Dawson in *The Great Mouse Detective*, the eponymous heroes of *The Fox and the Hound* (which Disney advertises as their 'tale about friendship'), the Merry Men in *Robin Hood*, Shere Khan's pursuit of Mowgli, the Lost Boys, and the Seven Dwarfs. This is not to say that Disney is full of closet homosexuality just waiting to be outed (although it sometimes is) but that homosocial desire, a phallocentric schema which at one and the same time excludes both women and the explicit expression of homosexuality, structures Disney's representation of hetero-patriarchal normativity. If there is something a bit queer about Disney, it is this equation of democracy as a natural law of brotherhood with the 'unnatural' passions of homosociality.

All the canonical taxonomies of the political (government, representation, sovereignty, citizenship and so on) are touched directly or indirectly in *The Hunchback of Notre Dame* by the question of friendship. Friendship runs through the narrative like a pink thread, joining each series of events. Quasimodo lives with his friends in the bell tower; Frollo tells Quasimodo that, 'I am your only friend ... be faithful to me'; Quasimodo repeats this line in chorus to Frollo's song 'You Are My Only Friend'; Phoebus tells Quasimodo that Esmerelda is 'lucky to have a friend like you'; when Esmerelda asks Quasimodo to hide the injured Phoebus she says, 'I must ask your help one more time, my friend'; when Quasimodo is reluctant to warn the gypsies about Frollo's attack, Phoebus upbraids him, 'I thought you were supposed to be Esmerelda's friend'; in order to find the gypsy safe haven Phoebus and Quasimodo, having previously warred over Esmerelda's affections, declare 'a truce' and provide one of the few buddy acts in these later films. These friendships play an organising role in the film's presentation of justice and democracy. When Esmerelda frees Quasimodo from mockery at the Festival of Fools she shouts across the heads of the gathered crowd in front of Frollo, 'You mistreat this poor boy [familial schema] the same way you mistreat my people [ethnic identity as brotherhood]. You speak of justice yet are cruel to those most in need of your help [your Christian brothers]'. With a theatrical flourish she cuts Quasimodo free and, raising a clenched fist, shouts 'Justice!' This friendship is constituted by justice and justice lies on the side of the Phoebus/Esmerelda/Quasimodo democratic alliance.

However, this friendship is asymmetrical. While Phoebus and Quasimodo can be friends and political allies, Esmerelda is more than a friend to both Phoebus and Quasimodo. To resolve this tension and to exclude the feminine from the 'democratic' resolution to the film, Esmerelda withdraws from the action when overcome by the flames as Quasimodo prevents her execution. This leaves Phoebus and Quasimodo to defeat Frollo, who was a one-time friend to both of them (as previous 'sons of Frollo' Quasimodo and Phoebus are brothers). At the close of the film, Phoebus and Esmerelda are a couple (not just friends) while Quasimodo is infantilised (a small girl cuddles 'the ugliest face in all Paris' as a fellow child with the proud parents, Esmerelda and Phoebus, looking on). This infantilisation turns the fraternal political alliance between the three lead characters into a familial schema structured by a similar phallogocentric logic. Within the fraternal alliance Esmerelda has only ever been a 'friend' and as such is a brother rather than a sister to Quasimodo (there being no difference which makes any difference for Disney between these gendered experiences). Esmerelda's friendships can only be with men, as an honorary man, and never with another woman. As soon as Esmerelda's femininity is marked, as a shared object of desire for Frollo, Quasimodo and Phoebus (an expression of heterosexual desire which ensures the homosocial bond between these men), she must retreat from the action and spend the closing section of the film unconscious. Like Notre Dame our leading lady must be an attractive backdrop to men of action.

Friendship or *philia* (love as friendship) plays a defining role in the organisation of political experience in this film as it does in both the Christian iconography which frames the narrative and the French republican tradition which predicates Hugo's source. The archdeacon commands Frollo not murder the infant Quasimodo because all men, as sons of God, are brothers (even though Quasimodo's mother has just been killed). The closing line of Esmerelda's song 'A Gypsy's Prayer' makes explicit reference to the elision between 'sons of God' and 'children of God', in which all children are sons and the feminine is just a special but non-different case of the masculine. In Esmerelda's song justice is determined by this phallocentric understanding of the social bond as fraternity. This is also the case in the French republican tradition which makes fraternity the *trait d'union* between freedom and equality. While this republican motto does not appear in the Declaration of Human Rights, the Constitution of 1793 or the Charter of 1830, it does appear in the addendum to the Constitution of 1791 and in the defining Constitution of 1848.[6] In essence, to be a brother and to be a democrat is to be French. It is not a coincidence that Disney in a moment of crisis for the Brotherhood of the New World Order (by this time looking rather old) should return to Paris as an overdetermined site of Western democracy.

Gay Paris

He [Peter Mandelson] may be a minister of the British government. But we are the Walt Disney Corporation – and we don't roll over for anyone.

Disneyland executive,
The Oxford Dictionary of Quotations, 1998

Topsy Turvy! Everything is ups-a-daisy.
The Hunchback of Notre Dame

Paris is at once a symptomatic site of Western democracy and Western sexuality. As the gargoyle Hugo, dressed in a Louis XIV–Shirley Temple wig, consoles Quasimodo in his song, 'Paris the city of love is glowing this evening / True, that's because it's on fire / But still there's *l'amour*.' The burning of Paris occurs after the Festival of Fools, 'when once a year, we turn Paris upside down', characterised by the carnivalesque refrain 'Topsyturvy'. With inversion as its mantra the festival has particularly resonant queer possibilities. Quasimodo desires to leave the closet of Notre-Dame, to escape the clutches of 'Our Lady' and Frollo's teachings about the penalties of revealing his own deformity. As Clochon the narrator tells us, his name literally means 'half-formed'. Quasimodo repeats his alphabet lesson in the garret with Frollo: ' A, Abomination, B, Blasphemy, C, Contrition, D, Damnation, E, Eternal Damnation', For F, however, he replies, 'Festival'. Frollo jumps: 'Excuse me?' 'Forgiveness, I meant forgiveness', stammers Quasimodo. The substitution of celebration for contrition marks the beginning of Quasimodo's coming-out party. He finally plucks up the courage to defy Frollo and join in the Festival of Fools/Mardi Gras, which he has watched each year from his hideaway, where all hierarchies and logics are inverted. The Festival of Fools is held on 6 January and is thus suggestive of Shakespeare's gender-bending in *Twelfth Night*.

Frollo's own attendance at the Festival every year, despite his injunction on Quasimodo, marks his own ambivalent sexual repression, which sits strangely in a Disney movie. Clochon underlines this in his opening song: 'Judge Claude Frollo longs to purge the world from vice and sin / and he saw corruption everywhere except within.' Whilst much of this purging is focused on Esmerelda, his tortured internal battles with his knowledge of his own perversity are matched by his evident delight in sexualised sadistic acts. In the caverns of the Palais de Justice we find him standing outside a torture chamber. Sounds of whipping and groaning can be heard. 'Ease up', he commands. 'Wait between lashes, otherwise the old sting will dull him to the new.' The torturer appears, clad in regulation SM gear like a medieval member of the Village People, with a drooping handlebar moustache, studded leather gloves and black tights. Frollo turns to Phoebus: 'My last captain of the guards was a bit of a disappointment to me. Well, no matter, I'm sure you'll whip my men into shape.' The Frollo, Phoebus, Quasimodo threesome, which appears to centre around their mutual desire for Esmerelda, serves as a denial of the more pressing competing claims each has upon the other. Frollo has secret liaisons with Quasimodo, whom he instructs to stay faithful and grateful to him, visiting him daily with food as his only friend. This secret relationship is betrayed when Quasimodo helps Phoebus and hides him under the dinner table in his garret, while he and Frollo eat lunch. In this way Phoebus and Quasimodo enter a secret relationship, whilst Quasimodo pretends to be loyal to Frollo. Frollo and Phoebus's legitimate public relationship has already been marked as having a sexualised potential in the dungeon scene. This public connection is broken *publicly* when Phoebus refuses to obey orders. Only when the triad is disrupted, Frollo dies and Esmerelda turns the relationships into a heterosexual familial unit, is this 'topsyturvy' logic inverted.

Paris as a site of possible inversions of bourgeois values may also be the place that Belle has in mind when she sings, 'There must be more than this provincial life' in *Beauty and the Beast*. This set-piece borrows heavily from the iconography of *The Sound of Music*, with Belle as Maria, and establishes her as one of Disney's gay divas. Belle's song of dissatisfaction with life in the sticks is a hymn to the as-yet-unknowable pleasures of an imagined elsewhere, framed as a teenage impatience with a small home town and aspirations to the metropolitan possibilities of the city. Belle doesn't ever leave the town; rather, she moves out of the bourgeois milieu by becoming the lady of the manor. However, her inability to fit in to the local culture stems from her being, as the townsfolk note, 'different from us all', and 'a pretty but a funny girl'. Belle reads books, longs for escape and doesn't find the attentions of the local macho hero Gaston at all flattering. Her horror of being 'his little wife', affirms that her desires are quite different from any understood in the town: 'Behind that fair façade / I'm afraid she's rather odd / Very different from the rest of us, that Belle.' Disney's desire to maintain the success of *The Little Mermaid* is evident in this portrayal of a girl trapped in a stifling environment and yearning for escape (in Ariel's case helped on her way by a mercenary drag queen). But Belle's desires are rather stranger than Ariel's unfortunate crush on Eric. Her rejection of Gaston and his offer of a hasty marriage suggests she has still to decide on an object for her affections; she tells him dismissively, 'What do you know of my dreams, Gaston?' As 'a most peculiar *mademoiselle*', her reading breaks town taboos for women, but the fact that she reads fairy tales rather than philosophy or literature also confirms her interest in narratives in which coded explorations of sexual taboos and desires are embedded.

The tragedy of the beautiful and clever girl who does not have an interest in men, her tragedy being all the greater because of it, is precisely how Freud begins his description of a lesbian in 1920.[7] Belle asks her father, 'Do you think I'm odd?' but he, as an asexual, eccentric inventor, is unable to offer reassurance about normality. The ineffectuality of her father as a masculine presence is further underlined when she offers herself in place of him as the Beast's prisoner, putting herself in the place of the father. In the Freudian paradigm this typifies the psychology of lesbian desiring, which is always reducible to the schema of heterosexual, familial monogamy. Hence a woman desiring another woman is, according to Freud, substituting herself in the role of the father and making her object of desire the mother. As romance blossoms between Belle and the Beast she sings in realisation of her desire, 'New and a bit alarming / who'd have ever thought that this could be /True, that he's no Prince Charming / but there's something in him that I simply didn't see.'

Belle's supplanting of the role of the father threatens the family unit with psychosis. Gaston decides that he can gain Belle only through threatening to have her father institutionalised in, as the Disney animators print on the awaiting carriage, the 'Asylum for Loons'. Such a disarming of phallic power demonstrates the threatening potential of lesbian desire to undermine the institution of family life. It is the image of her helpless father that inspires Belle to leave her relationship with the Beast and save the family. Gaston realises that his priviliged position in the town is endangered by this monstrous desire. He cries, 'If I didn't know better, I'd think you had feelings for this monster.' Belle replies, 'He's no monster, Gaston, you are.' In this way Belle suggests that there might be something queer about being straight. Whilst the Beast has been explained to the audience as a prince in disguise and is always referred to as master of the castle, in allowing for the possibility of monstrous desires the film constantly plays with the possibility of falling into a queer friendly narrative, where the Beast remains an undecidable sexual object, not '"neither/either/or", nor "both/and", nor even "neither/nor", while at the same time not totally abandoning these logics either', as Barbara Johnson has said, until the transformation to human form restores order in the closing moments of the film.[8] This closure is out of place with the rhythm of the rest of the film and this is confirmed by the numerous video sequels to the original film, in which the Beast returns to sing songs and have adventures with Belle without the need for the unambiguous return of heterosexual closure.

However, notwithstanding the wicked lesbians/drag queens Ursula the Sea Witch and her predecessor Cruella de Ville, who have their own substantial gay followings, Disney's most sustained creation of lesbian chic is its transvestite bonanza *Mulan*. A drag act is a highly appropriate vehicle for Disney's first foray into Chinese territory. A China-friendly Disney movie ought to be an ideological impossibility, but in this story of a woman disguised as a man to help fight the Hun invasion, one can read the figure of Disney itself, embarking on a piece of sustained ideological cross-dressing. Mulan/Disney confounds the capitalist/communist distinction, as an undecidable figure like the Beast, in order to further Disney's business interests in the region. The original poem of 'Mulan' as a choice of source material for this Disney production enables Disney to rehearse its respect for Chinese borders and the political status quo, whilst depicting a pre-Communist Chinese order which cannot confuse the sensibilities of a Western audience about Disney's role in the democratic West. Disney dissembles somewhat here, having previously been warned by Beijing over its Martin Scorsese directed film about Tibet, *Kundun*. Disney's economic interests in China were still being negotiated as *Mulan* was being made with a Chinese audience very firmly in mind. The corporation's plans for opening two theme parks in China are in an advanced stage and their children's radio show 'It's a small world' was launched in 1996 with an audience of 400 million Chinese. In hock to China, Disney finds itself in Queer Street.

The corporation may claim not to roll over for anyone, but they are quite happy to bend over backwards if the rewards are big enough. Reading the character of Mulan as Disney, it becomes clear that Mulan's cross-dressing is paradigmatic of Disney's own negotiation of seemingly impenetrable borders and mutually exclusive territories of gender, sexuality, economics and political sovereignty. Having decided to take her father's place at the front, Mulan takes his warrior's uniform out of the closet, reminding us that free-market Maoism also had a military costume in the closet. Mulan finds that wearing a battledress is not enough to 'make a man out of her'. Before entering the army camp (which turns out to be something of a camp army *à la* Sergeant Bilko) she practises walking in a manly way and attempts what she thinks are suitable tones of voice. Her entry to the camp causes mayhem, as a brawl erupts after she takes Mushu's advice about how to interact with other men and slaps one on the buttocks. As an explanation, Mulan offers the essence of masculinity: 'You know how it is when you get those manly urges, to kill something, fix things, cook outdoors.' She attempts to spit to underline her point but, unlike Gaston from *Beauty and the Beast*, she is not 'especially good at expectorating'. Captain Lee Shang's song confirms the ambiguous state of masculinity in the homosocial context of the army: 'Did they send me daughters when I asked for sons?' He repeats the chorus, 'I'll make a man out of you', to the recruits who perform very badly in training. It is only after Mulan in a last desperate attempt to make the grade before being sent home, and to prove herself a man, climbs to the top of the post to which Shang has shot an arrow, something no other soldier has done, that the whole camp's performance turns around.

The success of Mulan's drag act is confirmed as she adjusts to her new identity as Ping, her assumed sir-name. Her defeat of the Huns in the mountains assures her heroic status, but also the discovery of her secret. What follows is a grand coming-out scene. When Mulan has been abandoned by Lee Shang's troops, she sits in despair with Mushu, who confesses that he was not actually sent to protect her by the gods but has come to redeem his name after previous mistakes. On hearing this his companion the lucky cricket bursts into tears and confesses that he is not lucky after all. Mushu sums this up: 'I'm not a dragon, you're not lucky, and what are you [looking at Mulan's horse] – a sheep?' However, the significant political potential of transvestism is naturalised in the final rescue of the Emperor, as (at her suggestion) Mulan's former comrades-in-arms dress up as concubines to deceive the Huns. They attack the guards with fruit stuffed down their dress-fronts as cleavage. For Disney, drag offers an expedient means of performing itself – *Mulan* being that performance.[9] During the rescue there is a reprise of Lee Shang's song to the recruits, and its exordium that they must be 'as mysterious as the dark side of the moon', as a soundtrack to this performance of the masquerades of gender (Artemis, the goddess of the moon being sister to Phoebus). Resolving the impossible through this show Disney demonstrates that while it may *seem* to be unsuited for Chinese cultural wars, suitably disguised it can actually *seem* to be more pro-Chinese than the Chinese. Mulan is the perfect figure for Disney's queer relationship with the Chinese.

Mickey Mouse Democracy

When [Michael] Eisner visited Europe he insisted on a bullet-proof car.
                    Reported in the *Guardian*, 10 April 1999[10]

Winning the World Cup is the most beautiful thing to have happened to France since the Revolution.
                    Emmanuel Petit, quoted in the *Observer*,
                    19 July 1998

In Hugo's novel *Notre-Dame de Paris* the significance of the cathedral is the view which it affords over the city.[11] In Book Three of the novel Hugo takes time out from the story of Quasimodo and Esmerelda to give a detailed description of the architecture of the cathedral and of 'the view of Paris as it then appeared from the top of its towers' (p. 115). For Hugo the cathedral represents the concentrated site of the history of France with each new addition to the architecture signifying the historical moment of its construction: 'Notre-Dame is a structure in transition ... each face, each stone of this venerable monument is not only a page of the history of the country, but of science and art' (pp. 111–12). Hugo's historico-geographical map of Paris presents the city as a metonymic concentration of European history from the Roman Empire to the Renaissance and Reformation to the Enlightenment. Each district and building joins together to provide a genealogy of the political history of Europe and so presents the history of Western democracy structured by this genealogy. Within the city the greatest symptom of this history is Notre-Dame, situated on an island between the Palais de Justice to the west and the Louvre to the east:

> The greatest productions of architecture are not so much the work of individuals as of society – the offspring rather of national efforts than the outcome of a particular genius; a legacy left by the whole people, the accumulation of ages, the residue of successive evaporations of human society; in short, a species of formations. Each wave of time leaves its alluvium, each race leaves a deposit upon the monument, each individual lays his stone. Such is the process of beavers, such that of bees, such that of men. The great symbol of architecture, Babel, is a hive (p. 112)

Notre-Dame is a democratic building, the work of a people rather than one individual. The understanding of democracy which cements Hugo's description is that of democracy as brotherhood: 'each individual lays *his* stone', 'such is the process ... of *men*'. Babel is the figure of translation which unites the dispersed brotherhood of man just as Notre-Dame is the hub of the city of fraternity. Disney's Paris is also the place of the brother. Quasimodo sings that he wants to spend a day 'out there amongst the millers and the weavers and their wives' (woman being equivalent to a trade or fraternity) and of 'ordinary men who freely walk about there' (freedom being inextricably linked to fraternity in Paris, Esmerelda spending most of the film in hiding, seeking sanctuary, or unconscious).

Politics of Friendship as a book, says Derrida, 'sets itself up to work and be worked relentlessly ... close to the thing called France. And close to the singular alliance linking nothing less than the history of fraternisation to this thing, France – to the State, the nation, the politics, the culture, literature and language which answer for the name "France".'[12] Disney's francophilia is also a love for the brother. During the Cold War and especially during the years of Reaganism-Thatcherism Disney drew its inspiration from the 'special relationship' which enforced the global hegemony of English language cultural imperialism and London was its preferred site of democratic values in the Mother of Parliaments.[13] However, Disney's role in the construction of the new Europe involves a relocation across the channel to the phallocentric schema of fraternity rather than the familial paradigm implied by its previous colonial relation.[14] Hugo's text 'L'avenir' seems prescient in its description of what was to come for Disney at Le Marne:

In the twentieth century, there will be an *extraordinary nation*. It will be a great nation, but its grandeur will not limit its freedom. *It will be famous, wealthy, thinking, poetic, cordial to the rest of humanity. It will have the sweet gravity of an older sibling ... The legislation of this nation will be a facsimile of natural law, as similar to it as possible.* Under the influence of this motive nation, the incommensurable fallow lands of America, Asia, Africa and Australia will give themselves up to civilising emigration ... The *central nation* whence this movement will radiate over all continents will be to other societies what the model farm is among tenant farms. It will be more than a nation, it will be a civilisation; better than a civilisation, it will be a *family*. Unity of language, currency, measure, meridian, code; fiduciary circulation to the utmost degree, money bills making anyone with twenty francs in his purse a person of independent means; an *incalculable surplus-value resulting from the abolition of parasitical mechanisms* ... The illiterate person will be as rare as the person blind from birth; the *jus contra legem* [will be] understood ... The capital of this nation will be Paris, and will not be named France; it will be called Europe. Europe in the twentieth century, and in those following, even more transfigured, will be called Humanity. *Humanity, definitive nation* ... What a majestic vision! There is in the *embryo-genesis* of peoples, as in that of beings, a sublime hour of transparency ... Europe, one with itself, is germinating there. *A people, which will be France sublimated, is in the process of hatching. The profound ovary* of progress, once fertilised, carries the future, in this presently distinct form. This nation to come is palpitating in present-day Europe, like the winged being in reptile larva. In the next century, it will spread both its wings: one the wing of freedom, the other of will.

The fraternal continent is the future. May everyone enrol now, for this immense happiness is inevitable. Before having its people, Europe has its city. The *capital* of its people that does not yet exist exists already. This seems a prodigy; it is a law. The foetus of nations behaves like a human foetus, and the mysterious construction of the embryo, at once vegetation and life, always begins *with the head*.[15]

At the centre of the centre of the 'fraternal continent' is Notre-Dame, the ill-named site of Disney's phallogocentric schema of friendship. 'Ill-named' in so far as it names the feminine at all, not in its monumentalisation of primary narcissism.

Each brick in Notre-Dame is testament to the presence of the value of presence in the political genealogy of Europe. It is a suitable symbol for the Disneyfication of Europe as the fraternal continent of world democratic values. The archdeacon sings to Frollo, 'You never can run from / Or hide what you've done from / The eyes, the very eyes, of Notre-Dame' (the eyes watching Frollo are the all-male lines of apostles, saints, popes and Kings of France which see everything). For Quasimodo seeing is everything as he keeps watch over 'the histories they [the Parisians] have shown me'. In the Western logomachy of presence seeing is believing just as Disney relies on viewing for its very existence. Hugo's vision of Paris is analogous to the Disney Corporation's view of EuroDisney as the centre of a new European order.[16] Disney's visibility in Paris, standing on the towers of Notre-Dame and looking over the whole of Europe, connects Disney to the phallogocentric schema of democracy as brotherhood.

Disney's idea of democracy is that of the structure of the Mickey Mouse Club. The fraternal ideology, presented as the natural relations between children, who are all 'sons' of Walt, is a facsimile of the natural law of brotherhood as it is understood in the history of a certain concept of friendship which structures the history of the bulk of European political philosophy. With Disneyland as 'the central nation' the Disney Empire will 'radiate over all continents' and represent a model of civilisation figured as 'a family'. The blind shall see and the illiterate learn by sing-along videos in 'an incalculable surplus value' in a continent whose name will no longer be Europe but Humanity. Humanity here is nothing less – but also nothing more – than a brotherhood. Fraternity as democracy is the future and Disneyland Paris presents itself as the *capital* city of this Western global hegemony.

Given such eloquence on the part of Hugo and the pleasure afforded to millions by the Disney fraternity, why should we criticise this schema of friendship? We do so in the name of a more inclusive democracy which might find a place for those subjects without subjectivity that are excluded from Disney's Magic Kingdom and from the principles of liberal economics and liberal democracy which cement the Disney religion. It is this model of democracy as the inscription of a homo-fraternal (homosexual-homophobic) and phallogo-centric schema which obscures the effects of capital within the process of globalisation and which determines the unequal implementation of international law in today's televisual wars such as in Kosovo. This universal democratic model and the effects of international law have their origin in the history of European political philosophy *qua* the history of the schema of democracy as brotherhood: the 'humanitarian intervention' as a defence of the brother masks the global ambitions of capital. Disney's *The Hunchback of Notre Dame* reinforces this schema in profound and powerful ways while offering itself as a postfeminist-queer-friendly film.

From *Steamboat Willy*, the seven dwarves and Walt's all-male studio to this cartoon version of Hugo's democratic fraternity and the all-male executive of Team Disney, the corporation has always been concerned with the rights of the phallus and the death of Mother. The 'democracy' it has been keen to promote has only ever been the law of the Father (Walt was never one for democratic representation in the workplace) and the sedimentation of a phallogocentric European law as international law. The American genie sings to Aladdin that, 'You've Never Had a Friend Like Me', while Woody and Buzz Lightyear unite in the end-title song 'Friend In Me'. Democracy as friendship for Disney is always structured as male, even when it is female, and as a homo-virile virtue excludes the possibility of a homosexual relation.[17] Frollo's ethnic fraternity and Phoebus's homosocial friendship are both constituted in the same way and both involve the double exclusion of the feminine and the homosexual. According to *The Hunchback of Notre Dame* the 'friends of Dorothy' may be Disney's best friends but they are no friends of democracy. The question which remains to be asked is in what ways do these Disney films deconstruct the transcendental position allotted to the phallus by the ideological terms but in play within this schema? Can these films be read so as to encounter the possibility of a radically inclusive democracy which, like Quasimodo (referred to throughout the film by the nickname 'Quasi'), is quasi-transcendental, neither stubbornly immanent within the Paris throng nor permanently aloft in the towers of Notre-Dame?

8
Democracy Limited: Impeaching Disney

'Bill Clinton is the closest thing we have to a black president.'

Toni Morrison

slingit owryir shoodir then
go izza petrol pump
  Tom Leonard, 'Hercules Unzipped'

Hercules Unzipped

The two public engagements which Bill Clinton made in the immediate aftermath of his televised confession that he had lied about his relationship with Monica Lewinsky were attendance at an all-black southern Baptist church and appearing on stage at the end of a performance of the Broadway production of Disney's *The Lion King*. The correspondence between these two events as part of the presidential penitential process speaks volumes about the racial and religious entanglement between Clinton and Disney.[1] With the economy booming and Wall Street enjoying the biggest bull market in history Disney's explicit support for Clinton is not hard to fathom, while Clinton has managed to present himself at one and the same time as a man-about-town and as pro-family. If *The Lion King* is a demonstration of Disney's disavowal of race through anthropomorphism, then the figure of Bill Clinton represents an alternative strategy for this disavowal, namely to encode black experience as white. Clinton's personal image negotiates a path between white-southerner-as-Washington-apparatchick and underdog-sympathiser-apologiser-for-slavery-as-lover-of-black-cultural-forms. Between his love of the saxophone and

151

his Baptist Christianity, Clinton presents a jazzy presidency whose affirmative action programmes encouraged black voters to come out in sufficient numbers during the 1998 mid-term elections to derail the Republican-led impeachment process and claim the political scalp of Newt Gingrich. Offering himself as neither black nor white, Clinton deconstructs the racial binary of American politics which neither the Republican presidential hope, General Colin Powell, nor the Clinton family's personal pastor, Jesse Jackson, have been able to undo. This deconstruction, as a situation, is the topic of Disney's 1997 film *Hercules*.

Hercules is a more or less explicit character reference for the Clinton defence team. It is the only Disney feature-length animation in which African-Americans appear as themselves. The Muses who provide a narrative frame to the film (they are still outside of the full-colour animated text, but they are nevertheless present for the first time) are drawn as yellow and black reliefs on two-tone Grecian pottery and presented as a gospel choir. The Muses take over the telling of the story from a white-voiced narrator who ponderously asks, 'What is the measure of a true hero? Now, that is what our story is about.' This is the same question around which Clinton's lawyers constructed their defence: both that a president's true worth should not be judged by private failings, thus imposing a public–private distinction within political experience, and that the president should be forgiven because he is just a man, thus undoing the same public–private distinction. This opening scene takes place in the Pantheon, calling to mind both Athens as the origin of democracy (and also the architectural model for the US Senate and House of representatives) and the Acropolis as an important site in the history of colonial appropriation and Western art. The film then connects the question of democracy as representation and the first representation of African-Americans in a Disney film around the mythic origins of the West and the ontogenesis of Bill Clinton's political career.

The opening lines of the film, 'Long ago in the far-away land of ancient Greece', put us in mind of both the start of *Star Wars* (whose image-repertoire *Hercules* will happily dip into) and Bill Clinton's own initials, BC. The Muses describe themselves as 'goddesses of the arts and proclaimers of heroes'. While still excluded from the central narrative, African-American women are invoked here to give their blessing to the story and to provide a testimonial as to the sexual potency of its hero: 'Hunkules – I'd like to make sweet music with him.' They bring the audience up to speed on the necessary Greek mythology, in a song the chorus of which might be a refrain for the Clinton lawyers: 'Honey, though it seems impossible, that's the gospel truth.' At Hercules' 'christening' on Mount Olympus the infant god's hairstyle is clearly recognisable as that of the American president.

Hercules, as an inscription of Clinton, is the victim of a massive right-wing conspiracy. Hades, god of the Underworld, is planning a 'hostile take-over bid' and is told by the Fates that 'should Hercules fight, you will fail'. Hades is charac- terised by both his smoking habit and his crass 1980s commercialism (Zeus jokes with him, 'Slow down, you'll work yourself to death', while the River of Death has a customer counter at its entrance recording 'Over 5,000,000,001 Served'). Hades, voiced by James Wood, smokes a suitably capitalist cigar and has a blue flame for hair; as god of the Underworld his lair is a place of death and smoke. Like the chain-smoking conspirator in *The X-Files* this use of tobacco as a metonym is quite different from the retro-chic of Fidel Castro or the healthy appetites of President Clinton. The conspiracy narrative favoured by the more distraught democrats during Clinton's impeachment process was that Kenneth Starr's politically motivated prosecution was also underpinned by the tobacco industry which was suffering as a result of Clinton's health policies and which retained Starr as lead-counsel in the civil actions brought against them by dying smokers. Here Hades, a fellow-god and Hercules' uncle, manages to combine a republican disdain for social issues ('Memo to me: maim you after my meeting') with Bob Dole's zeal for the vested interests of the tobacco industry as a metonym for the unhealthy interests of capital. Placing a Clintonised Hercules in opposition to the god of Death is certainly one way in which to make the flawed president seem more attractive.

Hercules in contrast has an idyllic family background, the stuff spin-doctors' dreams are made of. Having been kidnapped from Mount Olympus and then turned mortal by Hades' henchmen Pain and Panic, Hercules grows up the only adopted son of a farming couple with Midwest accents. Here the familiar motif of innocent farm-boy who longs for adventure is invoked (we might think of Luke Skywalker and Clark Kent, to name only two of America's most enduring myths about its own innocence). However, like Luke Skywalker and Superman – and President Kennedy – Hercules has a famous dad and is a member of a politically powerful family. Combining homespun virtue with genetic political acumen Hercules–Clinton knows that he has a greater destiny: 'Sometimes I feel like I really don't belong here. Like I'm supposed to be someplace else.' His first song, 'I Can Go the Distance', is testament to his political and sexual staying power, while his visit to the temple of Zeus to discover his true identity marks him as one of the political élite. The figure of Zeus recalls King Triton's affable paternalism, Laurence Olivier in *Clash of the Titans*, as well as Disney's much earlier portrayal of Zeus in *Fantasia* (the images map almost exactly).[2] However, his statue also resembles the monument to Abraham Lincoln on Capitol Hill. Having made the connection between Hercules and the presidency, the film sends its hero on the campaign trail so that he can prove himself a true hero on earth and have his godhood restored. Being immortalised for his display of 'godhood' may be Hercules' ambition; sadly, Clinton will be best remembered for displaying his manhood.

Hercules seeks out Philatites the trainer of heroes. Phil, voiced by Danny DeVito, is a sort of cross between Dick Morris (he even shares Morris's penchant for nymphs) and Burgess Meredith's role in *Rocky*. Phil is a baby-boomer who has experienced too many disappointments and broken promises ('I trained all those would-be heroes – Odysseus, Theseus, Perseus. A lot of yuses') and is reluctant to take on this 'rookie'. However, Hercules – like Clinton's campaign image as the heir of Kennedy – is the one who will restore hope: 'Haven't you ever had a dream? Something you wanted so bad you'd do anything?' Phil's song over the by-now familiar images of Hercules' 'Jedi training' recalls Clinton's origins, making constant reference to the word 'hope' (the name of Clinton's home town in Arkansas). One of the enduring images of the 1992 election campaign was a photograph of the adolescent Clinton (awkward and too big for his body, like the teenage Hercules) shaking hands with Kennedy next to a signpost which simply said 'Hope'. Hercules–Clinton is the great white hope and Phil takes him on: 'You need an advisor / A satyr but wiser / A good merchandiser.' Like that abiding spirit of good who is always there for us in our most troubled moments, Obi-Wan Kenobi, Hercules is 'our only hope'. Phil's song concludes: 'You're my one last hope / So you'll have to do.'

Before making it to Olympus and to the pantheon of presidents Hercules must perform well in the primaries. Phil plans to take him to Thebes, a 'good place to start building a rep', but on the way they encounter their first 'bimbo eruption'. Hercules has a predictable Achilles' heel and his campaign is temporarily derailed by the appearance of Megera (who has the singing ability of Jennifer Flowers, the urban sophistication of Hillary Clinton, the big hair of Paula Jones, and the sexual availability of Monica Lewinsky). Hades uses this weakness to plan Hercules' downfall, employing Meg (who has sold her soul to Hades) as a metonym of all the President's women to entrap our handsome hero: 'He's got to have a weakness, everybody has a weakness.' The rows of erect columns in this film have more than archaeological significance. Meg is an unwilling participant in Hades' Starr plan – 'I've sworn off manhandling' – but she is offered immunity: 'Give me the key to bringing down Wonder-breath and I give you the thing you crave most in the entire cosmos – your freedom.' Faced with no option but to co-operate with this scheme Meg does the only decent thing and falls in love with Hercules, for who could resist him? And his weakness is understandable, given the number of women who throw themselves at him.

After being distracted by Meg ('a D.I.D. – damsel in distress'), Phil warns Hercules, 'Rein it in, rookie, you can get away with mistakes like those in the minor decathlons but this is the big leagues. Next time don't let your guard down for a pair of goo-goo eyes.' However, having survived the Jennifer Flowers incident in New Hampshire, Clinton went on to secure the presidential nomination at the Democratic conference. Hercules arrives in Thebes, 'One town, a million troubles, the Big Olive', and proceeds to clean up this 'city of turmoil'. Like Mayor Giuliani's New York, Hercules' Thebes turns from the haunt of millennial prophets and flashers selling sundials to a violence-free oasis of family entertainment.[3] Once he has proven that he is not 'just another chariot chaser' by killing the hydra (once the many-headed figure of communist conspiracy, now the symbol of right-wing machinations) prepared by Hades, Hercules wins the popular vote 'by a landslide'.[4] It is at this point that the Muses return to provide a lyrical analysis of Hercules' popularity in the song 'A Star is Born': 'Bless my soul, Herc was on a roll / Person of the week in every Greek opinion poll.' Having his mandate underwritten by this excluded–included black caucus allows Hercules to be figured, like Clinton, as the nearest thing Disney has to a black hero.

The song details an extended comparison between Hercules–Clinton and black athlete superstars like Michael Jordan (Hercules, like Clinton, is resolutely white and in keeping with myths of European origins is a blonde Aryan rather than a pigmented Greek).[5] In part this a self-referential parody of Disney's own practice of merchandising – which can only be parodied because it is so readily accepted (Meg has already made the joke that Pain and Panic are 'two rodents in search of a theme park'). However, the choice of Hercules products is significant. There is Herc-aid, a soft drink served in McDonalds-type containers, an advert for American Express using a Grecian relief (reminding us of Disney's debts and where Hercules' credibility lies), and best-selling Air-Herc trainers. Pain and Panic incur Hades' wrath by wearing the trainers and consuming the drink. Air–Herc maps onto Air–Jordan while tours of Hercules' villa suggest a connection with Gracelands and Elvis Presley's racial hybridity. The song itself follows a gospel pattern and invokes explicitly black religious imagery: 'Say Amen, there he is again', changing pace halfway through with the shake of tambourines to ask, 'Who put the "glad" in "gladiator"? Hercules!' Hercules brings back the feelgood factor to Thebes and in another moment of self-referential gesture Hercules has his 'daring deeds ... recreated' on stage, providing a *mise-en-abyme* to the film. The song does not miss the opportunity to make another connection between Hercules–Clinton and Kennedy with a constellation of stars in the shape of Marilyn Monroe's breezy encounter with a subway train in *The Seven Year Itch*. Like Clinton's star-struck presidency Hercules leaves his trace outside a recognisable Chinatown cinema, while the booming trade at his 'Pex and Flex Gift Shop' reminds us of Hercules' role in kick-starting the *oikonomia*.

Despite being imaged as a black superstar – 'I'm the most famous person in the whole of Greece, I'm an action figure' – fame alone is not enough to merit godhood for Hercules, 'Being famous isn't the same as being a true hero', Zeus tells him. Hercules will eventually prove his heroism by enduring the plot to bring him down and saving his loved ones from the threat posed to them by extremist conspirators. The film manages to resolve the aporias of Clinton's mediatic image through straightforward reversal and attribution of Clinton's more difficult characteristics to his enemies. It is Hades rather than Hercules who has 'got this major deal in the works, call it a real estate venture if you will'. The impeachment process having begun with an investigation into the Clintons' role in the Whitewater property deal, Hercules redeems the heroic virtue of the presidency by exposing Hades' dark deeds and bringing justice to bear upon corrupt government. After giving up his strength for 24 hours to rescue Meg (who he later discovers has betrayed him by co-operating with Hades–Starr) Hercules proves he is 'the Comeback kid' (Phil refers to Hercules as 'Kid' throughout the film) by defeating Hades and saving Mount Olympus. As a hero it is Hercules' task to make several comebacks in the film (escaping Pain and Panic, fighting the River Guardian, and killing the hydra). The deal Hades made with Hercules is broken when Meg is injured by a tumescent column from Hercules' villa. With his strength restored Hercules saves Olympus but only proves his heroism by entering the River of Death to rescue Meg.

Once again Disney's 'spirited and independent' (to quote the trailer for the *Hercules* home video) heroine is excluded

from the democratic resolution to the film by spending the
vital moments in a state of unconsciousness, perhaps an apt
metaphor for the 'soccer mum' that Meg will become when
she marries Hercules after the final credit has rolled. However,
this film presents us with serious questions about the mediatic
construction of the political space in the 1990s. It relates
demos, economy, aporia and justice to *eros* and a myth which
occupies a privileged position in the history of Europe.
Clinton's impeachment represents an aporia for the Left. His
guilt confessed, with countless other offences to be taken into
consideration, the question which presents itself is this:
should a democratic (read this both ways) president be
impeached by a politically motivated right-wing senate? As
an aporia this difficulty overruns logical confines and can
only resolve itself in the form of a narrative which offers an
imaginary resolution to its real and pained contradictions.[6]
Disney's *Hercules* is one such narrative ('A true hero isn't
measured by his strength but by the strength of his heart')
following the same aesthetic process as Hillary Clinton's
conspiracy narrative and the 'Monica: Her True Story' option
taken up by Clinton's lawyers during the impeachment trial.
The irresolvable question for the Left – Christopher Hitchens
aside – is whether it is better that truth be the preserve of the
best-paid legal team and the democratic process of
impeachment, as a constitutional right, be circumvented in
the interests of a higher justice, namely, not giving the scalp
of a 'centre-left' president to the religious Right and its
business allies who had themselves extracted the perjury
under contrived circumstances? This is a mediatic event (we
might well) ask (what political circumstances in the 1990s
would not constitute a media event?) which touches on
questions of the law, justice, economy, democracy, truth,
sexuality, sovereignty, confession, friendship, freedom, social
responsibility, citizenship, the state, the body, sexual
difference, the public, the private, and tele-technology. In
short, the entire field of political philosophy.

The fact that Disney sides with Clinton in this film ought
to alarm anyone prepared to welcome unequivocally the
defeat of the impeachment motion (which as far as the Left
is concerned is the desired outcome). This might be said, para-

doxically, to place Disney 'on the left' and in light of all that we have said up till now this would be a deeply troubling formulation. What such a proposition does suggest, however, is the profoundly unstable nature of the political space in this mediatic age. If politics is caught up in the structures of reproduction and recitation which constitute the spectral media event then it is precisely the hauntological status of meaning which determines the political space. It is the infinite complexity and radical instability of the trace which is the possibility of politics as such. The political is only possible because any politics while attempting to put an end to every other politics as its intended goal cannot do so. This is because despite the closure promised by the metaphysical discourse of political philosophy there can never be a limit to or a politics which fully attends to the effects of the trace. What remains in the political space, the very constitution of which depends upon the possibility of a Disney–Clinton type reversal for its existence, is the non-messianic messianic structure of hope produced by the trace's interminable path of alterity.[7] Not the Hope which has its boundaries set out in Arkansas and as the nominal effect of Philitites' disappointment, but a radical hope which is permanently open to the arrival of the other as such. This hope, as a demand for democracy, is the event of deconstruction.

Mulan Rouge

> JON SNOW: Tell us about the dress.
> MONICA LEWINSKY: Yeah, that was a big misconception.
> *Monica: The Interview*, Channel 4

> 'There is an old Vulcan saying: "Only Nixon could go to China."'
> Spock, *Star Trek VI: The Undiscovered Country*

This book begins and ends with a wall. Kafka's short story 'The Great Wall of China' offers a commentary on the politics of Disney's 1998 film *Mulan*.[8] The wall in Kafka's story is constructed ideologically as a barrier against the enemies of China. Kafka's faux-naïf narrator accepts this liminal function without question and is convinced of the hellishness of those non-Chinese the Wall will keep out (p. 73). However, the 'beyond' of the Chinese border and the transgression of that border presupposed by the building of the Wall is not mere conceptual speculation, it is the everyday reality of the Wall's existence. The Wall is built following a 'principle of piecemeal construction':

> It was done in this way: gangs of some twenty workers were formed who had to accomplish a length, say, of five hundred yards of wall, while a similar gang built another stretch of the same length to meet the first. But after the junction had been made the construction of the wall was not carried on from the point, let us say, where this thousand yards ended; instead the two groups of workers were transferred to begin building again in quite different neighbourhoods. Naturally in this way many great gaps were left, which were only filled in gradually and bit by bit, some, indeed, not till after the official announcement that the wall was finished. In fact it is said that there are gaps which have never been filled in at all, an assertion, however, which is probably merely one of the many legends to which the building of the wall gave rise, and which cannot be verified, at least by any single man with his own eyes and judgement, on account of the extent of the structure. (p. 67)

Even when the Wall is officially finished it is still not completed and rumours of its partiality would seem to be a necessary condition of its ideological function. With no end in sight to the building of this folly the architects and managers become depressed at their never-ending task. The narrator, one such manager, remembers that during its construction the Wall was heralded by an academic publication as 'a secure foundation for a new Tower of Babel' (p. 71). However, he realises that as southern Chinese the wall is as remote and meaningless to him and his fellow villagers as the Emperor, Peking, and the enforcement of Imperial legislation.

The problems of the Wall in this story remind us of the complacency of a logic of inside and outside which must always be guarded against, if that metaphor itself does not reintroduce just such a logic. The Wall is presented in ideological terms as a myth of origin for the Chinese nation and so cements the familiar myth of the origin and of the myth itself as origin of the nation. We might think here also of Disney's Notre-Dame (née EuroDisney) at the centre of 'the fraternal continent'. Such a pattern trains the citizens of China's attention on what is 'inside' the Wall and what lies at the centre or origin of the nation, namely, the Emperor and feudal government, just as China's size makes such government strictly impossible. 'Inside' is a difficult term here since strictly nothing can be said to be inside an open surface: 'How could the wall, which did not even form a circle, but only a sort of quarter or half-circle, provide the foundation of a tower?' (p. 71). However, as a border the Wall touches the other nations it seeks to exclude and so is a reminder that there are other nations which China cannot help but depend upon. The Wall as the origin of the nation (here the border becomes the centre) is neither originary nor simple but depends upon a differentiation of nations which pre-exist the Wall as origin.[9]

If this parable of difference as a pre-condition of identity is true of the Wall then it is true by analogy of all such constructions of inside–outside, including politics. 'The end of politics', notes Geoffrey Bennington, 'is the end of politics'.[10] Political ideology presents itself as a form of closure in which the continuation of the political process *qua* contest would no longer be necessary given the successful implementation of a particular set of policies or legislations. This is as true of Marxism as it is of Fukuyama's terminal 'democracy'. It is the destiny of politics which Kant identifies as 'perpetual peace' and which Disney seeks to enact in its policy of total merchandising. In this respect the political model which predicates Disney's role in the globalisation of capital is the same understanding of the political which informs the maintenance of the bamboo curtain, perhaps the prescient object of Kafka's short story. While Disney's incursion into communist China as the expeditionary force of Western capitalism might seem like a millennial encounter between immovable object and irresistible force both the Disney

executive and the Beijing politburo share the same belief in
the priority of centres over margins, inside over outside, and
the essentially closed nature of nations and institutions. If, as
Kafka suggests, the nation is always open to its others and is
constituted only in this opening which is, in principle,
violent then it is a political necessity (political in the sense of
a closed ideological system) for the nation to turn to the
radical fiction of narration to ensure the integrity of its
borders. Narration as a process offers a simulacrum of closure
which constitutes identity against difference.[11] The *rapprochement* between Disney and China characteristically takes
place in a narrative, *Mulan*.

It is the impossibility of the closure promised by narrative
which makes it readable and which opens *Mulan* to its own
deconstructive potential against the legislative effects it offers
through its narrative structure of repetition. *Mulan's* narrative
about the integrity of China's borders, which serves as a cover
for Disney's entrance into those borders, provides us with an
act of double legitimation. As a form of double jeopardy, the
competing interests of the film cannot be separated or, in this
way, be said to be properly 'competing'. The *a priori* openness
of the institution, and nation *qua* institution, means that
China is open to Disney just as the institution (the Chinese
state or the Disney corporation) is always already prepared to
extend its autonomous realm by acting as legislator to other
institutions and other nations. As Bennington notes of
Rousseau:

> The doctrine of the social contract is essentially intolerant
> of national differences, and will attempt to absorb them
> in the creation of an autonomous 'humanity', for
> example. The American and French declarations duly
> formulate a confusion between the names of their
> respective nations and postulated universal 'rights of man',
> on the basis of which they have felt able to play the
> legislator the world over.[12]

Such a confusion is also the principle which informs Disney's
global marketing and the Marxist-Leninist doctrine of International Socialism, as well as the 'social contract' of

international law which underpins the interventions of the New World Order. As a confusion it substitutes the singularity of the Other for a schematic model of humanity as brotherhood, taking the openness of the nation as a reason for desiring its closure. As metaphysical inscriptions within political discourse, both 'International Socialism' and 'socialism in one country' (both models being simultaneously extolled by the present Chinese government in the form of 'market reform' and a 'Greater China' policy) rely on this same slippage which subsumes singularity into schema. Both Disney's 'enlightened colonialism' and China's Great Wall presuppose the innate superiority of their own insides over what is outside. In this legislative structure narration is never far away. Perhaps this is Kafka's monumental lesson.

Mulan is Disney's attempt to 'open' the vast potential of the Chinese market. Following the Bush and Clinton administrations' failure to suspend China's most-favoured-nation trade status after the Tiananmen Square massacre, Disney want to open China only to close the door behind them, barring entry to their European and Asian competitors. As we have suggested, this is a film in which the lead character offers a paradigm for the actions of Disney in China, transvesting itself to gain access to the trade war from which it was in danger of being excluded. The film opens with the Hun army breaching the Great Wall and the Emperor telling his general to 'send your troops to protect my people'. As Kafka's narrator suggests, the majority of China's vast population does not require protection from Northern invaders, but building the Wall is an attempt to convince them that they do. This emblematic force defends a symbolic wall and the general will in effect be sending his troops to bestow identity on the Emperor's people. Disney attempts to sell itself to China as fulfilling a similar role. A film made in the 1990s which reprises a myth of Chinese national origins, simultaneously invoking the People's Liberation Army's defence of China's borders, in a more or less unequivocal way, has an explicit agenda. The film's action takes place in the north of China but its ideological operations are directed at the country's southern borders where the troubled regions of Hong Kong, Tibet and Taiwan endure Beijing's policies of nationalist aphorism: 'one country, two systems', 'reunite the Motherland' and so forth. The film makes the promise that China's borders will be in safe hands if aligned to the Wonderful World of Disney.

Disney, as a serial seducer, is well versed in the best strategies to encourage the resisting Chinese to open up their golden gates, but Beijing is also well practised in extracting a price for its favours. Accordingly, this film as a Disney film, with all that this entails for Western culture, offers the integrity of China's borders and its dictatorial system of government as a necessary condition of both regional stability and, perhaps paradoxically, the expansion of capital. The film's central song opens with Lee Shang, the captain of the later victorious Chinese army, singing, 'Let's get down to business to defeat the Huns.' In an irony almost too tragic to bear, communist China has become a 'safe haven' for Disney's much criticised labour practices.[13] The inscription on Buzz Lightyear's sleeve is a reminder of the plastic nature of capitalism and Disney's ability to strongarm its way into even the most resistant of consumer bases. There are Disney factories in the West and on mainland China but the majority of merchandise to be found in Disney shops from Moscow to Los Angeles is made in Taiwan. Taiwan as a site of international contest between the world's last superpowers provides a suitable location for the manufacture of Disney's products. Taiwan represents the overlap between two spheres of influence, as if it were the intersection of a Venn diagram, in which Chinese Maoist nationalism comes into proximity with Western capitalism. Both systems compete over the island, convinced of the superiority of what lies within their own sovereign identity while the 'inbetweenness' of Taiwan works to inter any such notions of autonomy and national integrity. Disney sets up its stall on this never-never island, exporting to the West while enjoying the economic benefits of the East. The actions of Disney overrun the national borders – spilling out into China as a logical extension, while returning manufactured goods to the West where 'good' is culturally manufactured – which the action of its film seeks to defend as a natural boundary. The *rapprochement* between

Disney and free market Maoism is a case of 'getting down to business' to protect each other's vested interests.

With *Mulan* Disney makes a dramatic relocation – its business plan suggests that Disney's interests will lie in China for some time.[14] The film has been considerably less successful at the box office in the West than previous films in the new Disney *oeuvre* but there is a sense in which such a failing is of no consequence to Disney. Like EuroDisney this film is a loss-leader, which Disney can well afford, intended to open up a new continental market. With the exception of Eddie Murphy's streetwise dragon Mushu, who could be easily dubbed out in the Chinese language version(s) of the film, *Mulan* is a remarkably solemn approach to Chinese cultural practices. Firstly, Mulan has both a father and a mother, as well as a grandmother – the symmetry of this extended nuclear family stands out against the absence of the mother in Disney's previous films and is designed to appeal to mainstream Chinese familial sensibilities. With the exception of Mulan's 'drag show' the women in the film know their place: either brides-to-be or picking rice while the army marches past. Announcing herself as a woman, rather than as a woman dressed as a man, Mulan is ignored by men and at the end of the film asks the Emperor to be allowed to return home. Inevitably Lee Shang follows her home ('You don't meet a girl like that every dynasty') to seek Mulan's hand in marriage. Her grandmother upbraids Mulan for not returning with a husband: 'She should have brought home a man', and is delighted when Lee Shang arrives, 'Would you like to stay for dinner, would you like to stay forever?' As ever, the reimposition of the patriarchal order at the end of the Disney film serves to undo the liberating potential of its central female character. A woman might be allowed to save China but she voluntarily gives up her place as a member of the Emperor's council to return home to look after her father and take a husband.

Repelling the Hun invasion is in fact an elaborate test of Mulan's suitability as a bride. Having failed to impress the village matchmaker at the start of the film, Mulan must redeem her value as a commodity on the marriage market and so make herself the object of desire for the most privileged bidder on that market, Lee Shang. This courtship does not follow the usual Disney formula of romantic ballad and 'magic carpet ride' but rather is as chaste as the potential libidinal economy between these two 'male' soldiers is uncomplicated. On hearing that Mulan has run off to join the army, one of the ancestors who watch over the Fa family suggests that 'traditional values will disintegrate'. With Disney as a moral guardian this fear may be misplaced. However, such a complaint is also a common response to the 'market reforms' currently taking place in China. Disney's response to this is more ambivalent because the complaint is undoubtedly true. This, after all, is the *raison d'être* of Disney's desire to play the global legislator on behalf of Western capitalism. The answer is to bring the spectrality of the ancestors on line.

Mushu conjures the ancestral spirits by sounding a gong. When he does so the family temple becomes electrified and each of the ancestors' statues and tablets is digitalised with a blue light which zips from tomb to idol. Brought to life by the flow of computerised capital (perhaps suggestive of the Eastern practice of burning counterfeit money known as 'spirit money') and brought within a tele-technological circuit, the ancestors come to terms with the place of Mulan–Disney within the phallocentric schema of familial culture. The lead ancestor is voiced by George Takei, Mr Sulu in *Star Trek*, as if to confirm that the final frontier of capitalism means the electrification of China. By the end of the film the ancestors are happy to accommodate the digitalised flow of capital within traditional values when they promote Mushu to the role of guardian, having brought honour to the family through his careful handling of both libidinal and financial economies. They celebrate their new-found sense of value by having a disco; a disco being a noticeably 'unhip' thing to have in the West but electrifying news to these Chinese ghosts who, like the Eastern European mer-people of *The Little Mermaid*, have been isolated from the irresistible strains of Stevie Wonder and Vanessa Mae.

Disney is able to offer China this neon future because the corporation has been respectful of the country's dark past. Perhaps the most arresting image from the film is the interruption of the song 'A Girl Worth Fighting For' by the discovery of a burnt-out village. After a metaphorically long march, the song comes to an abrupt halt as the soldiers come across an atrocity carried out by the Hun army – we know this village to have been the home of young children. There are no civilian dead in view but the houses have been burnt out, the snow stained red, and a doll lies abandoned; over the hill lies the massacred army of Lee Shang's father. On the one hand, such pathetic images are in keeping with a Western audience's understanding of the contemporary 'humanitarian mission' of Nato. On the other hand, it plays directly to a certain Chinese nationalist ideology of blood and soil, the same ideology which legitimates martial law in Tibet – the Chinese region most synonymous with blood-stained snow – and which unites the crowd in Tiananmen Square for the closing scenes of Mulan's military campaign. The crowd bows down to Mulan in honour of what she has done for the Emperor and what she has done for China. Images of supplication in this particular arena have an especially poignant resonance which provides a somewhat chilling edge to Mushu's emotional outburst, 'My little baby is all grown up and saving China.' It is the transvested doubleness of Mulan–Disney as neither communist nor capitalist which enables the massacre at the Tung Shu Pass to be read with equal but different sentimentality by Chinese and Western audiences. It is the formal duplicity of the Disney film which enables it to present itself as both saviour of China and the Westernising influence which will abjure the world's last spectres of marxism. The student dissidents who occupied Tiananmen Square in 1989 used a *papier-mâché* replica of the Statue of Liberty as the symbol of their struggle for democracy. This explicit appeal to American values has been supplanted, with Beijing's approval, by the figure of Mickey Mouse – the sorcerer's apprentice, conjurer of ghosts and object of laughter.

Epilogue: Disney Work

> But how to distinguish between the analysis that denounces magic and the counter-magic that it still risks being?
>
> Jacques Derrida, *Specters of Marx*, p. 47

> On the whole this distant prospect of the Castle satisfied K.'s expectations. It was neither an old stronghold nor a new mansion, but a rambling pile consisting of innumerable small buildings closely packed together and of one or two storeys; if K. had not known that it was a castle he might have taken it for a little town. There was only one tower as far as he could see, whether it belonged to a dwelling-house or a church he could not determine. Swarms of crows were circling round it.
>
> Franz Kafka, *The Castle*[1]

Let us conclude where we began, with deconstruction. This book has been concerned with the deconstruction of the *oeuvre* of Disney films from *The Little Mermaid* to *Mulan* and in so doing has sought to demonstrate that there is 'nothing outside' of these texts. Our reading of this limited corpus has required an investigation of the social, historical, cultural, political and philosophical contexts of these films which has overspilled into a consideration, at varying times and to varying degrees, of Kant, Hegel, Marx, Freud, Kafka, Hugo, phenomenology, economics, psychoanalysis, colonialism, postcolonialism, neo-colonialism, Europe, America, Africa, China, television, nuclear war, apartheid, theme parks and cigarettes, to name only a few of the minimal indices which form the direction of this book. In short, these films open themselves onto the entire history of the West and act as a symptomatic concentration of all the ideological contests which are currently being fought in our world today. If, as

Nicholas Royle has argued, 'there is no "limit" to deconstruction' we would like to add that there is no 'limit' to
Disney.[2] Here the term 'limit' might be read as meaning a
boundary to the work which both Disney and deconstruction
demand of their reader.

In writing this book it has become impossible for us to keep
pace with Disney's corporate output. Leaving aside the merchandising, the stage musicals, the ice hockey team, the
Internet company and the real estate ventures, in the last few
weeks Disney have released the feature-length computer
animation *A Bug's Life* and the live-action movie *Mighty Joe
Young*; it will release its thirty-seventh feature-length
animation, *Tarzan*, in July 1999, with an augmented version
of *Fantasia* to follow, as *Fantasia '99*. Michael Eisner's autobi-
ography, *Work in Progress*, will have been published by the
time this book is in print. Given that there can be no good
conscience with respect to the political and that one can
never give up on the twin tasks of distinguishing and
analysing presented to us by 'the Disney text' (the films
providing an opening to all corners of the Disney empire)
then in writing the epilogue to this book we must recognise
that the singular commitment its work represents is already
out of date. We might say that it is 'out of date' in the sense
that Hamlet speaks of time being 'out of joint'. The Disney
empire continues to grow but this book must come to an end
and in its ending rehearse its own limitations. However, in
being already 'out of date' it immediately has no date, it is
with-out a date. Subsequently, and conversely, it is both dated
by its relation to its contemporary context, here and now
today, and makes an appeal to the future dates of any Disney
product. The broad ambit of the initial themes which come
out of the book asks to be worked through with every new
Disney film and every encounter its readers have with the
Disney corporation. This task is potentially without limit, for
even when empires inevitably decline and fall their consequences reverberate throughout history.

The date of the release of *A Bug's Life* is of particular significance. The film is a paradigmatic case of all of the issues we
have raised in relation to Disney and it was a unnerving
experience to watch this film in the UCI cinema at the

Trafford Centre, Manchester while Nato planes were conducting another bombing raid over Belgrade. When visiting the cinema at Trafford, a shopping mall in the vulgar postmodern style, patrons walk through a pastiche of the Brandenburg Gate before entering the 'Centre' itself, the catering area of which has been constructed to resemble the *Titanic* – exhausted shoppers even have the chance to take a seat in one of the *Titanic*'s proverbial deck-chairs. The cinema lies on the top floor, beyond the Aztec Casino, Rainforest Café, the Eygptian-themed Pizzaland, 'New Orleans' and 'The Orient'. At this late stage we would like to note that despite appearances there is nothing in this book which says anything against the postmodern as such – maligning the postmodern is just another way of continuing its history and in a number of practical and intellectual ways we are inextricably bound up with the fate of the postmodern. However, watching the latest Disney film in the orientalist pastiche of the Trafford Centre offers an uncanny experience of what Freud would call the *Nachträglichkeit* constitutive of the narratives which construct Western culture's understanding of itself. The Trafford Centre as part of the mall culture which Fukuyama blithely identifies as the terminus of human history might be read as the cemetery in Kant's formulation of 'perpetual peace', with the casino, café and Pizzaland marking memorials to the history of colonial appropriation which predicates the Late Capitalist venture of a 'shopping centre'. This centre is on the edge of Manchester (the city which had been Engels's object of study in *The Condition of the English Working Class*) and at the opposite fringe of Europe from where the latest 'humanitarian intervention' by the powers of old Europe was taking place that night.[3]

A *Bug's Life* is unsettling in its schematic simplicity. It is a computer-animated remake of *The Magnificent Seven* – itself a remake of *The Seven Samurai* – or, more accurately, it is a recitation of *The Three Amigos*. A colony of ants sends one of its number, Flik (a name which suggests the policing function of cinema), to find warriors who will help defeat the gang of grasshoppers who terrorise the colony and eat all the food. With due irony Hopper, the lead grasshopper, explains, 'The ants gather the food, the grasshoppers eat the food, it's a kind of Circle of Life thing.' Flik accidently hires a troop of circus insects (including a caterpillar called Heimlich) who despite their limitations as a fighting unit and natural cowardice ultimately overcome the grasshoppers through ingenuity and juggling. Again the grasshoppers are presented in the contemporary vocabulary of State Department briefings as local thugs abusing the ants' 'human rights'. When they arrive at the colony to collect the food left for them on the 'offering table' the ants take shelter in their nest; and the camera focuses on the faces of worried ants as the sound of helicopter blades (the grasshoppers' wings) can be heard overhead. The grasshoppers form a mobile guerrilla force who break into the anthill and threaten the ants with brutal reprisals – including killing babies and old women. While the Woody Allen vehicle *Antz* made a distinction between worker ants and soldier ants, all the ants in the Disney film are peaceful farmers who are held back by their naïvety and communistic approach to living (a panic is created whenever a gap appears in the line of ants carrying food to the offering table). The ants require outside help to protect their way of life. The one thing that the grasshoppers are afraid of is the aerial power of birds, so Flik and the circus insects build a giant bird from leaves and twigs which they hide in the hollow of a tree and plan to release when the grasshoppers arrive. This stealthy simulacrum of power is eventually set to work dive-bombing the grasshoppers but is shot down in flames. Finally it is not aerial power which defeats the grasshoppers (although their leader Hopper, voiced by Hollywood 'heavy' Kevin Spacey, is ultimately eaten by a real bird) but the cultural intervention of the circus insects. Their performance distracts the grasshoppers long enough to rescue the queen ant and release the bird, while their circus skills prove more than a match for Hopper's trained assassins. Following standard CIA counter-insurgence procedures the intervention of the circus raises the ants' group consciousness against the outnumbered grasshoppers. However, the postcolonial moment is short-lived when the gathered ants are scattered by the aerial bombardment which comes with the first rains of autumn. The moral of this story, if this story can be said to be moral, is that only the cultural imperialism of Disney can guarantee the security of the minority populations of the globe. Ant Island requires Uncle Sam – it's a small world after all.

As a sort of Franz Kafka's *It's A Wonderful Life* this film provides an uneasy dream of the political space in which the powers of the New World Order are transformed into gigantic insects.[4] The colony of ants exchange their postcolonial moment for a place within a wider neo-colonial movement. The 'out-takes' which accompany the end credits remind us that film, as a privileged form of narrative in the mediatic space of *fin de siècle* politics, is never far away from the legislative foundations of this neo-colonial order. These comic asides, in which Woody from *Toy Story* has a cameo appearance, turns the simulacrum of animation inside-out, presenting the computer-generated characters as real actors capable of 'human error' in the delivery of their lines: the stick insect (David Hyde Pierce, Niles in *Frasier*) has to stop filming because he swallows a bug. In Plato's philosophical colony mimetic arts – animation presumably included – are excluded because they constitute the danger that imitation of fiction, and fiction as imitation, is formative.[5] Such imitation is an ambivalent form of colonisation, both *to be* colonised *and* colonising.[6] As a colonial appropriation – swallowing a bug – this film is ambivalent about its subject, both fearing and desiring the metaphor of the ant as a model for its neo-colonial practice.[7] The ant, like the bee, is a traditional image of an oppressed proletariat, the term 'drone' suggesting the dehumanising effects of capital. As an image for the colonial subjects of Ant Island who discover strength through unity (even if it is finally no match for the aerial power of the rain which scatters the colony) it has the potential to undermine the authoritative discourse of Disney's legislation.

By the end of the film Flik has introduced techno-scientific methods of farming to the colony and integrated the figure of the entrepreneurial individual into the colony's communistic structure but the ants, in Bhabha's words, retain a logic of 'the same but not quite'.[8] While Disney (following the model of the Magnificent Seven and their Mexican peasant hosts) colonise the ants in the name of defending their indigenous culture, desiring and fearing that the ants *qua* minority population be Americanized (they have always already been Disneyfied), the visual presence of the ants imitating the American way of life disrupts Disney's colonising discourse and reveals its inherent absurdity. If Disney are following Kafka's injunction in 'In the penal colony' to 'be just' then this justice is only on the minute scale of ants.[9] Under the microscope Disney's projection of international law in this film, and the ideas of democracy and human rights it presupposes, does not extend beyond the limited simulacrum of Ant Island into the political, economic and social fields which constitute the actions of the Disney Corporation. Disney's Chinese workforce, for example, may have an all-too-sympathetic relation to the metaphor of the ant. Sometimes it can be an uncannily small world.

There are no humans in this film, excluding the possibility that Disney's ants will meet the insect's usual fate of being crushed by a giant. However, the superpower of giants remains inscribed in this film in the constant Disney motif of the dwelling-place of giants, the castle. Here the anthill is the latest in a long line of architecural encodings of Disney's corporate trademark. King Triton lives in a castle, as does Prince Eric; the Beast owns a castle; Princess Jasmin lives in a palace; Pride Rock is the castle of the Lion King; the fort in Jamestown is a mock castle; Notre-Dame is the white castle to Frollo's black Palais de Justice, as Andy's bedroom is to Eric's; Mount Olympus is the castle of the gods, and the Emperor of China lives in a walled city. Each of these castles is haunted by the spectres of old Europe while the image of the castle itself *is* a spectre of old Europe. The castle is a singularly European invention bearing testimony to a history of siege and oppression, of Christianity and kingship, and of the secure defence of the logic of inside-outside. 'America' as a state-nation, founded with a constitution, does not have castles of its own because, as any schoolgirl knows, America is a democracy and has no place for such feudal signifiers. However, the castle is Disney's chosen trade mark and *A Bug's Life* is noticeable for the elaborate computer-generated castle, with flags flying from every turret, which replaces the usual Disney insignia of Sleeping Beauty's fairy-tale castle in the opening titles.

At the centre of EuroDisney stands a replica of the Sleeping Beauty castle. This is an imaginary centre since it is actually nearer the park's entrance than anything else. The castle cannot be entered but instead a crossroads leading to different zones runs underneath the castle's founding arches and the castle stands above the park's skyline as a constant reminder to lost children of where they are. The Disney castle is, then, like the castle in Kafka's novel, deceptively grand from a distance but inaccessible and in the cold light of day 'only a wretched-looking town, a huddle of village houses ... K. had a fleeting recollection of his native town. It was hardly inferior to this so-called castle, and if it were merely a question of enjoying the view it was a pity to have come so far' (p. 10). The castle as an emblem for the power of Disney's Magic Kingdom is, when confronted *volte face*, disappointing both as a spectacle and as a destination – a cartoon ideology in which the term 'Mickey Mouse' is synonymous with an experience of diminutive value. The power of the castle lies in its distance and as a site of desire the effects it produces are all constituted by the journey to it. Ariel wants more than anything to live in Eric's castle even if she is only substituing one patriarchal order for another; Scar's desire for Pride Rock reduces the countryside to a desert; Quasimodo longs to be 'out there' but finds himself mocked at the Festival of Fools. The power of Disney, as an ambassador of Late Capitalism and American strategic interests, lies in its ability to make itself an object of desire, the pleasure of which is to be found only in the construction of the desire, never in its possession. Disney is the *objet petit a* of the late twentieth century.

The 'illusory emptiness' (p. 3) of the castle provides another of those uncanny parallels between Disney and Kafka as voices at opposite ends of the twentieth century. For Harold Bloom the twentieth century is 'the age of Kafka'; it could also be said with an equally straight face that it is also the age of Disney,[10] the age of Disney now stretching from the bombing of Guernica in 1937 (*Snow White*) to the bombing of Belgrade in 1999 (*A Bug's Life*). The increasing patterns of similarity between the films in the new Disney *oeuvre* might be a sign that Disney is beginning to show its age, as surely as the hysterical pronunciations of the end of history have been a demonstration that Late Capitalism and Western hegemony are showing theirs. However, there is undoubtedly a relation between this age of Disney and what we cautiously called in our introduction 'the age of deconstruction'. If the text of Disney incorporates all the contradictory signs of Western culture, and the minimal trait of each film gathers in the greatest potentiality of historical, cultural and philosophical knowledge, then deconstruction itself – given that this is the metaphysical name we attach to the discursive effects of a political situation – cannot help but be related to Disney, just as deconstruction is always already in the Disney text. The Walt Disney Concert Hall in Los Angeles (home of the Los Angeles Symphony Orchestra and memorial to Walt Disney) is a 'deconstruction' of Disney's trademark castle. Designed by the 'deconstructive' architect Frank Gehry, the building seemingly follows a certain understanding of the deconstruction of those values to which architecture has been subjugated (utility, occupation, technical necessity and so forth) but which are not themselves architectural.[11] Undoubtedly it is an impressive monument which, although suspiciously similar to a number of other look-a-like 'deconstructive' buildings, merits its adjectival honorific as 'deconstructive'. At last, some might say, deconstruction has come of age by openly serving the reactionary interests it has always covertly represented. Certainly, Disney's deconstructive architecture should lead us to ask serious questions about the architecture of the term 'deconstruction' and the meanings it has become associated with in a specific area of contemporary culture. Perhaps Disney's appropriation of the term ought to tell us that it is time to abandon a word which was only ever a provisional nominal strategy.

However, it would be a pity to have come so far in this book merely to conclude that, like K., we have been standing in the castle all along, for as Derrida suggests: 'Deconstruction is not simply the decomposition of an architectural structure; it is also a question about the foundation, about the relation between foundation and what is founded; it is also a question about the closure of the structure, about a whole architecture of philosophy.'[12] Despite Disney's desire to buy its own deconstructive monument to its founder, the task of deconstructing Disney goes beyond the limitations placed upon it by the multiple but finite walls of the Walt Disney Concert Hall. We have sought to deconstruct Disney not to Disneyfy deconstruction, by offering the simple decomposition of a set of films as an exercise in critical methodology. Rather, we have tried to open up a question about the relation between Disney and the contemporary political space and about which, if any, is founded and which, if any, is foundational. In so doing the initial questions which we have succeeded in asking here call attention to the scandalous formal negativity of the term 'Disney' itself. As the projection of a series of aporias within 'the whole architecture of philosophy' this formal negativity might just be another name for the political.

Today, as we write these final lines, Nato has threatened to target television stations in Serbia unless they agree to broadcast six hours of Western television programmes every night.[13] It is a salutory reminder of what this European war is all about and how important a company like Disney is to the maintenance of what we have perhaps too hurriedly referred to here as the New World Order. In an early dispatch from Serbia, before the majority of Western journalists were expelled from Belgrade, the *Guardian* reported a scene from the New World Order Café in Belgrade in which beseiged Serbs sat watching *Aladdin* on video while their country was at war with America.[14] If Disney could be said to be the continuation of war by other means, then perhaps this episode is a case of a spoonful of sugar helping the bombs go down.

Filmography

Disney Films (in chronological order)

Snow White and the Seven Dwarfs, 1937, dir. David Hand, wr. Ted Sears *et al.*

Pinocchio, 1940, dir. Ben Sharpsteen and Hamilton Luske, wr. Ted Sears *et al.*

Fantasia, 1940, dir. Ben Sharpsteen, wr. Joe Grant and Dick Hiemer

Dumbo, 1941, dir. Ben Sharpsteen, wr. Joe Grant and Dick Hiemer

Bambi, 1942, dir. David Hand, wr. Larry Morey

Saludos Amigos, 1943, dir. Norman Ferguson, wr. *various*

The Three Caballeros, 1945, dir. Norman Ferguson, wr. *various*

Make Mine Music, 1946, dir. *various*, wr. *various*

Song of the South, 1946, dir. Harve Foster, wr. Dalton Raymond

Fun and Fancy Free, 1947, dir. *various*, wr. *various*

So Dear to My Heart, 1948, dir. Harold Schuster, wr. John Tucker Battle

Melody Time, 1948, dir. *various*, wr. *various*

The Adventures of Ichabod and Mr Toad, 1949, dir. Jack Kinney, Clyde Geronimi, James Algar, wr. *various*

Cinderella, 1950, dir. Wilfred Jackson, Hamilton Luske, Clyde Geronimi, wr. *various*

Alice in Wonderland, 1951, dir. Wilfred Jackson, Hamilton Luske, Clyde Geronimi, wr. *various*

Peter Pan, 1953, dir. Wilfred Jackson, Hamilton Luske, Clyde Geronimi, wr. *various*

Twenty Thousand Leagues under the Sea, 1954, dir. Richard Fleischer, wr. Earl Felton

Lady and the Tramp, 1955, dir. Wilfred Jackson, Hamilton Luske, Clyde Geronimi, wr. *various*

Sleeping Beauty, 1959, dir. Clyde Geronimi, wr. *various*

One Hundred and One Dalmatians, 1961, dir. Wolfgang
Reitherman, Hamilton Luske, Clyde Geronimi, wr. Bill Peet

The Sword in the Stone, 1963, dir. Wolfgang Reitherman, wr.
Bill Peet

Mary Poppins, 1964, dir. Robert Stevenson, wr. Bill Walsh and
Don DaGradi

The Jungle Book, 1967, dir. Wolfgang Reitherman, wr. *various*

The Aristocats, 1970, dir. Wolfgang Reitherman, wr. Larry
Clemmons *et al.*

Bedknobs and Broomsticks, 1971, dir. Robert Stevenson, wr. Bill
Walsh and Don DaGradi

Robin Hood, 1973, dir. Wolfgang Reitherman, wr. Larry
Clemons *et al.*

The Many Adventures of Winnie the Pooh, 1977, dir. various, wr.
various

The Rescuers, 1977, dir. Wolfgang Reitherman, John
Lounsberry, Art Stevens, wr. Larry Clemons, Ken Anderson

Pete's Dragon, 1977, dir. Don Chaffey, wr. Malcom
Marmorstein

The Fox and the Hound, 1981, dir. Art Stevens, Ted Berman,
Richard Rich, wr. *various*

The Black Cauldron, 1985, dir. Ted Berman, Richard Rich, wr.
David Jonas *et al.*

The Adventures of the Great Mouse Detective, 1986, dir. John
Musker *et al.*, wr. Pete Young *et al.*

Good Morning, Vietnam, 1987, Touchstone, dir. Barry
Levinson, wr. Mitch Markowitz

Oliver and Company, 1988, dir. George Scribner, wr. Jim Cox,
Timothy J. Disney, James Mangold

The Little Mermaid, 1989, dir. and wr. John Musker, Ron
Clements

The Rescuers Down Under, 1990, dir. Hendel Butoy, Mike
Gabriel, wr. Jim Cox *et al.*

Beauty and the Beast, 1991, dir. Gary Tousdale, Kirk Wise, wr.
Linda Woolvertoon

Aladdin, 1992, dir. and wr. John Musker, Ron Clements, Ted
Elliot, Terry Rossio

The Lion King, 1994, dir. Roger Allers, Rob Minhoff, wr. Irene
Meechi, Jonathan Roberts, Linda Woolverton

Pocahontas, 1995, dir. Mike Gabriel, Eric Goldberg, wr. Carl Binder, Susannah Grant, Philip Lazebnik

Toy Story, 1995, dir. John Lasseter, wr. Joss Whedon *et al.*

The Hunchback of Notre Dame, 1996, dir. Gary Tousdale, Kirk Wise, wr. Cab Murphy *et al.*

101 Dalmatians, 1996, dir. Stephen Herek, wr. John Hughes

Hercules, 1997, dir. and wr. John Musker, Ron Clements

Kundun, 1997, Touchstone, dir. Martin Scorsese, wr. Melissa Mathison

Mulan, 1998, dir. Barry Cook, Tony Bancroft, wr. Rita Hsiao *et al.*

A Bug's Life, 1999, dir. and wr. John Lasseter, Andrew Stanton

Mighty Joe Young, 1999, dir. Ron Underwood, wr. Ruth Rose, Merian C. Cooper

Other Films (in alphabetical order)

Antz, 1998, Dreamworks, dir. Eric Darnell, Jim Johnson, wr. Todd Alcott, Chris Weitz, Paul Weitz

Bullets over Broadway, 1994, Mirimax/Magrolia, dir. and wr. Woody Allen

Chimes at Midnight, 1966, Internacional Films Española/Alpine, dir. and wr. Orson Welles

Clash of the Titans, 1981, MGM, dir. Desmond Davis, wr. Beverley Cross

Dances with Wolves, 1990, Guild, dir. Kevin Costner, wr. Michael Blake

The Empire Strikes Back, 1980, TCF/LucasFilm, dir. Irvin Kershner, wr. Leigh Brackett, Lawrence Kasdan

Hamlet, 1948, Rank, dir. Laurence Olivier, wr. Alan Dent

Hamlet, 1964, Lenfilm, dir. Grigori Kozinstev, wr. Boris Pasternak

Hamlet, 1991, Warner, dir. Franco Zeffirelli, wr. Christopher de Vore, Franco Zeffirelli

The Hunchback of Notre Dame, 1939, RKO, dir. William Dieterle, wr. Sonya Levien, Bruno Frank

Husbands and Wives, 1992, Columbia, dir. and wr. Woody Allen

Indiana Jones and the Last Crusade, 1989, UIP/Paramount/LucasFilm, dir. Steven Spielberg, wr. Jeffrey Boam

Indiana Jones and the Temple of Doom, 1984, Paramount/LucasFilm, dir. Steven Spielberg, wr. William Huyuck, Gloria Katz

Jurassic Park, 1993, UIP/Universal/Amblin, dir. Steven Spielberg, wr. Michael Crichton

La Belle et la Bête, 1946, Discina, dir. and wr. Jean Cocteau

The Last Days of Disco, 1999, Westerly Films, dir. and wr. Whit Stillman

Lethal Weapon, 1987, Warner, dir. Richard Donner, wr. Shane Black

The Little Colonel, 1935, Fox, dir. David Butler, wr. William Conselman

The Magnificent Seven, 1960, United Artists, dir. John Sturges, wr. William Roberts

The Man from U.N.C.L.E.: To Trap a Spy, 1966, MGM, dir. Don Melford, wr. Sam Rolfe

The Name of the Rose, 1986, TCF, dir. Jean-Jacques Annaud, wr. Andrew Birkin *et al.*

Raiders of the Lost Ark, 1981, Paramount/LucasFilm, dir. Steven Spielberg, wr. Lawrence Kasdan

The Return of the Jedi, 1983, TCF/LucasFilm, dir. Richard Marquand, wr. Lawrence Kasdan, George Lucas

Rocky, 1976, UA, dir. John G. Avildsen, wr. Sylvester Stallone

Romeo and Juliet, 1936, MGM, dir. George Cukor, wr. Talbot Jennings

Romeo and Juliet, 1968, Paramount, dir. Franco Zeffirelli, wr. Franco Brusati, Masolino D'Amico

Schindler's List, 1993, Universal/Amblin, dir. Steven Spielberg, wr. Steven Zaillian

The Seven Samurai, 1954, Toho (Shojiro Motoki), dir. Akira Kurosawa, wr. Akira Kurosawa, Shinobu Hashimoto, Hideo Oguni

The Seven Year Itch, 1955, TCF, dir. Billy Wilder, wr. Billy Wilder, George Axelrod

The Sound of Music, 1965, TCF, dir. Robert Wise, wr. Ernest Lehman

Space Jam, 1996, Warner, dir. Joe Pytka, wr. Leo Benvenuti *et al.*

Star Trek VI: The Undiscovered Country, 1991, UIP/Paramount, dir. Nicholas Meyer, wr. Nicholas Meyer, Denny Martin Flynn

Star Wars, 1977, LucasFilm, dir. and wr. George Lucas

Superman, 1978, Warner, dir. Richard Donner, wr. Mario Puzo *et al.*

Tarzan the Ape Man, 1932, MGM, dir. WR. S. Van Dyke, wr. *various*

Three Amigos, 1986, Orion, dir. John Landis, wr. Steve Martin, Lorne Michaels, Randy Newman

Thunderbird Six, 1968, UA, dir. David Lane, wr. Gerry Anderson, Sylvia Anderson

Twelfth Night, 1996, Renaissance Films, dir. and wr. Trevor Nunn

William Shakespeare's Romeo and Juliet, 1997, TCF, dir. Barry Luhrmann, wr. Craig Pearce, Barry Luhrmann

The Wizard of Oz, 1939, MGM, dir. Victor Fleming, wr. Noel Langley, Florence Ryerson, Edgar Allan Wolfe

The X-Files: Fight the Future, 1998, TCF, dir. Rob Bowman, wr. Chris Carter

Select Bibliography

Andersen, Hans Christian, 'The little mermaid', in *Hans Christian Andersen's Fairy Tales*, trans. Reginald Spink (London: Everyman, 1960), pp. 75–103.

Armstrong, Nancy, *Desire and Domestic Fiction: A Political History of the Novel* (New York: Oxford University Press, 1987).

Bachelard, Gaston, *The Poetics of Space*, trans. Maria Jolas (Boston: Beacon Press, 1994).

Baudrillard, Jean, *The Illusion of the End*, trans. Chris Turner (London: Verso, 1993).

Baudrillard, Jean, 'Disneyworld Company', *Liberation*, 4 March 1996.

Bell, Elizabeth, Lynda Haas, Laura Sells (eds.), *From Mouse to Mermaid: The Politics of Film, Gender, and Culture* (Bloomington and Indianapolis: Indiana University Press, 1995).

Bennington, Geoffrey, *Legislations: The Politics of Deconstruction* (London: Verso, 1994).

Bennington, Geoffrey, 'X' in *Applying: to Derrida*, eds. John Brannigan, Ruth Robbins, and Julian Wolfreys (London: Macmillan, 1997).

Bhabha, Homi K., *The Location of Culture* (London and New York: Routledge, 1994), p. 67.

Bloom, Harold, *The Western Canon: The Book and The School of Ages* (London: Macmillan, 1994).

Bryman, Alan, *Disney and His Worlds* (London: Routledge, 1995).

Butler, Judith, *Gender Trouble, Feminism and the Subversion of Identity* (Routledge, London and New York, 1990).

Butler, Judith, *Bodies that Matter: On the Discursive Limits of 'Sex'* (London: Routledge, 1993).

Butler, Judith, *Excitable Speech: A Politics of the Performative* (New York: Routledge, 1997).

Canemaker, J. (ed.), *Treasures of Disney Animation* (New York: Abbeville, 1982).

Cixous, Hélène and Mireille Calle-Gruber, *Hélène Cixous, Rootprints: Memory and Life Writing*, trans. Eric Prenowitz (London and New York: Routledge, 1997), p. 119.

Cripps, Thomas, *Slow Fade to Black: The Negro in American Film, 1900–1942* (Oxford: Oxford University Press, 1977).

de Man, Paul, *Allegories of Reading: Figural Language in Rousseau, Nietzsche, Rilke and Proust* (New Haven: Yale University Press, 1979).

Derrida, Jacques, 'Speculations – On Freud', trans. Ian McLeod, *Oxford Literary Review*, 1978, 3(2), pp. 80–98.

Derrida, Jacques, 'The *retrait* of metaphor', *Enclitic*, 1978, (2).

Derrida, Jacques, 'The Law of Genre', trans. Avital Ronell, *Glyph 7*, 1980, pp. 176–232.

Derrida, Jacques, *The Post Card: From Socrates to Freud and Beyond* (Chicago: University of Chicago Press, 1984).

Derrida, Jacques, *The Ear of the Other*, ed. Christie Macdonald, trans. Peggy Kamuf (Lincoln: University of Nebraska Press, 1985).

Derrida, Jacques, 'Racism's last word', trans. Peggy Kamuf, *Critical Inquiry*, 12, 1985, pp. 290–9.

Derrida, Jacques, 'Fors: the Anglish words of Nicolas Abraham and Maria Torok', trans. Barbara Johnson, in Nicolas Abraham and Maria Torok, *The Wolf Man's Magic Word: A*

Cryptonymy, trans. Nicholas Rand (Minneapolis: University of Minnesota Press, 1986).

Derrida, Jacques, 'Pas', in *Parages* (Paris: Galilée, 1986).

Derrida, Jacques, 'The laws of reflection: Nelson Mandela, in admiration', in Jacques Derrida and Mustapha Tlili (eds.), *For Nelson Mandela*, (New York: Seaver Books, 1987).

Derrida, Jacques, 'The ghost dance: an interview with Jacques Derrida', trans. Jean-Luc Svobada, in *Public*, no. 2, 1989.

Derrida, Jacques, *Given Time. I. Counterfeit Money*, trans. Peggy Kamuf (Chicago: University of Chicago Press, 1991).

Derrida, Jacques, *A Derrida Reader: Between the Blinds*, ed. Peggy Kamuf (Hemel Hempstead: Harvester Wheatsheaf, 1991).

Derrida, Jacques, *Aporias*, trans. Thomas Dutoit (Stanford: Stanford University Press, 1993).

Derrida, Jacques, *Specters of Marx: the Work of Mourning, the State of the Debt, and the New International*, trans. Peggy Kamuf (London and New York: Routledge, 1994).

Derrida, Jacques, 'The deconstruction of actuality', *Radical Philosophy*, 68, Autumn, 1994.

Derrida, Jacques, *The Gift of Death*, trans. David Wills (Chicago: University of Chicago Press, 1995).

Derrida, Jacques, *Points: Interviews 1974–1994*, ed. Elizabeth Weber, trans. Peggy Kamuf *et al.*, (Stanford: Stanford University Press, 1995), p. 252.

Derrida, Jacques, *Monolingualism of the Other or the Prosthesis of Origin*, trans. Patrick Mensah (Stanford: Stanford University Press, 1996).

Derrida, Jacques, *The Politics of Friendship,* trans. George Collins (London and New York: Verso, 1997).

Derrida, Jacques, *Cosmopolites de tous les pays encore un effort!* (Paris: Galilée, 1997).

Dorfman, Ariel and Armand Mattelart, *How to Read Donald Duck: Imperialist Ideology in the Disney Comic*, trans. David Kunzle (New York: International General, 1984).

Dunlop, Beth, *Building a Dream: The Art of Disney's Architecture* (New York: Harry N. Abrahams Inc., 1996).

Elam, Diane and Robyn Wiegman (eds.), *Feminism Beside Itself* (London and New York: 1995), pp. 71–93.

Eliot, Marc, *Walt Disney, Hollywood's Dark Prince: A Biography* (Secaucus, NJ: Carol/Birch Lane Press, 1993).

Ellison, Ralph, *Invisible Man* (Harmondsworth: Penguin, 1965).

Engels, Friedrich, *The Condition of the Working Class in England: From Personal Observation and Authentic Sources* (London: Grafton Books, 1986).

Fanon, Frantz, *Black Skin, White Masks* (London: Pluto, 1986).

Finch, Christopher, *The Art of Walt Disney: From Mickey Mouse to the Magic Kingdoms* (Harry N. Abrahams Inc., 1975).

Fjellman, Stephen M., *Vinyl Leaves: Walt Disney World and America* (Boulder: Westview Press, 1992).

Freud, Sigmund, *The Standard Edition of the Complete Psychological Works of Sigmund Freud*, trans. and ed. James Strachey (London: Hogarth Press, 1964).

Fukuyama, Francis, *The End of History and the Last Man* (London: Hamish Hamilton, 1992).

Fuss, Diana (ed.), *Inside/Out: Lesbian Theories, Gay Theories* (New York: Routledge, 1991).

Gates, Henry Louis (ed.), *'Race', Writing, and Difference* (Chicago: Chicago University Press, 1986).

Gates, Henry Louis, *The Signfiying Monkey: A Theory of African-American Literary Criticism* (Oxford: Oxford University Press, 1988).

Gill, Carolyn Bailey (ed.), *Bataille: Writing the Sacred* (London: Routledge, 1995).

Grant, John (ed.), *Encyclopedia of Walt Disney's Animated Characters* (London: Harper and Row, 1987).

Hiassen, Carl, *Team Rodent: How Disney Devours the World* (Toronto: Ballantine, 1998).

Hugo, Victor, *The Hunchback of Notre-Dame*, trans. Walter J. Cobb (Harmondsworth: Penguin, 1996).

Hugo, Victor, 'L'avenir', in *Paris* (Introduction to the Paris Guide), Paris 1867.

Hulme, Peter, *Colonial Encounters: Europe and the Native Caribbean 1492–1797* (London: Routledge, 1985).

Johnson, Barbara, *A World of Difference* (Baltimore: Johns Hopkins University Press, 1987).

Kafka, Franz, *Metamorphosis and Other Stories*, trans. Willa and Edwin Muir (Harmondsworth: Penguin, 1961).

Kafka, Franz, *The Castle*, trans. Edwin and Willa Muir (London: Everyman, 1992).

Kant, Immanuel, *Kant's Political Writings*, ed. Reiss (Cambridge: Cambridge University Press, 1970), p. 106.

Klein, Richard, *Cigarettes are Sublime* (Durham and London: Duke University Press, 1993).

Kurtz, Druce D. (ed.), *Keith Harring, Andy Warhol and Walt Disney* (Munich: Prestel, 1992).

Leebron, Elizabeth and Lynn Gartley, *Walt Disney: A Guide to References and Resources* (London: G. K. Hall and Co., 1969).

Leonard, Tom, *Intimate Voices: Selected Works 1965–1983* (London: Vintage, 1984).

Lévi-Strauss, Claude, *From Honey to Ashes: Introduction to a Science of Mythology, Volume Two*, trans. John and Doreen Weightman (Chicago: Chicago University Press, 1973).

Lloyd, David, *Anomalous States: Irish Writing and the Post-Colonial Moment* (Durham, N. Carolina: Duke University Press, 1993).

Lyotard, Jean-François, *The Inhuman: Reflections on Time*, trans. Geoffrey Bennington and Rachel Bowlby (Cambridge: Polity Press, 1991).

Marx, Karl, *Capital*, trans. Ben Fowkes (New York: Vintage: 1977).

Marx, Karl, *The Communist Manifesto* (Oxford: Oxford University Press, 1992).

Mauss, Marcel, *The Gift: The Form and Reason for Exchange in Archaic Societies*, trans. W. D. Halls (London: Routledge, 1990).

Maynard, Richard, *The Black Man on Film: Racial Stereotyping* (New Jersey: Hayden, 1974).

McQuillan, Martin, Graeme Macdonald, Robin Purves and Stephen Thomson (eds.), *Post-Theory: New Directions in Criticism* (Edinburgh: Edinburgh University Press, 1999).

Merrit, Russell and J. B . Kaufman, *Walt in Wonderland: The Silent Films of Walt Disney* (Baltimore: Johns Hopkins University Press, 1993).

Miller, J. Hillis, *Ariadne's Thread: Story Lines* (New Haven: Yale University Press, 1992).

Miller, J. Hillis, 'Derrida's Topographies', in *South Atlantic Review*, 59 (1), 1994, pp. 1–25.

Mosely, Leonard, *The Real Walt Disney: A Biography*, (London: Grafton, 1985).

Plato, *The Collected Dialogues of Plato, Including the Letters*, eds. Edith Hamilton and Huntington Cairns (New Jersey: Princeton University Press, 1961).

Poster, Mark (ed.), *Politics, Theory, and Contemporary Culture* (New York: Columbia University Press, 1993).

Project on Disney, *Inside the Mouse: Work and Play at Disney World* (London: Rivers Oram Press, 1998).

Ronell, Avital, *The Telephone Book: Technology, Schizophrenia, Electric Speech* (Nebraska: University of Nebraska Press, 1994), p. 90.

Royle, Nicholas, 'Nor is deconstruction: Christopher Norris, *Deconstruction: Theory and Practice*', *Oxford Literary Review* 5:1–2 (1982).

Royle, Nicholas, *After Derrida* (Manchester: Manchester University Press, 1995).

Rybczynski, Witold, *Home: A Short History of an Idea* (London: Heinemann, 1998).

Schickel, Richard, *The Disney Version: the Life, Times, Art, and Commerce of Walt Disney* (New York: Simon, 1968).

Sedgwick, Eve Kosofsky, *Between Men: English Literature and Male Homosocial Desire* (New York: Columbia University Press, 1985).

Sedgwick, Eve Kosofsky, *Epistemology of the Closet* (Harvester: Hemel Hempstead, 1991).

Sedgwick, Eve Kosofsky, *Tendencies* (London: Routledge, 1991).

Shakespeare, William, *Hamlet, Henry IV, Romeo and Juliet, Timon of Athens, Twelfth Night*, in The Riverside Shakespeare (Boston: Houghton Mifflin, 1974).

Smith, John, *Works 1608–1631*, ed. E. Arber (Birmingham, 1884).

Smith, John, *The Generall Historie of Virginia, New England, and the Summer Isles* (1624), facsimilie edn, Cleveland, 1966.

Smoodin, Eric (ed.), *Disney Discourse: Producing The Magic Kingdom* (London and New York: Routledge, 1994).

Snead, James, *White Screens, Black Images, Hollywood from the Dark Side*, eds. Colin MacCabe and Cornel West (London and New York: Routledge, 1993).

Thomas, Bob, *Walt Disney: A Biography* (London: W. H. Allen, 1981).

Weber, Samuel, *Institution and Interpretation* (Minneapolis: University of Minnesota Press, 1987).

Welsh, Irvine, *The Acid House* (London: Vintage, 1995).

Young, Robert, *White Mythologies: Writing History and the West* (London: Routledge, 1990).

Zizek, Slavoj, *Looking Awry: An Introduction to Jacques Lacan through Popular Culture* (London: MIT Press, 1995).

Notes

Introduction

1. Ariel Dorfman and Armand Mattelart, *How to Read Donald Duck: Imperialist Ideology in the Disney Comic*, trans. David Kunzle (New York: International General, 1984), p. 95. Originally published as *Para Leer al Pato Donald* (Ediciones Universitarias de Valaparaîso, 1971).
2. Richard Schickel, *The Disney Version: the Life, Times, Art, and Commerce of Walt Disney* (New York: Simon, 1968); Marc Eliot, *Walt Disney, Hollywood's Dark Prince: A Biography* (Secaucus, NJ: Carol/Birch Lane Press, 1993); *From Mouse to Mermaid: the Politics of Film, Gender, and Culture*, eds. Elizabeth Bell, Lynda Haas, Laura Sells (Bloomington and Indianapolis: Indiana University Press, 1995).
3. Figure quoted in *From Mouse to Mermaid*, p. 2.
4. This argument owes more than merely this phrase to Geoffrey Bennington, 'Inter', in *Post-Theory: New Directions in Criticism*, eds. Martin McQuillan, Graeme Macdonald, Robin Purves and Stephen Thomson (Edinburgh: Edinburgh University Press, 1998).
5. See Jacques Derrida, 'Signature, event, context', trans. Alan Bass, in *A Derrida Reader: Between the Blinds*, ed. Peggy Kamuf (Hemel Hempstead: Harvester Wheatsheaf, 1991), pp. 106–109.
6. See Derrida's comments on *J'Accuse!* in 'The deconstruction of actuality', *Radical Philosophy*, 68, Autumn, 1994, p. 38.
7. Interview with Michael Eisner, *60 Minutes*, CBS, 23 November 1997.
8. Disney Television first showed the outing of Ellen DeGeneres on her sitcom *Ellen*. However, the show was later decommissioned after a ratings slump (*Guardian*, 21 April 1998, G2, p. 5).
9. See Susan Miller and Greg Rode, 'The movie you see, the movie you don't', in *From Mouse to Mermaid*, p. 89.
10. See ArabicNews.Com, 20 August 1997 and 23 September 1997.
11. US Treasury department ruling, quoted in 'Donald Duck vs. Chilean socialism: a fair use exchange', John Shelton

Lawrence, contained as an appendix to *How to Read Donald Duck* (1984).

12. The Edinburgh author Irvine Welsh plays on this pun in the short story 'Disnae matter', in *The Acid House* (London: Vintage, 1995, pp. 118–19.

13. 'One can never know too much about Hitchcock' is the title of the second part of Slavoj Zizek's *Looking Awry: an Introduction to Jacques Lacan through Popular Culture* (London: MIT Press, 1995).

Chapter 1

For a full account of this, see Marc Eliot, *Walt Disney, Hollywood's Dark Prince*.

1. On the subject of speculation, see Jacques Derrida, 'Speculations – On Freud', trans. Ian McLeod, *Oxford Literary Review*, 1978, 3(2), pp. 80–98; see also the fuller text 'To speculate – on Freud', in *The Post Card: from Socrates to Freud and Beyond* (Chicago: University of Chicago Press, 1984).

2. More will be said in Chapter 4 about Francis Fukuyama, *The End of History and the Last Man* (London: Hamish Hamilton, 1992).

3. Speech in Moscow, 17 September 1995, *New York Times*, 18 September 1955, p. 19.

4. Jacques Derrida, *Specters of Marx: the Work of Mourning, the State of the Debt, and the New International* trans. Peggy Kamuf (London and New York: Routledge, 1994).

5. Jean Baudrillard offers a similar reading of Western triumphalism after the collapse of communism in *The Illusion of the End*, trans. Chris Turner (London: Verso, 1993).

6. Sigmund Freud's 'The acquisition and control of fire', *The Standard Edition of the Complete Psychological Works of Sigmund Freud*, vol. 22, trans. and ed. James Strachey (London: Hogarth Press, 1964), is a reading of the myth of Prometheus which should be thought of as an extended footnote to *Civilization and Its Discontents*, as might the entire Disney corpus.

7. As a red sidekick to the Eastern European King Triton we are tempted to read Sebastian as an inscription of Cuba. This interpretation would be supported by the Spanish-language version of the film in which, as in all Spanish versions of Disney, the characters have South American accents and Sebastian's Caribbean identity is marked by a Cuban accent.

8. For a fuller account of quasi-transcendentality, see Geoffrey Bennington, 'X' in *Applying: to Derrida*, eds John Brannigan,

Ruth Robbins and Julian Wolfreys (London: Macmillan, 1997).

 9. See Jean Baudrillard, 'The strategy of dissolution', in *The Illusion of the End*.

10. Jacques Derrida, 'To speculate – on Freud', in *The Post Card: from Socrates to Freud and Beyond*, p. 410.

11. Hans Christian Andersen, 'The Little Mermaid', in *Hans Christian Andersen's Fairy Tales*, trans. Reginald Spink (London: Everyman, 1960), pp. 75–103.

12. The trident is the classic emblem of sea power, being associated with the imperial figure of Britannia and Nato's nuclear capacity. In Greek mythology Triton is the son of Poseidon and Amphitrite; this lineage is perhaps suggestive of Triton's non-originary status in *The Little Mermaid*.

Intermission

1. Jacques Derrida, *The Gift of Death*, trans. David Wills, (Chicago: University of Chicago Press, 1995), p. 8.

 2. See Geoffrey Bennington's comments on the phrase: 'Applied Derrida', in 'X', p. 5.

 3. On the subject of secrets, see Jacques Derrida, 'Fors: the Anglish words of Nicolas Abraham and Maria Torok', trans. Barbara Johnson, in Nicolas Abraham and Maria Torok, *The Wolf Man's Magic Word: A Cryptonymy*, trans. Nicholas Rand (Minneapolis: University of Minnesota Press, 1986) and J. Hillis Miller 'Derrida's topographies', in *South Atlantic Review*, 59 (1), 1994, pp. 1–25.

 4. On the issue of responsibility, see Chapter 1, 'Secrets of European responsibility', of Jacques Derrida's *The Gift of Death*.

 5. The Spanish newspaper *El Pais* reported on 27 February 1999, p. 35, that the children and parents of Catalonia recently took to the streets in protest at Disney's decision, motivated by costs, to stop producing separate Spanish and Basque language versions of each film. Instead the film would be distributed in Catalonia dubbed only in Spanish. Such are the aporias of postmodernism, this children's crusade took to the streets dressed as Disney characters to demand oppression, but to have it in their own language!

Chapter 2

1. Michael Eisner, quoted in *Disney Discourse: Producing The Magic Kingdom*, ed. Eric Smoodin (London and New York: Routledge, 1994).

2. Sigmund Freud, *Civilization and Its Discontents*, trans. and ed. James Strachey, in *The Standard Edition of the Complete Psychological Works of Sigmund Freud*, vol. 21 (London: Hogarth Press, 1973), p. 88. Hereafter refered to as *CD*.

3. Avital Ronell, *The Telephone Book: Technology, Schizophrenia, Electric Speech* (Nebraska: University of Nebraska Press, 1994), p. 90.

4. Derrida uses the term 'encondomize' in the interview 'The rhetoric of drugs' in relation to the inability of nation-states to seal their borders against the Aids virus; see Jacques Derrida, 'The rhetoric of drugs' in *Points: Interviews 1974–1994*, ed. Elizabeth, trans. Peggy Kamuf et al. (Stanford: Stanford University Press, 1995), p. 252.

5. For a discussion of the four terms 'politics', 'friendship', 'hospitality' and 'democracy', see 'Politics and friendship: a discussion with Jacques Derrida', Centre for Modern French Thought, University of Sussex, 1 December 1997, http://www.susx.ac.uk/Units/frenchthought/derrida.htm. Derrida also proposes the 'deconstructive effects' of capital in response to a question about hospitality.

6. On the subject of hospitality, see Jacques Derrida, *Cosmopolites de tous les pays encore un effort!* (Paris: Galilée, 1997), or 'Politics and friendship: a discussion with Jacques Derrida', and *Specters of Marx*.

7. The gift is that which is given without return, the impossibility of giving without implying some form of debt makes the gift relation strictly impossible; see Jacques Derrida, *Given Time. I. Counterfeit Money*, trans. Peggy Kamuf, (Chicago: University of Chicago Press, 1991).

8. Samuel Weber, 'The debts of deconstruction and other related assumptions', in *Institution and Interpretation* (Minneapolis: University of Minnesota Press, 1987); this is just one of the texts to which we are indebted for our reading of Disney.

9. Maurice Chevalier being Disney's standard metonym for France, as in Chevalier's own title-song to *The Aristocats* (1970) and the garbled mention of his name during the chef's pidgin-French soliloquy in *The Little Mermaid*.

10. David Ginola, the French footballer, having undergone dramatic transformations of his own recently when he replaced the late Diana, Princess of Wales, as patron of the international anti-personnel landmine campaign.

Chapter 3

1. Gaston Bachelard, *The Poetics of Space*, trans. Maria Jolas (Boston: Beacon Press, 1994). Hereafter refered to as *PS*.

2. See *The Little Mermaid: Ariel's All New Undersea Adventures* Vols. 1 and 2, *Beauty and the Beast: The Enchanted Christmas*, *Belle's Magical World*, *Aladdin II: The Return of Jafar*, *Aladdin and the King of Thieves*, *Around the World with Timon and Pumbaa*, *The Lion King II: Simba's Pride*, *Pocahontas II: Voyage to a New World* (forthcoming).

3. While the editors identify the circumvention of the corrosive cynicism of theory with respect to Disney as a problem within the discipline of Film Studies –

> The high theories of film as art not only ignore the Disney canon, but render suspect and expose the biases of their critical intervention. Not unlike certain relatives forcing their feet into Cinderella's shoe, Disney film is the ugly stepsister unfit for the glass slipper of high theory. (p. 3)

– they also suggest that their book has been written 'because we too are admiring fans who look forward to each new film release or theme park addition, [therefore] the naturalised Disney text [i.e something only for children] suggests that we as cultural critics should recognise and ask questions about our own pleasures and participation in Disney film' (p. 4). Accordingly, the 'glass slipper' attitude they describe above runs through their own political quietism which always seems to fall short of an engagement that would be something more than a mere application of semiotic methodology to tacitly admired films.

4. Witold Rybczynski, *Home: A Short History of an Idea* (London: Heinemann, 1998), p. 77. On the subject of domestication, see Rachel Bowlby, 'Domestication', in *Feminism Beside Itself*, eds. Diane Elam and Robyn Wiegman (London and New York: 1995), pp. 71–93, and Nancy Armstrong, *Desire and Domestic Fiction: A Political History of the Novel* (New York: Oxford University Press, 1987).

5. On molluscs in general, see also Nicholas Royle's *After Derrida* (Manchester: Manchester University Press, 1995), p. 16ff.

6. Rachel Bowlby, 'Domestication', p. 75.

7. Minimal references to Derrida's use of this term might be Jacques Derrida, *Aporias*, trans. Thomas Dutoit (Stanford: Stanford University Press, 1993), p. 6; 'The Retrait of Metaphor', *Enclitic*, 1978 (2); 'Pas', in *Parages*, (Paris: Galilée, 1986).

8. For a considerable length of time this was the standard 'critical' reading of Disney, for example, see Richard Shickel's *Walt Disney* (1968). However, this instinct remains a preoc-

cupation of new Disney as well. It has recently built a town called Celebration in Florida, an experiment in social engineering which consists of houses with picket-fences that belong only in a Disney film.

9. Rachel Bowlby, 'Domestication', p. 75.
10. Jacques Derrida, *Aporias*, p. 61.
11. In *The Aristocats* (1970) we have a mother with three young kittens. As in *One Hundered and One Dalmatians* (1961), anthropomorphism allows Disney to screen out many troubling effects of human gender roles. However, in this film Duchess sets out as a single mother but ends as a wife through a process in which she is sexualised, with the complicity of her children, by her relationship with Thomas O'Malley.
12. One of the dictionary definitions quoted by Freud in 'The uncanny'. See Sigmund Freud, 'The uncanny', trans. James Strachey, in *Literary Theory: An Anthology*, eds. Julie Rivkin and Michael Ryan (Oxford: Blackwell, 1998), p. 156.
13. Jacques Derrida, *The Ear of the Other*, ed. Christie Macdonald, trans. Peggy Kamuf (Lincoln: University of Nebraska Press, 1985), p. 38.
14. Karl Marx, *Capital*, trans. Ben Fowkes (New York: Vintage: 1977), vol. 1, Chapter 1, sect. 4, pp. 163–4. Derrida discusses this passage in *Specters of Marx*, pp. 149–53.
15. Jacques Derrida, *Specters of Marx*, p. 150.
16. Jacques Derrida, *Specters of Marx*, p. 150. This is offered by Derrida as a translation of Marx's *'verwandelt er sich in ein sinnlich übersinnliches Ding'*.
17. We might think here of Mary Shelley's *Frankenstein* as an example of this.
18. Jacques Derrida, 'The ghost dance: an interview with Jacques Derrida', trans. Jean-Luc Svobada, in *Public*, no. 2, p. 61.

Chapter 4

1. Francis Fukuyama, *The End of History and the Last Man*, pp. xii, 108.
2. Source: http://www.informatik.uni-frankfurt.de/~fp/Disney/Features.html
3. Jean Baudrillard, 'Disneyworld company', in *Liberation*, 4 March 1996.
4. This term is used with a due note of caution. We recognise that it is shorthand for a political and philosophical engagement which cannot be reckoned with in the nominal effects produced by the term itself. Furthermore, the phrase

as it appears throughout the book is not a unified or self-identical thing. For example, during the Gulf War the term meant an alliance between America, Russia, the European Union and Arab states; in current usage it usually refers to a 'Western alliance' only. Invoking this term runs the risk of falling into the restricted forms of thinking implied by the metaphysical vocabulary of Politiology but we hope that the contradictions inherent in this term will be rehearsed by our readers every time it is used in this book.

5. *Specters of Marx*, Chapter 2, 'Conjuring Marxism'.
6. In this sense Disney, as heirs of Marx, are working with a standard marxist hypothesis that change in the economic base results in transformations in the political and cultural superstructure.
7. 'A spectre is haunting Europe – the spectre of Communism'. What haunts the powers of old Europe is the fear that communism will 'appear' at some point in the future: Karl Marx and Friedrich Engels, *The Communist Manifesto* (Oxford: Oxford University Press, 1992).
8. The song 'Never Had a Friend Like Me' also refers to Aladdin as the 'Shah'.
9. Robert Young, *White Mythologies: Writing History and the West* (London: Routledge, 1990), p. 13.
10. This is the basis of Derrida's critique, in so far as it is a critique, of Marx in *Specters of Marx*.
11. Under the control of Jafar the genie assumes enormous proportions and has dark-rimmed eyes. Jafar's incarnation as a genie is similarly disturbing. These characterisations would seem to point towards the figure of the djinn in Islamic mythology (a class of spirits formed by fire which encircle the world, sometimes assuming the form of men of enormous size and hideousness) which is often confused in Western accounts with the benign figure of the genie.
12. Jean-François Lyotard, 'The wall, the Gulf, and the sun: a fable', in *Politics, Theory, and Contemporary Culture*, ed. Mark Poster (New York: Columbia University Press, 1993).
13. *Specters of Marx*, p. 58.
14. When Aladdin retrieves the lamp from the Cave of Wonders his monkey Abu defies the instructions they have been given by touching the gold and jewels lying around in the cave. Immediately, all the gold turns to liquid and nearly drowns Aladdin and Abu. They escape this oil slick, presented here as a lava flow, with the help of the magic carpet. These scenes, reminiscent of the assault on the Death Star in *Star Wars*, formed the basis of the video game which accompanied the film.

15. Such a response would involve a recognition of America's responsibility as the 'last superpower', one which the genie ambiguously refers to when he shoots off like a cruise missile at the end of the film, declaring, 'I'm history, no, I'm mythology, I don't care what I am, I'm free.'
16. Quoted (with approval) in Francis Fukuyama, *The End of History and the Last Man*, p. 89.
17. Jacques Derrida, *Specters of Marx*, p. 139.
18. Karl Marx and Friedrich Engels, *The Communist Manifesto*, p. 2.
19. Jacques Derrida, 'Racism's last word', trans. Peggy Kamuf, *Critical Inquiry*, 12, 1985, pp. 290–9; see also Jacques Derrida, 'The laws of reflection: Nelson Mandela, in admiration', in *For Nelson Mandela*, ed. Jacques Derrida and Mustapha Tlili (New York: Seaver Books, 1987).
20. It is with breath-taking audacity that Francis Fukuyama suggests that Pinochet's electoral defeat in 1989 was the result of the inevitable link between liberal economics and liberal democracy (Francis Fukuyama, *The End of History and the Last Man*, pp. 14, 21, 42, 104, 112). One of the primary reasons why Pinochet's regime was so enthusiastically endorsed by the West was because Pinochet used the Chilean economy to experiment with the neo-liberal theories of Milton Freedman and the Chicago School. As Dorfman and Materlatt have demonstrated, one of the major interests which set out to undermine Allende's Popular Unity Government and empower the military oligarchy was Disney itself. It is often very difficult to tell the difference between the covert operations of the CIA and the encoded significations of a Disney film. It is not without significance that the 1973 film *Robin Hood* is also a film about autocracy in which the corrupt civilian King John (Allende) is replaced by the good military King Richard (Pinochet) through the intervention of Disney's domesticated animus. In this film Robin Hood is, ironically, a fox.
21. Along with Rowan Atkinson as the king's majordomo (Polonius), Disney appreciate that only the British really understand what it means to be part of the irrational social organization of monarchy.
22. Baden Powell spent his early years in South Africa and the paramilitary discipline of the Boy Scouts might have something to tell us about his experiences during the Boer War.
23. The image of Jafar as cosmic genie is also strikingly similar to Soviet propaganda posters of the hero-worker and the electrification of the Soviet Union.

24. *Timon of Athens* is the Shakespeare play quoted most often by Marx and is the subject of some analysis by Derrida in *Specters of Marx*, pp. 43–4.
25. *Lion King II: Simba's Pride* repeats this haunting by staging the next generation of lions as a version of *Romeo and Juliet* in which Simba's son and Scar's daughter come together.
26. Jacques Derrida, *Specters of Marx*, p. 16.
27. We are thinking here along the lines of Lyotard's use of the 'post' in (post)modernity. See Jean-François Lyotard, 'Rewriting modernity', in *The Inhuman: Reflections on Time*, trans. Geoffrey Bennington and Rachel Bowlby (Cambridge: Polity Press, 1991), p. 25.

Chapter 5

1. Thanks to Dick Hebdige, whose story of his use of this phrase in reference to Bob Marley entertained us in Glagow in 1996.
2. Ralph Ellison, *Invisible Man* (Harmondsworth: Penguin, 1965), p. 7.
3. Frantz Fanon, *Black Skin, White Masks* (London: Pluto, 1986), p. 112.
4. For a detailed account of this period, see Thomas Cripps, *Slow Fade to Black: The Negro in American Film, 1900 –1942* (Oxford: Oxford University Press, 1977).
5. James Snead, *White Screens Black Images, Hollywood from the Dark Side*, eds. Colin MacCabe and Cornel West (London and New York: Routledge, 1993), pp. 81–99.
6. We are of course referring here to Henry Louis Gates's study of tropes in African-American Literature, *The Signifying Monkey: A Theory of African-American Literary Criticism* (Oxford: Oxford University Press, 1988).
7. Clifford Mason, 'Why does White America love Sidney Poitier so?', *New York Times*, 10 September, 1967, collected in Richard Maynard, *The Black Man on Film: Racial Stereotyping* (New Jersey: Hayden, 1974), p. 79.
8. See Snead, *White Screens Black Images*, p. 99, and Maynard, *The Black Man on Film: Racial Stereotyping*, pp. 19–21.
9. See http://www.informatik.uni-frankfurt.de/~fp/Disney/ Features.html. This web site also includes a still from this scene.
10. *The Aristocats*, 1970.
11. The film *The Last Days of Disco* (1998) is indicative of the confusion between race and class which structures standard analyses of *Lady and the Tramp*. In the later film the character Josh expounds upon the topic:

It's not really about dogs except for some superficial bow-wow stuff at the start. The dogs all represent human types which is where it gets into real trouble. Lady, the ostensible protagonist, is a fluffy blonde cocker-spaniel with absolutely nothing on her brain. She's great-looking but let's be honest is incredibly insipid. Tramp, the love interest, is a swarmy braggard of the most obnoxious kind, an oily jail bird out for a piece of tail or whatever he can get ... He's a self-confessed chicken thief and all-round sleazeball. What's the function of a film of this kind? Primarily its a prime around love and marriage directed towards very young people. Imprinting on their little psyches the idea that smooth-talking delinquents, recently escaped from the local pound, are a good match for nice girls from sheltered homes. When in ten years the icky human version of Tramp shows up around the house their hormones will be racing and no-one will understand why. Films like this programme women to adore jerks ... The only sympathetic character, the little Scottie who is so loyal and concerned about Lady, is mocked as being old-fashioned and irrelevant and is shunted off to the side ... Perhaps he [Tramp] wanted to change or tried to change but there's not a lot of integrity there. First he'd be hanging around the house drinking, watching ball games, knocking Lady about a bit but pretty soon he'd be back at the town dump chasing tail.

As a commentary on the relationships in *The Last Days of Disco* the audience might have an ironic distance to this conservative reading. As an analysis of *Lady and the Tramp* it subsumes race to a class issue without acknowledging that what separates Tramp from the Scottie is the mark of racially acceptable citizenship, the collar. The fact that Tramp gains a licence by the end of the film is significant in itself regardless of any 'future' activity.

12. Homi Bhabha, 'The other question: stereotype, discrimination and the discourse of colonialism', *The Location of Culture* (London and New York: Routledge, 1994), p. 67.
13. Franz Kafka, 'Investigations of a dog', *Metamorphosis and Other Stories*, trans. Willa and Edwin Muir (Harmondsworth: Penguin, 1961), pp. 83–126.
14. The dachshund and bulldog present further paradoxes in the logic of this film in that Tramp is on good terms with a German family, the Schulzes, and the British were unlikely to have as many problems entering America as Russian Jews. However, rather than representing the poltical actualities of

access to America we would argue that the film produces and participates in a discourse of American identity that involves a disavowal of Englishness. Furthermore, the existence of Germans inside and ouside the walls of the dog pound suggests the ambivalent status of postwar Germany in Europe and America.

15. Jacques Derrida, 'Racism's last word', trans. Peggy Kamuf, *'Race', Writing, and Difference*, ed. Henry Louis Gates, Jr. (Chicago: Chicago University Press, 1986), pp. 329–38.

16. Jacques Derrida, 'But, beyond ... (Open letter to Anne McClintock and Rob Nixon)', *'Race', Writing and Difference*, pp. 354–69.

17. For example, when told by Rafiki that he knows where his father is, Simba has to make his way through a tunnel of thick undergrowth to confront his own reflection. There is a remarkable similarity between this scene and Luke Skywalker's encounter with a ghostly Darth Vader during his jedi training in *The Empire Strikes Back*. Skywalker kills the spectral Vader only to discover his own face behind Vader's mask. By the end of the film we learn that Vader is Luke's father. The connection is made all the more resonant by James Earl Jones's presence in both films. There are profound racial implications in this citation from a film called *The Empire Strikes Back* in an African setting with a black-voiced father, who has previously been the only black man in the universe.

18. There is a 3-D film show at EuroDisney featuring Michael Jackson and directed by George Lucas in which Jackson performs heroic feats cloned from *Star Wars*.

19. See Henry Louis Gates, Jr., *The Signifying Monkey*. Esu is the 'inbetween' figure who interprets between the gods and the people. He is usually figured as a monkey with two faces, moving between the world of the gods and the people. Gates reads him as the first African textual analyst.

20. Jean Baudrillard uses this term in 'Disneyworld company'.

21. 'On the never-never' used here in the colloquial sense to mean 'on credit'.

22. Jacques Derrida, *Monolingualism of the Other or The Proesthesis of Origin*, trans. Patrick Mensah (Stanford: Stanford University Press, 1996), p. 39.

Chapter 6

1. 'Pocahontas Information', http://www.informatik.uni-frankfurt.de/~fp/Disney/PocaInfo.html

2. We are grateful to Peter Hulme's book *Colonial Encounters: Europe and the Native Caribbean 1492–1797* (London: Routledge, 1985) for a more or less factual account of Pocahontas. Even if some of the facts he chooses to distinguish from the fiction seem to be grounded in political and rhetorical expediency rather than 'history'. In his introduction Hulme says of deconstruction that, politically 'such a position can lead only to quietism' (p. 6). If we are allowed to quietly reject the 'position' offered to us here, we would like to dedicate the first half of this chapter to Peter Hulme with grateful thanks for his 'deconstruction' of the Pocahontas myth.

3. *A True Relation of such occurrences and accidents of noate as hath hapned in Virginia since the first planting of the Collony* (1608), in John Smith, *Works 1608–1631*, ed. E. Arber (Birmingham, 1884), pp. 1–40.

4. John Smith, *The Generall Historie of Virginia, New England, and the Summer Isles* (1624), facsimile edn, Cleveland, 1966, p. 49.

5. Smith's account of his meeting with Pocahontas in England seems to demonstrate both Smith's own non-understanding of (as well as fascination with) the gift relation and Pocahontas's dismay at the ways in which the colonists contravened the rules of that relation:

> Hearing shee was at *Branford* with diuers of my friends, I went to see her: After a modest salutation, without any word, she turned about, obscured her face, as not seeming well contented; and in that humour her husband, with diuers others, we all let her two or three houres, repenting my selfe to haue writ she could speake *English*. But not long after, she began to talke, and remembered mee well what courtesies shee had done: saying, You did promise *Powhatan* what was yours should bee his, and he the like to you; you called him father being in his land a stranger, and by the same reason so must I doe you: which though I would haue excused, I durst not allow of that title, because she was a Kings daughter; with a well set countenance she said, Were you not afraid to come into my father Countrie, and caused feare in him and all his people (but mee) and feare you here I should call you father; I tell you then I will, and you shall call mee childe, and so I will bee fore euer and euer your Countrieman. They did tellvs alwaies you were dead, and I knew no other till I came to *Plimoth*; yet *Powhatan* did command

Vttmatomakkin to seeke you, and know the truth because your Countriemen will lie much. John Smith, *The Generall Histoire*, pp. 122–3.

6. Quoted from Jacques Derrida, *Given Time: 1. Counterfeit Money*, p. 109.

7. Jacques Derrida, *Given Time: 1. Counterfeit Money*, p. 87.

8. We are using 'sublime' here in the strict Kantian sense as Richard Klein describes it: 'That aesthetic satisfaction which includes as one of its moments a negative experience, a shock, a blockage, an intimation of mortality', in his study *Cigarettes are Sublime* (Durham and London: Duke University Press, 1993).

9. Marcel Mauss, *The Gift: The Form and Reason for Exchange in Archaic Societies*, trans. W. D. Halls (London: Routledge, 1990), pp. 70–71. Derrida offers a commentary on this passage in *Given Time*, pp. 99, 114. However, on the anthropology of both food and tobacco, see also Claude Lévi-Strauss, *From Honey to Ashes: Introduction to a Science of Mythology, Volume Two*, trans. John and Doreen Weightman (Chicago: Chicago University Press, 1973).

10. For a reading of Irish history which tackles this reductionism, see David Lloyd's *Anomalous States: Irish Writing and the Post-Colonial Moment* (Durham, N. Carolina: Duke University Press, 1993).

11. In the live-action remake of *101 Dalmatians* (1996) Jeff Daniels plays Roger, the American owner of Pongo and struggling computer game designer. At the end of the film he designs a best-selling game based upon the dogs' adventures. No killing is involved.

12. On the cautiously used phrase 'absolute exteriority' and on the discussion which follows, see Geoffrey Bennington , 'Introduction to Economics I: Because the world is round', in *Bataille: Writing the Sacred*, ed. Carolyn Bailey Gill (London: Routledge, 1995), pp. 46–57.

13. Immanuel Kant, *Kant's Political Writings*, ed. H. Reiss (Cambridge: Cambridge University Press, 1970), p. 106.

14. Immanuel Kant, 'Idea for a Universal History from a Cosmopolitan Point of View', in *Kant's Political Writing*, p. 47n.

15. We are grateful to the above essay by Geoffrey Bennington for our understanding of Kant and also to an unpublished conference paper by him, 'In Memoriam', given at 'Criticism of the Future', University of Kent (Canterbury), 1997.

16. Geoffrey Bennington, 'Introduction to Economics', p. 54.

Chapter 7

1. In effect this is the same understanding of Fascism which predicates *Schindler's List*, which in its aesthetic portrayal of the Holocaust and heroic-rescue narrative follows the rhythm of the Indiana Jones films.
2. For all that follows in the rest of this chapter, see Jacques Derrida, *Politics of Friendship*, trans. George Collins (London and New York: Verso, 1997). For a reading of this text, see also Martin McQuillan's review of it in *Textual Practice*, Spring 1998, 12 (1), pp. 178–84.
3. 'To shove the queer' is a slang English expression meaning to be in debt.
4. Eve Kosofsky Sedgwick, *Between Men: English Literature and Male Homosocial Desire* (New York: Columbia University Press, 1985), p. 1.
5. Eve Kosofsky Sedgwick, *Between Men*, p. 25.
6. For a review of the fate of fraternity in French republicanism, see *Politics of Friendship*, Chapter 9.
7. Sigmund Freud, 'The psychogenesis of a case of homosexuality in a woman', *Sexuality and the Psychology of Love*, ed. Philip Rieff (Collier-Macmillan: New York, 1978), p. 133.
8. Barbara Johnson, *A World of Difference* (Baltimore: Johns Hopkins University Press, 1987), p. 12.
9. We understand 'performance' here in the sense that Judith Butler uses the term in *Gender Trouble*, in which gender is undertood as 'performative': 'gender is always a doing, though not a doing by a subject wbo might be said to pre-exist the deed'. Judith Butler, *Gender Trouble, Feminism and the Subversion of Identity* (Routledge, London and New York, 1990), p. 25.
10. Simon Hattenstone, 'Master of the Mouse', *Guardian*, 10 April 1999, Review, p. 6.
11. All quotations from the novel come from Victor Hugo, *The Hunchback of Notre-Dame*, trans. Walter J. Cobb, (Harmondsworth: Penguin, 1996).
12. Jacques Derrida, *Politics of Friendship*, p. 264.
13. Before *The Little Mermaid* Disney had a considerable investment in the British hegemony within children's literature: *Oliver and Company* (1988), *The Adventures of the Great Mouse Detective* (1986), *The Black Cauldron* (1985), *The Many Adventures of Winnie the Pooh* (1977), *Robin Hood* (1973), *The Jungle Book* (1967), *The Sword in the Stone* (1963), *One Hundred and One Dalmatians* (1961), *Peter Pan* (1953), *Alice in Wonderland* (1951). Disney's 1999 offering is *Tarzan*.

14. Disney has of course been in Paris before in *The Aristocats* (1970). This is a Paris occupied by the English, notably a queer butler, and the Americans. O'Malley the alley cat tells us that his full name is 'Abraham de Lacy Guiseppi Casey Thomas O'Malley'; Duchess remarks that, 'Monsieur, your name seems to cover all of Europe.' The American O'Malley offers the lost children of 1968 paternal authority and at the end of the film displaces the English butler in the household to establish a family unit with Duchess. Disney's ambition 'to cover all of Europe' might be traced back to this film in which the conservative corporation identify O'Malley as 'Prince of the boulevard / Duke of the avant [pronounced 'avon-t'] garde'. We might suggest at this late stage that everything that the Disney Corporation does is contained in this film, but you have to watch every film to appreciate this.

15. Victor Hugo, 'L'avenir', in *Paris* (Introduction to the Paris Guide), Paris 1867, pp. 5, 9, 11–15, quoted in Jacques Derrida, *Politics of Friendship*, pp. 264–5.

16. The *Time Out: Paris* guide for 1999 (Harmondsworth: Penguin, 1999) reports that EuroDisney now attracts more visitors per year than Notre-Dame, p. 239.

17. One might argue that the relationship between Pocahontas and Nakoma represents a determined encoding of female friendship. However, this friendship retards the experience of democracy in this film (Nakoma intervenes to stop the relationship with Smith developing) and is sidelined by the more important interaction between Pocahontas and Smith.

Chapter 8

1. Both Disney and Clinton have, in recent years, been hate figures for certain sections of the religious right in America. Christian fundamentalist pressure groups helped fund Paula Jones's legal team, while Disney films have been variously scrutinised and 'over-read' by the self-styled American Family Association as pornographic, violent, un-American, anti-family and un-Christian; while the Texas Board of Education sold its $45 million stake in Disney in protest at a perceived surfeit of sex and violence (reported in the *Guardian*, 13 July 1998, p. 19).

2. The image of the Titans in *Hercules* also corresponds almost exactly to the hellish figures in the 'Night on Bare Mountain' sequence from *Fantasia*.

3. Mayor Giuliani's public image is intimately connected to the Disney Corporation. A friend of Disney Chief Executive Michael Eisner, part of his 'clean up' of Times Square has involved a real estate venture by Disney on West 42nd Street similar to the social-engineering experiment Celebration in Florida.

4. The hydra was drawn by Gerald Scarfe, a right-wing British satirical cartoonist during the Thatcher years. Such a reversal (Scarfe and Disney in defence of Clinton) is suggestive of the overturning of established political orders characteristic of the mediatic space of *fin de siècle* politics.

5. Michael Jordan is contracted to Warner Brothers and appeared as himself alongside Bugs Bunny (in a reprise of the 1930s formula of black male and cartoon character) in the basketball film *Space Jam*, also released in 1997.

6. On the subject of the aporia, see Jacques Derrida, *Aporias*, trans. Thomas Dutoit (Stanford: Stanford University Press, 1994).

7. On this formulation of the messianic without messianism, see Jacques Derrida, *Specters of Marx*, Chapter 2 'Conjuring Marxism'.

8. Franz Kafka, 'The Great Wall of China', in *Metamorphosis and Other Stories*, trans. Edwin and Willa Muir (Harmondsworth: Penguin, 1961). All page references are to this edition.

9. For a productive account of borders, see Geoffrey Bennington, 'Postal politics and the institution of the nation' and 'The frontier: between Kant and Hegel', in *Legislations: the Politics of Deconstruction* (London: Verso, 1994).

10. Geoffrey Bennington, *Legislations*, p. 248.

11. To offer just a few minimal references on narrative see Jacques Derrida, 'The law of genre', trans. Avital Ronell, *Glyph 7* (1980), pp. 176–232; *Parages* (Paris: Galilée, 1986), Paul de Man, *Allegories of Reading: Figural Language in Rousseau, Nietzsche, Rilke and Proust* (New Haven: Yale University Press, 1979); J. Hillis Miller, *Ariadne's Thread: Story Lines* (New Haven: Yale University Press, 1992); and Geoffrey Bennington, 'Postal politics and the institution of the nation'.

12. Geoffrey Bennington, 'Postal politics and the institution of the nation', p. 252.

13. For an account of such, see *The New Internationalist*, no. 308, December 1998, special issue on Disney, 'The mousetrap: inside Disney's dream machine'. The *Guardian* reported on 5 November 1998, 'Taking the Mickey', that the average age of workers in Disney factories in the Far East was 15 years. These employees are said to work 10- to 16-hour shifts and

sleep 16 to a room in dormitories between shifts. Disney has a factory in Vietnam which produces toys for Disney–McDonalds promotions and until recently owned a factory in Burma in which the military junta shared a 45 per cent stake. Disney also owns factories in Indonesia. Michael Moore reports that while technicians at the Disney-owned ABC television station were on unpaid industrial action (protesting at having worked for one and a half years without a contract) Michael Eisner earned $60,000 per minute. The ABC workers are still without a contract (*The Awful Truth*, Channel 4, 17 March 1999).

14. *Toy Story* broke box-office records in Shanghai, attracting a million viewers out of a 13 million population; while the Chinese state television company currently uses Disney's sports network, ESPN, to provide almost 50 per cent of all programming on its sports channel ('The mousetrap: inside Disney's dream machine', p. 19).

Epilogue

1. Franz Kafka, *The Castle*, trans. Edwin and Willa Muir (London: Everyman, 1992), p. 9–10. All subsequent quotations come from this edition.
2. Nicholas Royle, 'Nor is deconstruction: Christopher Norris, *Deconstruction: Theory and Practice*', *Oxford Literary Review* 5:1–2 (1982), p. 173.
3. Friedrich Engels, *The Condition of the Working Class in England: from Personal Observation and Authentic Sources* (London: Grafton Books, 1986).
4. The opening line of Franz Kafka's 'Metamorphosis' is of course 'As Gregor Samsa awoke one morning from uneasy dreams he found himself transformed in his bed into a gigantic insect.' In *Metamorphisis and Other Stories*, p. 9.
5. *The Collected Dialogues of Plato, Including the Letters*, eds. Edith Hamilton and Huntington Cairns (New Jersey: Princeton University Press, 1961), p. 832. We might also think of the parable of the cave in Book XXV of *The Republic* as a Platonic analysis of animation.
6. For this connection we are grateful to Andrew Bennett and Nicholas Royle's *Introduction to Literature, Criticism and Theory*, 2nd edn, (Hemel Hempstead: Prentice Hall, 1999), p. 212. They also provide an excellent reading of Kafka's short story 'In the penal colony' in the preceding pages.

7. Both Jacques Derrida and Hélène Cixous provide extensive commentary on the metaphor of the ant. In her *'Une théorie de fourmis'* Cixous writes:

> Across a path, here is a single-file line of ants. The ants carry burdens on their backs. The child sees the relationship and the resemblance: procession of indigenous porters in the bush and the maquis. One cannot say who resembles whom exactly. There is reciprocity. She herself an isolated ant on the sand, but not forever: a line of porters is formed in the paths of her dream: it is her first discontinuous continuous line. The words move, take turns, go around each other, climb.

From 'Avantposte' in *Post-Theory: New Directions in Criticism*, eds. Graeme Macdonald, Martin McQuillan, Robin Purves and Stephen Thomson.

In 'Fourmis' Derrida suggests that the ant [*un fourmi*] 'is already the adventure of reading and interpretation, it crawls with thousands of meanings, with a thousand and one images, with a thousand and one sexes, it cuts itself in the middle (four/mis)', 'Fourmis', excerpt from *Lectures de la différence sexuelle*, trans. Eric Prenowitz, in Hélène Cixous and Mireille Calle-Gruber, *Hélène Cixous, Rootprints: Memory and Life Writing* (London and New York: Routledge, 1997), p. 119.

8. Homi K. Bhabha, 'Of mimicry and man', *The Location of Culture*, p. 86.
9. Franz Kafka, 'In the penal colony', in *Metamorphosis and Other Stories*, p. 192.
10. Harold Bloom, *The Western Canon: The Book and the School of Ages* (London: Macmillan, 1994), p. 448.
11. Interestingly, although Frank Gehry designed the building Disney did not allow him to complete the work. He was removed from the project and the concert hall was constructed by a design and build group. See 'Nobody messes with the mouse', *Guardian*, 16 June 1997, G2T, p. 10.
12. Jacques Derrida, '"There is no *one* narcissism" (Autobiographies)', in *Points: Interviews, 1974–1994*, p. 212.
13. 'Yet more artists on the war', *Guardian*, 10 April 1999, p. 22.
14. Maggie O'Kane, 'Dancing with rage at the New World Order', *Guardian*, 30 March 1999, p. 3.

Index